MY LIFE IS GREAT. WHY DO I FEEL SO AWFUL?

MY LIFE IS GREAT. WHY DO I FEEL SO AWFUL?

Steve Pieczenik, M.D., Ph.D.

WARNER BOOKS

A Warner Communications Company

Warner Books, Inc., 666 Fifth Avenue, New York, NY 10103

W A Warner Communications Company

Printed in the United States of America
First printing: April 1990
10 9 8 7 6 5 4 3 2 1

Library of Congress Cataloging-in-Publication Data

Pieczenik, Steve R.
  My life is great. Why do I feel so awful?
Steve R. Pieczenik.
    p.   cm.
  ISBN 0-446-51458-6
  1. Women—Psychology.   2. Self-realization.   3. Success.
4. Psychotherapy—Case studies.   I. Title
HQ1206.P48   1990
158'.1'082—dc20   89-39118
                                                              CIP

Designed by Giorgetta Bell McRee

To Birdie, my wife, a complete woman.
For a lifetime of love, devotion, and support—
all the while growing within herself.
This book belongs to her.

To Sharon and Stephanie, my daughters.
In time the future will be yours;
take from us what you may, and be all
that you can be—without regrets.

To Those whom I have treated and loved.
Beyond Gratitude.

ACKNOWLEDGMENTS

Special thanks to all the gracious, encouraging professionals at Warner Books.

To my editor, Joann Davis, who in her quiet but unsparing way shepherded the idea into an exciting book. Many thanks.

To Margaret Wolf, who worked on the manuscript and made it presentable.

To Nansey Neiman, who never once faltered in her support of the writer on this project. A demanding publisher with a full spirit and a gentle heart.

To Mel Parker, a compassionate editor whose critical judgments have made my efforts so much more worthwhile.

To Larry Kirshbaum, who always made me feel at home at Warner Books.

And to Robert Gottlieb, my literary agent at the William Morris Agency—my advisor, my confidant, and, most of all, my trusted friend who never once failed me.

CONTENTS

Contents ——————————————————————— xiii

PREFACE

I wrote this book to describe a group of women whom I have treated over a twenty-year period for what might have appeared at first glance to be clinical depression. In fact, what I had discovered was a category of women, all of whom in one way or another had achieved a significant degree of success in their lives (by both objective and subjective criteria), who also felt incomplete or discontent. They all shared one common complaint—something was missing in their lives. They couldn't quite pinpoint what that something was, but they all agreed that whatever was missing would have to be dealt with from within.

Many of these women would come into my office and say "My life is great. Why do I feel so awful?" Changing external factors in their lives (jobs, friends, hobbies) only ameliorated the problem slightly. The majority of these successful women felt that their feelings of incompleteness stemmed from something they were not doing for themselves. They felt that they were not in touch with that part of themselves that had been discarded in the pursuit of success—a self filled with all types of hidden emotions or hidden passions. And so I began to formulate a therapeutic strategy that addressed the fundamental question that many successful women could not answer for themselves: what do *I* want?

The basic starting point of this book is that many women who strive for success often find that they attain an incomplete life. They acquire all the accoutrements that one commonly associates with success—wealth, power, prestige. But I found that one very important part of their life had been completely ignored, if not discarded—the sense of self. Many women I treated in my practice were unable to determine who they were and what they wanted, not for others—but for themselves. It was this absence of self in the pursuit of modern success that drove their ultimate search.

By asking herself the three key questions of this book—"What do I want?" "How do I get it?" "What will it cost me?"—the Successful Woman narrows the focus of the yearning for the self into a finite world of personal choices and consequences. In this book I have tried to help women discover and examine hidden passions (passion for living, creating, feeling) so that they can fulfill this yearning. The feelings, emotions, and passions uncovered in the exercises I provide give expression and legitimacy to a sense of self that is lost in the classical socialization process of a childhood that is designed to nurture others.

I highlight this yearning for self because I believe it is so important in understanding the questions asked and the techniques that need to be applied. To find oneself in the expression of a written word or a painted image or the embrace of a loved one is what I would call the ultimate success. But, each woman must ask herself what in her past has stopped her from finding that part of herself that was lost during the pursuit of success? Was it the fear of risk? Was it the inertia of laziness? Or was it the routine numbness of habit? Why has everything and everyone taken precedence over the yearning for her self? I believe that as children many women were taught to subsume their desires to those of others. They were taught that their primary goal was to nurture the family—their father, brother, husband, boyfriend, children. But who was there to nurture that particular woman? Who was there to ask, "What do you want?" And, more important, "How may *I* help *you* attain it?" Instead, I believe that women were instructed to disguise their personal desires and emotions within the acceptable rubric of nurturance and caring for others.

As adults, the women I have treated were taught to break the shackles of that learned dependency and encouraged to acquire the male-dominated values of success—power, prestige, money. I found that they had learned to achieve and compete but without a clear sense of what it was they were competing for. Somehow, more became less, and the treadmill of achievement made them hostages to success. The pursuit of success was intertwined with a sense of want, a desire for passion—a yearning for the self. Therefore, to everyone around them they could honestly proclaim that their life was, indeed, great. But, within themselves, they felt incomplete, and awful. And that was something they could admit to no one.

In this book I have tried to provide a roadmap that will allow you to proceed on the odyssey of expressing that self through the passion for living, passion for creativity, passion for love. I believe the journey begins by asking three basic questions—"What do I want?" "How do I get it?" "What will it cost me?" Once you have found the answers to those questions, you will feel yourself empowered to express those hidden passions. Only then can you feel completely ready to accept and value the genuine successes you've achieved and stop looking for the one final validation you need—finding rather than yearning for the self.

Then, you can affirm the three basic tenets of the self: *I am. I need. I want.* Therefore, I am complete.

INTRODUCTION

Yearning for Self: Awakening the Hidden Passions

Donna woke up one night in a blanket of cold sweat. Unlike her other sleepless nights, she found this one absolutely frightening. She got up from the bed, tiptoed quietly to the bathroom, swallowed an anti-anxiety medication, went back to bed, and lay there with her eyes wide open, staring up at the ceiling and listening to the deep breathing of her husband, Roy. Her mind was racing. Thoughts, fears, anxieties, images all collided as if signaling the beginning of a nervous break-down. And yet, within this maelstrom of turbulence was a silent oasis of certitude. She knew that as terrifying as her thoughts might be, they were important. They reflected very deep feelings that were buried within her.

For some time now, perhaps as long as four and a half years, she had felt a gnawing sensation that she was not really happy. Because she wasn't a person who considered herself self-indulgent or whimsical, the feeling disturbed her even more so. She knew that she could no longer go on like this.

For four and a half years she had asked herself one annoying question—What do I want? And each time the answer was the same. She didn't want to be married to Roy. She was unhappy. How foolish, she thought; millions of women feel the same way every year but don't tear themselves apart over it. So what is wrong with me? How can I even think these horrible thoughts? She had two sons—one of whom was a teenager, the other preteen. Both would need her. They loved their father. They loved their mother. And they loved being in the warm, supportive family unit she and Roy had created. Objectively there was really very little she could complain about. Roy was a conscientious father. He drove the kids to their activities. He played baseball with them. He was even the baseball coach one year. He made an extremely handsome income and so did she. Together they had everything anyone could envy: a beautiful house in the most exclusive area of town; a second home in East Hampton; two cars; private school for the children. Was she simply a spoiled "princess" who could never be happy, no matter what she received? She felt that this wasn't the case. What she was missing had nothing to do with money. She was yearning for passion. To feel alive and enthusiastic. Engaged. Whole. Not simply a dedicated wife, mother, professional. She loved being both a mother and a wife, but there was something missing. She no longer loved Roy. He was kind, responsible, caring, smart, handsome. But for several years he had been unable, if not unwilling, to stimulate the passion for which she longed. At home after work, when things weren't going too well, all she wanted was for him to hold her in his arms and comfort her. But he would look at her quizzically or make a faint effort or simply turn away. She had tried to mobilize his emotions for her. God how she had tried. She asked him, pleaded with him, manipulated him, seduced him, and even fought with him. And she had to give Roy credit. He would respond. But it was so ethereal and short-lived that it made the situation even more frustrating for her. For two of the four troubled years they had been in couples therapy. The psychologist who treated them informed Roy that he thought the marriage was in trouble unless Roy tried to change. But again his efforts were short lived.

Then a few months later it happened. The very thing of which she was afraid. She started to have an affair with a man at work. Someone she felt was sensitive and caring. Someone who could give her the emotional sustenance for which she yearned. And the passion. But her lover only heightened the feeling of how cheated she felt at home. She began to feel alive, close, connected, sexy, funny. He made her feel wanted and special. He was sensitive, caring, sensual, and a wonderful friend. He was, in short, everything Roy was not. And through him she realized that in order to feel complete, to be true to her

Hidden Passions, she would have to leave Roy. In order to be true to herself she could no longer maintain a clandestine relationship. As it was, this surreptitious affair stood against everything she believed. She wanted to feel alive but out in the open.

During the period of time she was having the affair she found it increasingly difficult to have sex with Roy. Every time she wanted to deny him access to her body, she became frightened and anxious. And other practical concerns were pressing in on her as well. Foremost in her mind were the children. She adored them. And they, in turn, adored her. What would happen to them if she were to leave Roy? As she lay there in bed gazing up at the ceiling, she recalled the countless horror stories of how marital divorces could traumatize children for life. There was no doubt in her mind that a divorce would be perceived as the equivalent of a tornado—both the kids and her husband would be stunned.

Then there were economic considerations. Although she was making a six-figure salary, she was working in her father-in-law's business. She had no doubt that he had suspected something was wrong in their marriage and had given his daughter-in-law a job as a way of controlling her. She would have to give up the job and begin again. And how would she support the kids? She would want joint custody. But considering her markedly diminished income, compared to Roy's, she was scared. What would they do with the house? In all likelihood they would have to sell it. My God, the problems were mounting rapidly. Breaking up a family. Losing income. Acquiring a new job or new job training. Trauma to the kids. Trauma to her husband. Not to speak of her own feelings of psychological devastation. New home. New school. Joint custody, lawyers. Accountants, new tax forms. And of course, a "shrink."

Donna's primary reaction? *Panic!* You bet! Many of you who have had to live through this scenario know exactly what I am talking about. But she was resolved that the up-front expenses were going to be far less costly to her than the long-term stress she was enduring with Roy. In therapy, Donna wondered whether her concern with solving all these practical issues wasn't a rationalization for her being afraid to leave Roy. It wasn't.

I broke down the therapy sessions into three basic parts. During the first part, I reality-tested her concerns. Were they real? Or were they simply a projection of her own anxiety and fear? If they were real, what could be done about them? She went to an accountant, talked to a lawyer, evaluated alternative careers (including a job as director of personnel in a small high-tech start-up firm), and met with friends and friends of friends who had been divorced and had already gone through this process. She talked to them extensively, asking for advice and the names of necessary professionals including the name of a psychiatrist. By going out and reality-testing her fears, she was able to put them in perspective.

The second part of therapy involved examining certain assumptions that she had made about marriage in general. Together we examined the common beliefs usually associated with marriage.[1]

1) Marriage is until death-do-us-part.

Donna grew up in an upper-middle-class household. Her mother was a devoted churchgoer who remained with her nondemonstrative husband for thirty years because she wasn't about to destroy the institution of marriage. Love was always a secondary consideration. It was intended primarily for the young at heart.

2) Marriage is an institution based on mutual respect, caring, and commitment.

Donna's father told her when she had just gotten married that marriage was a wonderful place to hang your hat if you have nowhere else to go. He added solicitously, "Remember, you don't have to love one another. You only have to like and respect each other. Love is what gets you into the marriage; caring is what keeps you in."

3) Whatever problems exist in a marriage can be worked out if two people care enough about each other.

Donna's parents worked out their differences through long periods of silence. In many ways, Donna's marriage was far healthier than her parents'. She was able to talk about her problems with Roy. That's what made it even harder for her to leave Roy.

4) A failure in marriage reflects a personal weakness.

Donna was repeatedly told by her women friends that if a woman didn't keep her husband happy and at home, there would always be another woman to take over.

5) A bad marriage is better than no marriage.

Similarly, her friends reassured her, as did Roy, that everyone needs someone and that it is better in the long run to put up with the problems than to live alone.

6) Marriage is an institution that gives children a sense of legitimacy and mental health.

If you destroy your marriage, you run the risk of ruining your children's mental health.

Donna knew that an impending divorce would affect her children. Our discussion of this issue could not be satisfied without some further reality-testing of the actual problem. I suggested that her children be evaluated by a child psychiatrist (I didn't want to bring in my own clinical prejudices) who could better determine what the impact of divorce might be on them. I know what you are thinking, dear reader. No, I am not a mind reader nor is the child psychiatrist to whom I sent Donna's children. Neither one of us can predict the future. But what psychiatrists are trained to do is to evaluate children in terms of their needs, ego defense mechanisms, and psychological trauma. The child psychiatrist was able to assure Donna that the divorce would not be easy on the children, but that they had a strong psychological constitution and would be able to tolerate the trauma. He did add a note of concern about the youngest boy. He would have to be monitored very carefully. At that point, Donna's reluctance to leave the marriage increased markedly. I explained to her that her younger son's response shouldn't dictate her actions within the marriage. Her increasing despondency wasn't going to make it easier for her younger son. In fact, if anything, he might become more upset as he saw his mother grow more dissatisfied with her marriage.

After examining some of the practical concerns involved in divorce I reality-tested the origins of those beliefs. Where did they come from? Were they really relevant to Donna now? Could she substitute other belief systems? After several intensive sessions focusing on these problems Donna realized that Roy and she were no longer compatible. Furthermore, she began to accept the sad truth that no matter how much she wanted the marriage to succeed, it might still not work out. She had to learn how to mourn the loss of her fantasy that the marriage might improve if only she tried harder. Why is it that the woman in the relationship always feels that she should have tried harder? I'm convinced it's a carryover from the socialization process that fosters women to be nurturant, caring, and worried about the man more than about herself. But after six months, Donna went on to deal with two other equally important issues—her increasing anger toward Roy and her loss of a twenty-year marriage.

She was surprised to see how much resentment she was building up toward Roy. She resented the fact that he had done very little to nourish the relationship. In fact, the longer she lived with him the more she realized how emotionally starved she had been. For that reason alone she was beginning to dislike him (this was not a woman who normally became angry at people). And, as one might imagine, she was beginning to dislike herself for having those feelings. In any case, she concluded that the best thing she could do was to leave him and the marriage and request joint custody.

Having confronted the reality-based issues and her belief systems, she finally had to come to terms in the third part of the therapy with what she wanted and decide whether it was really worth it. Here she became extremely frightened. She suddenly felt that she could not live without him. Even though she had her own professional life she felt that her identity was still very much tied to Roy's. She was Roy's wife, Roy's lover, the mother of Roy's children. You get the idea. But then, when I asked her what she wanted, she braced herself and replied that she wanted to leave the marriage and start a new life with both of her sons.

"How much is it worth to you?" I asked. She replied that she had no other choice. If she didn't leave, she would die of emotional starvation. So what was keeping her back? Why couldn't she break that final attachment? Fear. The fear of a child who will lose her sense of security, even though she recognized the fact that this sense of security was false, a carryover from her childhood when she hung on to her father whenever she was frightened. But even then it was not very rewarding. He was too distant, too aloof, too preoccupied. Just like Roy.

By asking her what it would take to get what she wanted, I helped Donna to realize that what she needed to do was to overcome her fears—of the past and the future. Once I encouraged her in the sessions to immerse herself in her imagined new life—a new job, new friends, and acquiring a new home, she was ecstatic. Having convinced herself that her fears of change were far less frightening than her mounting resentment toward Roy and her present "stagnant" situation, Donna decided to file for a divorce. Did she do the right thing? For herself? For her husband? For her children? The questions are easier to ask than to answer. Four years later, I think Donna would have answered, "Yes, definitely. For everyone concerned." But four years prior, when she asked herself the *"What do I want?"* question, the question was as terrifying as the potential answer. She had wanted a change. A change that would require a complete upheaval of her personal, professional, marital, social, financial, and religious lives.

Terrifying? You bet! The prospect of even entertaining the possibility of such wide-ranging change is enough to immobilize most women. But don't panic. First understand and appreciate the fact that the need for change is a continuous process, which does not suddenly stop or start. In a simplistic sense, think of change as a conveyor belt moving down the assembly line. At any point, you can jump on and off as you wish. If you jump off too many times, the product never gets made. But if you don't even try to jump off, then the product—you—may never have a chance to change.

The realization that you are not complete or whole, or that you may want more out of life, may strike you at the weirdest moments. During a daytime meeting or in the middle of the night. In any case, whenever it does occur—don't dismiss it. It's an inner voice that tells you there is something missing inside of you—I call it a Hidden Passion—which you know in your heart of hearts would make you feel alive and complete—if only it were uncovered. Respect it! It is a feeling that has been percolating inside of you for some time. Don't just dismiss it!

I believe there is no single truth or message that will allow you to feel complete or whole. It is not the words or the instructions in this book that you will remember. As in therapy, the patient rarely recalls specific words. What she responds to is the sense and texture of the relationship with her therapist. Can she trust me? Will I try to harm her or help her? Do I care enough about her? Does she feel that I understand her on an intuitive emotional level as well as an intellectual level? But all the good "feelings" in the world aren't going to amount to anything positive in therapy unless they can be articulated clearly and succinctly.

I have my own concerns about what I am offering you here. Not exactly second thoughts, but a certain hesitancy. Self-help books, of which this is definitely one, can only do so much.[2] Life is too convoluted, intricate, contradictory, and rich to confine its principles to a few universal statements, no matter how compelling or accurate they may appear. How do I avoid sounding like a cookbook, telling you that if you follow instructions one, two, three, and four you will be able to fashion for yourself the perfectly balanced life you deserve. This approach to self-growth is too rigid, unrealistic, and threatening. If you fail at "improving" within twenty-one days, have I failed? Has the "recipe" failed? Have you failed? Or is it a "Catch-22"? The "cook" (read psychotherapist) who designed the recipe is usually considered infallible. So if you fail, it can't really be his fault. It must be *your* fault. Even if you feel worse than when you started the book.

Well, my dear reader, I am not infallible. What is even more important to understand is that I don't want to be right all of the time (only some of the time). I don't need to be omniscient. I have no one technique or method that is correct. I work using different skills, many of which you currently possess or may be eager to develop. For example, as a client walks into my office, I form certain impressions about her. How? By the way she looks, walks, looks around, shakes my hand, or even arranges for her appointment. What is that skill? I may be simply acting as an observer. Just as you are in most of your daily interactions. You watch. You listen. You take mental notes. You don't necessarily record your impressions on paper, but they are certainly encoded in your mind for some future retrieval. True, I have been trained professionally. But it is my hope that I may be able to impart some of my knowledge and skills in this book. I hope to be able to sensitize you to observing yourself. In this way, my "cookbook" can give you the possibility to make a good "dish." But, of course, it's ultimately up to you to create the end product *you* want to achieve.

Please use this book as a guide. Not as a bible or a crutch. For even if you followed everything I said down to the final word, you might still not feel better. But don't take that as a sign of your failure. Assume, until proved otherwise, that it is my failure for not having made myself understandable, intelligible, or relevant. Furthermore, we both may have to accept another reality; that this book may not deal with your problem or may not deal with it in an appropriate way.

Becoming a Complete Woman is an easier concept to articulate than it is to realize. My thesis is a simple one. In order to become a Complete Woman, you must be able to uncover, release, and utilize in a creative, disciplined fashion your Hidden Passions. What do I mean by Hidden Passions? Simply those emotions that empower you to live life as it should be lived—to its fullest. The essential ingredient of my notion of passion is a positive one. A creative life force. A feeling that leads to a change, whether it is simply a change in sensibility or a more dramatic one like a change in life-style. More specifically (as you will read in chapter 4), I talk about different types of passion: passion for living, physical passion, passion for discovery, passion for growth, passion for fusion, passion for reaffirmation of self, passion for romance, passion for mature love.

A Hidden Passion is a rush of emotions you can experience on a sunny day or on the eve of your daughter's first ballet recital or in the embrace of a loved one. It is an intense feeling and sensation that you alone deserve to possess.

Remember, nothing is written in stone. There is no one right way of approaching a life problem. There is no one truth. Life is a complicated, ever changing, dynamic involvement that requires risk, courage, commitment, a tolerance for uncertainty, and an ability to distance yourself from the immediate situation. Above all else—trust your instincts. If it doesn't feel right, don't persist. If it sounds or feels right, try it, even if it hurts a little. You have nothing to lose except a little pride and a lot of fear. And be gentle. Gentle with others— but most important, with yourself. Remember, it's okay to have second thoughts about your desire for change. Change is one of the most difficult undertakings in life. I know! I have done it several times. And I assure you it does not get any easier. I always tell my patients that the simple fact that they have come into my office to seek out help is already quite revealing. It is not easy to walk through a stranger's door, no matter how impressive the degrees or reputation, and share your Hidden Passions. So I never take a patient's presence for granted. And I do not ignore your courage in buying and reading this book.

Most of my clients who have changed their lives recognized that the feelings they had about the need to change were agonizing, protracted ones. Only after countless sleepless nights, and interminable internal monologues assessing the pros and cons of change, did my clients come to the realization that they must do something about their feelings of incompleteness. So give yourself time. There is no right or wrong amount of time. You are not racing against some ticking clock. Take whatever time you *think* you might need. If you err, tend to err on the side of taking more time rather than less. And don't forget—be easy on yourself.

ORGANIZING OUR EFFORT

I have divided this book into two parts. In the first part, EXPLORING THE SUCCESSFUL WOMAN AND HER HIDDEN PASSIONS, I describe the phenomena of the Successful Woman who feels empty, incomplete, and hides her passion for living so that she does not have to reawaken old fears, concerns, and disappointments. Through the presentation of different cases I have treated, I will offer a blood-and-guts feeling of the range of problems that were presented to me, how they were handled in therapy, and what eventually happened to the women who were brave enough to undertake self-exploration. At the same time, I am hoping to share with you my own personal feelings and reactions so that the process of psychotherapy loses its mystique and is viewed on the human scale on which it works.

In the second part of the book, HOW TO BECOME THE COM-PLETE WOMAN, I will share with you some of the techniques that might be helpful to the already Successful Woman in regaining her Hidden Passions in order to become the Complete Woman. Some of these techniques can be tried alone, without the direction of a therapist. Many of them were developed in the various disciplines in which I had trained, including behavior therapy, cognitive therapy, crisis intervention, and short-term psychotherapy.

PART
I

EXPLORING THE SUCCESSFUL WOMAN AND HER HIDDEN PASSIONS

CHAPTER 1

The Problem of Becoming a Complete Woman

"I'm a forty-three-year-old publishing executive. My professional reputation is enviable. I travel as much as I want; I am busy and challenged all day long. My husband, Jeffrey, is a wonderful man and an excellent lawyer. We have two terrific children. Yet, I feel something is missing. I feel ashamed, almost embarrassed, to admit that too frequently I feel that there really has to be more to life. It's like I'm still waiting for something . . . someone to give it all meaning. *To make me feel whole . . . and alive.*"

Phyllis is an attractive, self-possessed woman who has an answer for everyone and everything. Except for one crucial question: *What do I want?*

She first came to me for therapy because she was having difficulty making up her mind about taking a new job. Although the new job offered her the opportunity to earn more money and would provide her with both intellectual challenge and upward mobility, she was totally conflicted about whether or not to take it. She seemed inordinately anxious.

"I'm unable to sleep. Each morning I wake up with a queasy feeling in the pit of my stomach."

"What are you afraid of?" I asked.

3

"I don't know. But I feel that for the first time in a very long time I am unable to make up my mind about something I think I really want."

"What do you really want?" I asked. She ignored my question and proceeded to enumerate her formidable accomplishments. She had entered Barnard at sixteen; graduated at nineteen. She received an M.A. in English literature that she parlayed into a job as an assistant copy editor at a major publishing house. Within four years she was a senior editor, and by the age of thirty-one she was a vice president in charge of her own division. After several protracted relationships she decided to marry Jeffrey, a bright, ambitious lawyer, soon to be made partner in a prestigious Wall Street law firm. She had decided to marry him partly because he was extremely bright, and partly because they shared "fun" interests in films and music. But most important to her was that Jeffrey showered her with the emotions she was searching for but rarely found in the men she dated: empathy, warmth, and consideration. Jeffrey was very supportive of her career aspirations. After several years of a comfortable marriage, they decided to have children because they felt it was "the right time." After the birth of each of their children, Phyllis took a three-month sabbatical. And during each sabbatical she felt a disquieting anxiety. A little voice inside her head quietly urged her to return to work lest she become too far removed from her "real" world. After a few fleeting pangs of guilt about staying at home to take care of her children, she would remind herself that the role of mother was equally important as that of a publishing executive.

Jeffrey was always caring and helpful. But by the time she appeared in my office, their sex life had lost a lot of its initial passion. It had become a highly ritualized expression of caring and tenderness, offering sexual release without fun or intense feelings. On her business trips she was often tempted to have a "one-night stand" but after experiencing the "frightening rush" of having come very close to realizing her fantasy, she would back away and discuss her feelings with her husband, who was, as she expected, totally understanding. He shared his own fantasies about sexual liaisons with several attractive women in his law firm. But his genuine concerns about violating the strong bonds of trust that he and Phyllis had carefully nurtured over the years always led him to conclude that having a "passionate fling" wasn't worth the risk. This ability to talk openly about their feelings was typical of their marriage. She concluded wryly: "This is a picture-book marriage and picture-book life. So why should I feel so distraught about the possibility of making lots of money in a challenging job?"

"What do you really want?" I wondered if she realized that this was the second time I had asked the question.

Her face bleached of all emotions except anger.

"What do you mean?"

"This is the second time that I have asked you what you really want for yourself."

"I'm sorry, I wasn't listening." She became more fidgety in her chair.

"What's the matter?"

"Nothing." Her face flushed red.

"You seem angry."

She didn't reply. I sat with her, patiently demonstrating that her anger didn't frighten or bother me. Would she respond to my question or would she walk out of the room?

"Why do you keep asking me that same question?"

"Which one?"

"You know, the one about what I really want."

"That seems to upset you."

She nodded her head in agreement. Then she began to cry.

"It is very hard to admit that we don't know something, particularly something important about ourselves."

She couldn't stop sobbing. She raised her hands to cover her face. I let her cry. For the first time in her life she was being asked to confront an issue that she had taken great pains to bury, discard, and avoid. She had become a successful wife, mother, and working professional. But along the path to success she had forgotten to inquire about the most important person in her life—herself.

"I knew what I had to do in order to become a success in publishing. The road map was clear—first you become an editor; then a senior editor; and then an executive in the corporation. And as a mother, you spend the time that's needed to make certain that your child is well taken care of and has a clear sense of trust that you will be there when he or she needs you. As a wife, you have to realize that there is a mutual give-and-take between you and your husband. The routine and boredom are traded off for the good times. Intimacy. Caring. Loving. Fun." She paused, trying to outguess my reaction to her outpouring. But I sat in silence, waiting for her to continue. "But there is no road map to . . . me! No principles. No guidelines. I'm supposed to have what I want. Not still be looking for it."

She paused again. I said nothing.

"Aren't the choices I've made a reflection of my desires? Then why do I feel as if I were missing something in me . . . as if I haven't really engaged life on my own terms . . . but simply learned to be productive and busy?"

"There's nothing wrong with being productive and busy."

"No. But I don't feel as if it's fulfilling *my* needs for something *I* want. Something *I* desire just for *me* that makes *me* feel good. Alive."

Even Phyllis was surprised at the intensity of her emotion and the sound of her own voice. Lurking within the meticulously tailored existence of this extremely successful professional woman was a woman of passion. A woman who desired more than the predictable, busy existence of her life. She felt that some inexplicable, amorphous event, person, or feeling was missing from her life. Although she knew "something" was wrong, she didn't know exactly what that "something" was. Given the fact that she was weeping and crying, I could have diagnosed her as depressed or having a mood disorder. Treatment, accordingly, would have meant an initial period of insight psychotherapy combined with some antidepressant medication. In fact, many of my psychiatric colleagues could have accused me of denying her a course of treatment frequently dictated by the mores of my professional community. But I decided to interpret her problems not as a pathology of personality, but as a missing link in the maturation of a woman. A link that had to be uncovered and investigated before she could feel whole, integrated, and "alive." The key problem that lay ahead of us was to uncover the cause of those feelings of emptiness and incompleteness (what I call missing or hidden emotions) and to teach Phyllis how to lead a successful and passion-filled existence.

I assured Phyllis that I would work with her, but that I needed her full commitment to a process that would take us through uncharted waters. It would be her responsibility throughout our working relationship to tell me what she was feeling and how much she was learning about herself. The primary objective of therapy was for her to be able to answer the question, "What do I want?"

As she left my office *I* was shaking. My hands were clammy and wet. My throat was dry. And the likely diagnosis was an entity I found hard to accept—anxiety reaction. But why was I anxious? Was I having some underlying countertransference problem? Psychiatrists often use their own reactions to a patient as an instrument to gauge what is transpiring in therapy. What was it about Phyllis that was eliciting an anxiety response? Did I find her attractive? Yes. But not unusually so. Was Phyllis a threat to me? I didn't think so. My own wife is a successful businesswoman. I have always felt comfortable in the presence of accomplished women. Could her problem be similar to mine? For months I had been seriously contemplating giving up my private practice for what amounted to an entirely new career on Wall Street. In retrospect, it was the problems I had been facing at home, rearing my two daughters, that crystallized the significance of Phyllis's life for me.

LIFE'S MAJOR QUESTIONS

How does a woman in a male-dominated society develop *self-esteem* and a *sense of self-worth*? By the time Phyllis was ready to terminate her therapy sessions she was able to answer the three most critical questions of her (and your) life:

> *What do I want?*
> *How can I get it?*
> *What am I willing to pay for it?*

The answers to each of these questions are related to childhood dependencies and lack of self-esteem, which invariably have their adult analogue in problems of intimacy, autonomy, initiative, entitlement, and self-worth. How these issues are resolved will decide whether the Phyllises of society, including their children and my daughters, can feel secure enough in taking a risk on themselves and their own desires and proclaim: *I want!*

The ability to take a risk on one's own desires, no matter how poorly defined or whimsically derived, is at the core of every woman's sense of self-worth and personal identity. She feels incomplete or, as yet, undefined, because she has suppressed her passions for living life fully out of fear of alienating her husband, lover, friend or, most importantly, of disappointing herself. Most women I have either seen in therapy or know on a social basis hold back their own desires or passions, fearful that if the full force of their emotions were realized they would literally frighten or drive away their partner. Or worse, if an attempt were made to meet these needs it would fall short of the goal and the woman would be left wanting. So she retreats into a posture of silence, or she faces the world with well-rehearsed pleasantries that gloss over the disappointments. Sounds arcane? A throwback to former decades?

Without a doubt, the feminist revolution of the seventies liberated women from gender stereotypes as passive, submissive, dependent, and nurturing, and allowed them to approach the yuppie eighties with a panoply of psychological insights and self-actualization techniques (i.e., assertiveness training, stress management). A career-woman mystique arose that boldly proclaimed economic and professional achievements could coexist with love, and that all of these were appropriate expectations for women.

The key question for the nineties is why so many successful women are having such a hard time feeling personally fulfilled. Why do so many women describe their lives as having flown by, or worse yet, say they have "sleepwalked" through them?

THE MODERN DILEMMA: WHO AM I?

The issue of what women want and how they can get it is tied into a more fundamental question: *Who am I?* The answer to that question is at best difficult to reach, especially for the woman of the eighties who has had time to internalize, but not resolve, two sets of conflicting values.

The traditional female role was conceived for someone who primarily took care of others. The emotional and physical "taking" care of a son or daughter or husband or friend was and still remains the foundation of the female identity.

No woman is born feminine. As no man is born masculine. Gender identity is learned through an elaborate, often unconscious, process called socialization. A woman is reared to be nurturant of others. She is taught that her primary identity arises from those values that allow her to relate effectively to a "significant other." By acquiring and internalizing "other-directed" values such as tenderness, understanding, caring, compassion, gentleness, and sensitivity she can better relate to men (and men will be less threatened by her). The argument goes that girls at the crucial age of the oedipal conflict learn to break away from their mothers through an elaborate psychological process involving separation and identification which allows each girl to establish some autonomy while still maintaining the prominent traits of her mother—femininity and dependency. When this is successfully managed, a female is able to avoid any direct threat of competing with her mother for her father's attention. Many of the women who are in the work world today have grown up with this traditional feminine role, where their primary fulfillment is derived from serving and nurturing others. Their identity, no matter how successful they are in their professional life, is "Dr. Jones's wife," "Mr. Richard's youngest daughter."

Where is the conflicting set of values? Over the last fifteen years, as women have entered the work world on increasingly equal footing with men many have had to act as if they had acquired male attributes: independence, aggressiveness, autonomy, assertiveness, competitiveness, achievement, and productivity. Unfortunately some haven't. But in joining the modern work world each woman has learned that in order to survive, she has to be wary of her need to be dependent on someone else. Should she be the nurturing and dependent figure, or should she assert her own need to be nurtured? Is she afraid that like her mother, who took care of her father, she will repeat a pattern that sets her up to be rejected, abandoned, and ridiculed for her "neediness"? The thought of relaxing the expectations on any one of her newly acquired "male" attributes makes her anxious, depressed, and confused. The simple realization that she is dissatisfied with both value systems—the passive, submissive dependency learned from her feminine socialization and the newly acquired masculine attributes of competition and independence has created a situation in which she learned to appear professionally competent, emotionally self-reliant, and concerned about the welfare and care of others; while, at the same time, she was numb to her own individual emotions and needs. Rather than feel anxious and uncertain, she preferred to feel nothing. Instead of asking herself what *she* might really want, she decided to ask what more she could do in her job or what more could she do for others.[1]

Most assuredly, not every woman who is dedicated to her job, or who enjoys taking care of her husband or lover, has a problem. I have met many women who are extremely satisfied with their careers—journalists, doctors, lawyers, secretaries, teachers, and housewives. They work very hard and genuinely enjoy what they are doing. It makes them feel accomplished and committed to something larger than themselves. These women can describe one period in their lives when they literally sat down with great trepidation and started to ask the hard question. What do I want for myself?

Most of the women I have treated, however, have reacted to the pull of values with anxiety, withdrawal, depression, numbness, and an inability to access those emotions which I have called *Hidden Passions*. These Hidden Passions include: the desire to want; the ability for self-love; the passion for physical pleasure; discovery, expansion; and mastery; creativity; fusion with people; the desire to take a personal risk; the willingness to tolerate failure and loss; and the desire to experience intensity, even if it entails releasing such feelings as jealously, envy, and possessiveness. In order to uncover these Hidden Passions, the modern woman must be willing to explore the unknown; afford herself the opportunity to experience what is new; and make herself emotionally vulnerable to rejection and failure. Feeling alive and rediscovering those Hidden Passions entail focusing on one's self-esteem as well as affirming ones desire to feel peak emotions. Letting go of proscriptions, inhibitions, and constraints requires a rigorous and courageous self-examination. It requires giving up old concepts. It requires a great deal of commitment and consistency to the process of self-discovery.

In the 1960s we had a permissive, self-indulgent ethos that espoused "doing your own thing." It frequently meant little more than a helter-skelter abandonment of financial and emotional obligations in order to focus attention and emotions onto yourself. The 1970s highlighted women's liberation (as yet an incomplete process), which unleashed all types of hostile emotions on women inwardly toward themselves and outwardly toward men. The 1980s brought in the yuppie values of upward mobility and material aggrandizement. Self-development centered around material acquisitions and the relevant questions were "How many?" and "How much?" Because America seems to be returning to a time of traditional values the 1990s will herald a return to a process of self-definition in which the sense of self is clearly and comfortably integrated into the collective good of the community. This could mean that one decides to leave the business world to take care of the family or vice versa. Which direction the choice takes becomes secondary to the hard task of making that choice. And, more important, the choice reflects the deep wishes and desires of that particular Successful Woman.

It's not going to be easy to address the first question—*"What do I want?"*—because throughout most of your life you have not been encouraged to address your own needs and wants. So this first question may be the most important question you ask all your life. Then the next two questions fall into a logical sequence. *"How can I get it?"* relates to the basic operational concerns of what personal attributes are required to obtain a particular goal. For most people, change, any change, is extremely difficult. And why shouldn't it be? Change requires an ability to break old habits, overcome the need for security, defy the imperatives of inertia and laziness, and master the fear of the unknown. Not easy tasks. However, lest you despair completely, like any new skill there are techniques that you can learn (later on in this book) that will allow you to take control of your own destiny, overcoming what once seemed like formidable obstacles.

"What am I willing to pay for it?" Many patients have been able to answer the question "What do I want?" But once they fully evaluated the consequences of their choice, that is, the cost that a drastic change would entail, they decided to stay where they were. Why? Because it was emotionally, physically, and economically less taxing. So serious consideration must be given to the different types of payments that one must make before embarking on a journey of change.

However, rest assured that the hardest part of becoming the Complete Woman, through uncovering your Hidden Passions, is the ability to ask and answer the three basic questions: What do I want? How can I get it? What am I willing to pay for it?

UNLEASHING PASSIONS

Lisa was a thirty-three-year-old attractive sales executive at a local television station. For five years she was the station's number-one salesperson, consistently booking seven figures in TV ads each year. Senior management was appreciative of her performance and on several different occasions offered her a position as a vice president in the holding company that owned the television station. She always refused, saying that she was happy in sales, where she loved the opportunity for hands-on experience. As she coyly added one day in therapy, she was really a "snake-oil salesman who could charm the pants off of any advertiser." She traveled a great deal and whatever free time she had she spent with her friends, a diverse group who enjoyed playing volleyball, skiing, and partying together.

Lisa came into therapy wanting to deal with the fact that she was not really satisfied with her life. By her own admission, and my observation, she wasn't unhappy or depressed. She just felt incomplete. She wanted a close attachment to someone or something that would make her feel alive. Intense. She wanted to feel passion. Unlike many of my other patients, she was very clear about what it was that she didn't want: another sexual relationship with the Sturm und Drang emotions of a runaway roller coaster. She had had enough of that. She had broken off a five-year affair with a divorced man whom she felt was on the verge of asking her to marry him. Although she adored him and respected his entrepreneurial talents, she correctly realized that marrying him would be a big mistake. He was basically too controlling and possessive. In many ways he reminded her of her father, a stereotypic alcoholic Irish policeman, who loved his "little girl" as long as she acted submissive. Needless to say, what she became was aggressive, assertive, and unwilling to brook any male domination. Her mother was a chronically debilitated housewife who spent the majority of her life confined to a wheelchair monitoring the police band on a shortwave radio. Lisa, the dutiful daughter, spent at least one weekend a month taking care of her family.

Just at the time that Lisa and I were beginning to explore issues relevant to her ability to answer the question "What do I want?" she decided that she had fallen in love with a thirty-eight-year-old divorced doctor with a nine-year-old son. She had met him at the beach while playing volleyball and from that point on they started to date seriously. One day she came to the therapy session certain that he was the right man for her and convinced that their impending marriage was *the answer* to her life's questions. She no longer needed therapy, she informed me. He was what she needed. A high-achieving, empathetic, noncontrolling Irish Catholic internist whose only peccadillo was the need to be a perfectionist. I tried to remind her that she had not answered the question of what she wanted for *herself*, and that the normal stress and strains of her marriage would merely heighten the issue even more. I tried to explain to her that she could not hide behind a new husband in order to avoid answering an old question.

Well, human nature is true to its own dynamics. Six months after her honeymoon, Lisa stormed into my office, furious that I had kiboshed her marriage with my prophetic statement. After her barrage of insults, she started to cry. And cry. Nothing had really changed. She was married, four months pregnant, and felt as incomplete and lacking as she had the year before.

I was not surprised. I was disappointed. She had married prematurely, avoiding the tough work of defining her own ego boundaries, her own needs, her own Hidden Passions. She had gone off to do what she always had done when she had to deal with her own desires; she became her father's "good little girl," nurturing and taking care of others at the expense of her own growth.

After the birth of her son, Andrew, Lisa spent a year and a half in therapy, part of it in couples therapy, analyzing and correcting the asymmetry in the power relationship in her marriage and more evenly aligning the distribution of responsibilities at home. We addressed those issues that were blocking her attempt at personal growth: dependency, need for attachment, anger toward her parents, sibling rivalry, fear of success, fear of failure, fear of taking a risk. And when she was finally able to answer that crucial question, she decided that she no longer wanted to remain in a corporate structure which, although encouraging in certain ways, inhibited her entrepreneurial and creative skills. Childbirth had helped her realize, "no pain—no gain." Anything worth obtaining was paid for with time and effort. She had long before suppressed her desire to become an interior designer because her father had always insisted that interior decorating was not what a proper Irish Catholic girl did.

Four years after ending therapy, Lisa is extremely happy with her marriage and her two children. She is a successful interior decorator, earning an attractive salary. She stopped playing volleyball, however, fearful that she might tear her Achilles tendon and end up an invalid in a wheelchair like her mother.

Lisa's history illustrates several important patterns that one typically finds in the Successful Woman with Hidden Passions. Despite an appearance of success, which can be easily confirmed by the existence of a comfortable salary, an interesting job, an assortment of active, interesting friends, she had a visceral feeling that she was missing something very important. She wasn't totally alive. Passion was missing from her life. Yet she sensed that passion for living life to its fullest was within her, buried beneath layers of other emotions. Dependency. Rage. Anger. Ambivalence. Each of these emotions scared her enough for her to hide them. And hiding them prevented her from focusing attention and energy on the key question: "What do I want?" Therapy allowed Lisa to get in touch with those emotions, and the result of her psychological journey was her being able to take the necessary risks required to confront the vagaries of everyday life and commit herself to an endeavor that expressed the desires and passions she had guarded since adolescence. To be creative. To be artistic. Throughout her race to maturity she was busy denying her own needs to be nurtured and encouraged, afraid she might become powerless, helpless, and crippled—just like her mother. She felt she had no other choice but to become "Papa's little girl," what prominent psychologists described as an overstressed, high-achieving woman who was caught in the self-created trap of trying to be everything to everybody.[2]

On the surface, Lisa defended against her need to be dependent on someone by becoming unduly self-reliant. But, the more she took care of herself, both physically and emotionally, the more incomplete she felt. Early in therapy, when Lisa was beginning to address the issue of what it was that she wanted, she bolted out the door (and therapy) and absorbed herself in a totally consuming relationship; a relationship unconsciously intended to divert the focus away from herself and onto the caring and nurturing of her future husband and children.

CHAPTER 2

The Successful Woman: Contradictory Realities— Why She Feels Incomplete

You can always recognize the Successful Woman. She looks and, yes, even smells, successful. She has an aura of being in control. Of herself. Of her circumstances. Of everyone around her. She always seems to know where she should be and for how long; whom she should meet, and what person is a waste of time. Her meetings are productive. Although she may say little, she projects self-assurance. The point to remember is that while everyone defines success differently, most of us can identify the Successful Woman.

It is interesting, if not directly on the subject, to note that the Successful Woman is always the object of envy. And envy is one of the most deleterious emotions I have ever encountered in or out of therapy. By definition, envy is the emotion that compels us to feel as if we should possess certain traits that a particular individual might have or become as good as the person whom we envy. In reality, envy forces us to take those attributes (beauty, wealth, prestige) away from the person whom we admire. Not only do we want what that envied person has; we also don't want that person to have it. The Successful Woman radiates something that you or I (yes, men do envy women) want, something we think that she may have. In some cases, the Successful Woman flaunts her success by driving a red 928 Porsche, or conspicuously dressing in designer clothes. Many Successful Women go out of their way to diminish the envy level of others. Paradoxically, doing so may raise it even more. The dynamics of success and envy are complicated.

What we don't see about the Successful Woman—despite the fact that her marriage, her profession, her accomplishments, her social set are the envy of her friends and colleagues—is that sometimes she is not content with her success. It is difficult to describe her discontent precisely. *Unhappy* is too strong a word; *depressed* too distant and pathological a concept. An unarticulated sense of incompleteness lurks immediately beneath her veneer. When pressed (the Successful Woman will rarely volunteer a discussion about her true feelings), she will admit to feeling empty, wanting. She will talk about a deeply buried emotional numbness in terms of what has *not* yet happened to her. The feeling of incompleteness is usually defined in terms of a life that is passing her by. The person we perceive to be the Successful Woman is waiting, like Sleeping Beauty, to be magically awakened to her "real" self. Self-discovery is out there, waiting . . .

Despite the façade of success, the Successful Woman is continuously trying to anesthetize (substitute "hide") her disquieting sense of incompleteness (substitute "passions"). Unfortunately, her attempts frequently drag her through a variety of ultimately unsatisfactory activities: excessive sleep, TV mania, alcoholism, drug addiction, overeating, undereating (the eating modality that has become "fashionable" in the eighties); increased or decreased sexual activity; or workaholism (the analogue of anorexia in the work setting).

Notwithstanding an appearance of confidence, and the draw of admiration, the Successful Woman is frightened. Not of success. Not of failure. Not of intimacy. Not of commitment. Not of liberation. Not of involvement. *She is frightened of her feelings of vulnerability*, despite all her successes. When questioned, she will admit to feeling trapped by her accomplishments, unable to derive an inner peace from them. She is confused by the fact that she has aggregated the feminist rhetoric and values of the seventies with the male-achievement oriented values of the eighties and—something is still wrong!

The sad truth is that despite her appearance of achievement and success, the Successful Woman is confused. Having made her choices as a free, independent, strong individual—a career, or a family, or both—she is confused and saddened to find that those choices don't add up to a sense of fulfillment. So she panics and buries her discontent in *avoidance behavior*—any activity that will distract her from facing herself and making some hard choices. As she buries herself in the "process" of work and/or family life, she feels increasingly more trapped, more incomplete, and more vulnerable.

IN CONFLICT WITH HERSELF

The tragedy inherent in the dilemma of being a Successful Woman with Hidden Passions is that no amount of achievement, connectedness, or busywork seems to alleviate the contradictory realities she confronts daily.

1. On the surface she appears self-assured. But within, she feels frightened and scared.

2. She can direct herself to achieve specific professional goals. But she remains unclear about how those goals fit into the larger picture of life's meaning.

3. She displays the material trophies of male-oriented success. But she wonders why they are unfulfilling.

4. She projects an image of a woman very much in control of her own destiny. But she feels both powerless and helpless when she tries to tap into her secret longings.

5. She appears alert, responsive, and articulate. But she frequently retreats into an emotional numbness so that she doesn't have to make any real demands on herself or others.

6. She is competent with men in both social and sexual settings. But she blames herself when the relationship doesn't work out.

7. The unattached Successful Woman may feel ready for an emotional commitment. But she finds it difficult to maintain one.

8. Probably the most paradoxical of all her conflicting psychological realities is that while the Successful Woman is industrious and conscientious, she believes she is basically lazy. Here is a woman who puts in an eight- to twelve-hour work day, additional hours as a mother, wife, companion, and household executive and, despite all this energy and time dedicated to work and home, she believes that she is not doing enough. And I concur, for she has consistently avoided the fearful and difficult task of uncovering her very personal set of needs and goals.

Once in therapy, it is obvious that the Successful Woman possesses an impressive array of psychological insights into her condition. As a matter of fact, because of her keen intelligence and incisive observations, she can intimidate many therapists into dismissing her as someone without significant problems. But her problems are real. She has lost perspective. What was it she really wanted from life? From a relationship? Because she has lost her perspective, she often needs help to find her way back into herself.

PROFILE OF THE SUCCESSFUL WOMAN

"Whatever I've done, I've done to the best of my ability. And then some. I'm twenty-seven and black—and I am extremely proud of being black—born off some back road in South Carolina. I left home at the age of sixteen to come to Los Angeles to work in the motion picture industry. Of course things were tough. Very tough. I didn't have a skill. All my friends would say 'You're crazy, Lucille, you're going to starve if you run away from home.' The crazy thing was that I knew I would starve if I didn't leave South Carolina. When I got to Los Angeles, I got jobs as a waitress, carhop, usher, and, you know, other things, nothing illegal, maybe just slightly immoral. But I saved enough money to enter a film school in Sherman Oaks, did very well, got a few jobs as an assistant to an assistant. You know, one of those direct, indirect connections. Eventually, slowly, I worked my way up to my present position, first assistant director. Hopefully, in a couple of years, I'll get my chance to direct a small-budget independent film. Then I'll know I will have made it. But I can't be sure in this business. I never stop learning. After work I take acting classes, and would you believe it, even screenwriting courses—just in case I don't make it as a director. It's fun, but very hectic. I barely have time for my boyfriend, who is jealous of my career. But that's another issue for some other time. I see my friends occasionally. I work out. But, even though I'm doing everything I want to do, I still can't help feeling that I'm not doing quite enough. And maybe what I am doing isn't good enough! So I have trouble sleeping. I wake up anxious every morning."

Lucille is a twenty-seven-year-old high achiever who came to see me because she felt as if she were a failure. When she first expressed this complaint, I had a hard time understanding exactly what it was that she was complaining about. By most standards of performance, she would have been considered a success; perhaps not fully developed, but nevertheless a success. She had single-handedly elevated herself from rural poverty to the glamorous world of movies. She had literally directed her own talents into a practical, tough, rewarding career. Yet by her own admission she felt incomplete, unfulfilled. She was frightened that what she had achieved up to this point "wasn't good enough." Throughout the sessions, she continuously reassured me that she would try hard to be a "good patient." I asked her what she meant by that. She replied, "You know. Someone who understands what you are saying and can really appreciate the insights you are revealing to them. And doesn't appear weak . . . or break down and cry."

Lucille's primary problem was one that is very typical of Successful Women. *They don't possess a clear image of themselves.* As convincing or self-assured as they may sound or appear, if asked, "How do you see yourself?" they are often confused or anxious. What they feel about themselves does *not* necessarily correspond to how they present themselves to the world.

MORE IS NOT ENOUGH

Anne, a thirty-five-year-old divorced mother of two, was a CPA at a major accounting firm. When I met her, she was managing forty-five million dollars' worth of business in a corporate division consisting of twenty-five accountants and twenty support staff. She worked fifteen hours a day, for which she received a good executive salary. When she came home, she cooked dinner for teenage sons who, like most adolescents, were rambunctious. On the weekends, she spent time with her boyfriend, Frank, a struggling entrepreneur who had never been married.

Anne came to me at a point in her life when her relationship with Frank was turning sour. She enjoyed coming home to her children, but she found Frank increasingly irritable, sardonic, and distant. After she had received her last promotion he was preoccupied, she felt, with what she would do with her newfound money. His jealousy was less than subtle. On more than one occasion she avoided his questions about investing in start-up companies. As much as she cared about him, she didn't trust his business acumen . . . with her money.

Here is the kicker. Despite his record of business failures, and her record of professional successes, Anne decided that there might be something wrong with her (not with him). Perhaps she was too harsh on him. She reasoned that after a day's work at the office, and then coming home to take care of her two boys, Frank might have a legitimate grievance that she was not available to him. Perhaps he had the right to expect some concrete evidence, such as her financial commitment, of her feelings for him. On the one hand, she knew better than to really believe that. Yet on the other hand, if she *were* to spend less time at work and more time with Frank . . . Of late, they had been having some sexual problems. Frank had been expressing some discontent over her ability to satisfy him. Anne, in true candor, admitted that on several occasions she was tempted to have an affair with a colleague in her office whom she had dated from time to time. But she was afraid of what the other men in the office might think. As a matter of fact, she added, she was increasingly concerned about her professional reputation in the office, the higher she was promoted. She was extremely sensitive to the criticisms of her colleagues. On several occasions, when she felt guilty about not having worked hard enough, she became more productive by staying later at work or by working at generating more business. And yet, she discovered that the more she accomplished, the less she was able to measure her accomplishments. Instead of feeling satisfied she felt compelled to work even harder. She found herself, as she described it, on a "treadmill" of self-destruction. She had lost her identity. She no longer knew what she really wanted. She was afraid that she was going to lose everything. It was, as she described, a "Catch-22."

Both Anne and Lucille shared many traits. They were overachievers for whom more was never enough. They needed to assume several different working roles in order to quell the underlying discontent resulting from their respective inabilities to answer the basic question, "What do I want?" They both had poor self-images that made them vulnerable to the emotional needs and entitlements of the people around them. They defined themselves primarily in terms of performance and accomplishments. Lucille in particular felt that she was a performance machine, someone with an endless capacity to obtain a goal no matter what the cost might be. Unquestionably Lucille was, and still is, an ambitious woman. And there is nothing wrong with ambition. On the contrary, without ambition I could argue that there would be no means by which to obtain some sense of self-worth or a forward momentum for self-definition. Ambition is a type of psychological energy needed to define the parameters of an ego, as well as a sense of self-worth. In the case of Lucille, the drive to define her sense of being was so strong that she overcame every conceivable obstacle in order to achieve a specific objective—in her case it was by becoming a director of an independently produced movie. On the surface, it sounded as if she had a clear, conscripted sense of what she wanted. She sounded self-assured and prideful of her black heritage. Very impressive. So why am I picking on her? Rest assured of one point, I don't look for trouble. Although I am paid to be skeptical, I also leave well enough alone.

In the case of Lucille, however, her ability to define a clear self-image was not that convincing. She continuously had a need to perform well—as a black woman, an aspiring director, and a patient. She could not tolerate any sense of failure. In her world view there was no such thing as an obstacle that could not be surmounted. Throughout therapy, she was reluctant to discuss such threatening concepts as dependency and control—equating them with such fearful concepts as passivity, submission, helplessness, paralysis, victimization. Like many Successful Women, Lucille talked and acted a good game. But inside she was frightened, anxious, and confused. She lacked the very thing she was trying to portray—self-confidence. She was, as it turned out, extremely grateful that there was a paid stranger who could do for her at this time what she had done to the rest of life—overcome her conscious and unconscious barriers. She welcomed the "uncomfortable intruder," as she affectionately called me.

She, like Anne, was very concerned about what her colleagues thought about her, always fearful that she might not perform up to some series of unstated standards. Frank had become the repository of standards and expectations by which Anne had to conduct her life. Rather than doubt his capability to perform as a breadwinner and lover, Anne immediately decided that whatever was wrong in their relationship was in large part due to her shortcomings. Only with great hesitancy would Lucille or Anne attribute any part of their discontent to their boyfriends' inadequacies. Instead, Anne felt that Frank was right, she should have placed a higher priority on improving their deteriorating relationship, even though Frank gave no evidence of even wanting, let alone trying to improve their relationship. Every time she brought up the subject of their relationship, Frank found himself suddenly preoccupied with work-related activities. At times in therapy, she mused how she suspected that Frank, despite his words to the contrary, never really understood the magnitude of her job.

Who are these Successful Women who try so hard to satisfy some internal burning desire while at the same time they lose their direction? And who disguise whatever passions are left so that they are not later rebuked or disappointed? For them, desiring more is tantamount to needing more, and having strong needs is a natural setup for disappointment. So the credo becomes—want less, expect less, and become disappointed less. But I'm ahead of my cases. For the moment, I want you to acquire a clear image of what I mean by a Successful Woman and the inherent contradictions that reside within her.

Lucille and Anne demonstrate the simple but important fact that you cannot take anything for granted—neither their physical appearance nor their self-assured presentations. What is in conflict is the image they hold of themselves in contrast with the image that they project in the everyday work world. There is a marked discrepancy between their internal self and the one they portray to the outside. They don't feel the way they know that they should feel. They don't behave the way they would like to. And most important, they are not, by any standards, whether it be their own admission or their unrelenting sense of incompleteness, anxiety, and sadness, content with their own lives. What is the source of such a discrepancy? We must look at the pattern through which women acquire a sense of self: through role models; idealized self; derived identities; internalized values, attitudes, and behaviors.[1]

Most men, unlike women, are socialized to compete. Compete at school, work, home, play. They think in terms of life as a *zero-sum game*. Win or lose. Men are taught that it's a rough-and-tumble world out there where only the fittest survive. The weakest are defeated. A simplistic image? Perhaps a bit overdrawn to dramatize the point. But a good point, nevertheless.

Men measure their success by the fact that their opponent is defeated and they have emerged from some real or imaginary encounter as the self-proclaimed victor. In their minds there is no doubt who was more successful. At work, look at the weekly paychecks; on the football field, read the scoreboard. In both cases, success is measurable, well-defined, and often entails a gain at someone else's expense. Don't misunderstand me. There is nothing wrong with the need to be competitive. Competition only becomes a problem when it is an end unto itself.

Most women, on the other hand, are socialized to measure their accomplishments on a *self-referential basis*. They measure success from standards that they have incorporated within themselves. The basis of comparison is *not* a zero-sum game. There are no winners and losers. Women were thought to be gentle, delicate, and kind. Women were not socialized to become aggressive or competitive in the man's sense of the term. This doesn't mean that there aren't tough, competitive women out there. On the contrary, there is mounting evidence to suggest that in a variety of spheres of influence women have become increasingly competitive and ruthless. But the basic socialization pattern rears women to have, and to value, compassion. To have, and to value, caring. To have, and to value, understanding. And these values do not lend themselves to a measurement system that pits one's self-worth against another person's self-esteem. Instead, women were taught to rely on standards of excellence that arise from within, from what psychiatrists call an *idealized self-image*.[2]

Women do not measure themselves against other women in order to establish their sense of self-worth. Don't get me wrong, a woman may want what another woman has (envy), or may want to make herself prettier than someone else (jealousy), or excel in a professional setting (competition), but, the history of women's rearing has predisposed her to take care of her dependency issue first and foremost. The idealized self-image of an independent, autonomous woman protects the Successful Woman against feeling dependent, needy, and emotionally clingy. It is important to understand how the issue of dependency plays into a Successful Woman's self-image and self-esteem.

Even in the 1980s, it is still safe to say that a mother, her role model, raises a daughter to become an emotional and physical caretaker of her children, her lover, her husband. A woman is taught to nurture everyone but herself. In contrast, boys are taught almost from the day that they are born that they will always be taken care of, usually by a woman. A mother takes care of her sons. A sister coddles her brother. A wife supports, encourages, and literally feeds her husband. In every stage of her development, from childhood unto adulthood, a woman is taught to take care of others first, and then, if she has enough energy, time, desire, or reservoir of emotion, she can take care of herself. Of course, by then most normal women are depleted or disgusted. So, in effect, what women are implicitly taught as a result of their socialization pattern is that they, themselves, have no needs. Or if they do have needs, they are, in fact, subordinate to the needs of almost everyone else around them. Lest you think I might be exaggerating, I can say that in the hundreds of cases of Successful Women I have treated, ranging in age from twenty-one to sixty-eight, *not one* could assure me that her basic needs for nurturance, caring, or dependency were fulfilled during her years of growth, or quite frankly, at any other time in her life. The normal reaction to this deprivation was to deny any need. Many of the women felt embarrassed by the fact that they had certain needs. Others had learned never to expect to have their feelings, passions, or needs recognized or fulfilled.[3]

DEPENDENCY—A DIRTY WORD

Dependency, or fulfilling one's own need for nurturance, protection, relatedness, has become a dirty word. Successful Women, at least the ones I have seen and treated, associated the concept of dependency as a one-way ticket into submission, passivity, helplessness, powerlessness, abandonment, loneliness, and destitution.

Janet, a single, thirty-three-year-old high-powered government bureaucrat, came to see me because she could not find the "right man." Every man she dated had a defect. I'm certain you know the type. Paul was tall, dark, and handsome. Janet couldn't tolerate him after a while because he was distant, aloof, and too silent (all traits, by the way, that had attracted her in the first place). Similarly, another boyfriend, Harry, was the sensitive type—caring, understanding, and, by her own admission, tried to anticipate her needs. Invariably, given enough time, Janet found fault with Harry. According to her, he was weak, indecisive, and lacked aggressiveness. The list of rejected men was long and getting longer. And there was no end in sight—either of her discontent or the failings that she could uncover in each of the men she dated. When asked what she was looking for in a man she responded flippantly, "An all-around American female."

"Female?" I replied. Her face turned a bright red.

"That's a Freudian slip, isn't it?"

"I would say so. But what's more important is that the slip covers over some deep-seated needs that you have that you are having a hard time expressing."

"I'm not a lesbian," she blurted out defensively.

"I didn't say you were."

"I meant to say . . . I want an all-American male: tough—yet tender, aggressive—yet compassionate, strong—yet yielding."

"I get the picture. Someone who exists in your fantasy."

"No, I'm sure he's out there . . . somewhere." She added somewhat indignantly, with a tone of voice that bordered on a threat, "You wouldn't want me to sell myself short, would you?"

"No. I simply want to know what it is that you need and want for yourself."

"I'm afraid to let these men see what it is I need. It's a setup. No sooner will I say to them that I need some warmth, some hugging, some tenderness; just someone to be there; to be supportive and encouraging, then I suddenly see the men scurrying away . . . like rats on a sinking ship."

"In other words, you are afraid to let the men see that you have needs. You've hidden your needs and your passions."

"Deep. I've hidden them very deep. Just coming here to this office, I took a big risk. I've never let any man see what I needed and wanted."

I asked her not to place me in such an elevated position because I, too, would invariably find myself failing her. She had to start some serious work on uncovering and defining her needs, and, equally important, realistically defining the limits of those needs.

EMOTIONAL ACCOUNTABILITY: NOTHING IS FOR FREE

I have always felt that in the world of human emotions, nothing is for free; including those needs, passions, and desires that we might have for someone or something but suppressed or denied. We pay for it exponentially! Sounds ominous, doesn't it? But believe me, it's true. Believe the aphorism: "You get nothing for nothing." Back to the problem of dependency. The emotional payment becomes increasingly costly the further we postpone the day of reckoning. Frustrations, resentment, anger, rage—all build up. A woman becomes hungry when she realizes that her basic appetite for connection, relatedness, nurturance isn't being met. She becomes ravenous when she has to postpone the possibility of having those emotions met. But she becomes frustrated and angry when she realizes that there is *really* no possibility at all to have her needs met. Tragically she is now paying the emotional equivalent of compounded interest. She not only has to suppress her dependency needs (as well as her passion for living a full life) but she must also bury the frustrations and resentment she feels over not having had her basic needs fulfilled. So what most women carry within themselves are smoldering emotions, which I call—Hidden Passions. Witness the following case of Laura, who is not atypical in the intensity of her repressed emotions.

NEVER RELY ON A MAN

Laura was a thirty-five-year-old divorcee without children. She was an extremely successful entrepreneur who owned a chain of fast-food restaurants, which she had single-handedly created out of a defunct diner. Her ex-husband, who had helped her develop the business, was bought out when he realized that there was really no place for him to go in the business. According to Laura, she had usurped all the key functions in the company because she could never trust her husband to carry through on any decisions he made. By her own admission, she found men to be "blowhards," and basically "little boys who were searching for their mommies." Although she was skeptical of most men's ability to deal with her on an equal footing, she was determined to find a man who could make her feel alive and stir up her "caldron of passion" (my terminology, not hers). Tony was just such a man. He was a forty-two-year-old, single, attractive architect who had a history of long-term relationships always falling short of marriage. For both Laura and Tony, the other was the long-awaited soul mate. Their first year of marriage was an "incredible honeymoon."

Each attended to the other's needs with remarkable alacrity and deep sexual fulfillment. They spent every free moment they had making love or exploring new avenues of interest. They discussed the possibility of her giving up completely the CEO functions of the corporation in order to develop some creative interests that she had always harbored. She was interested in going to art school to learn sculpting. But she had never pursued this Hidden Passion because she was too afraid of discovering that she might not have any talent. Tony was supportive and reassured her that between the profits of her company and his salary, they would be more than financially comfortable. For the first time in her life, she felt good about herself and eager to undertake a risky venture that directly involved her self-esteem (she never considered business a reflection of her own narcissism). Expectations were high on both sides.

Unfortunately events started to unravel their "honeymoon" existence. Just as Laura began to undertake her new artistic life, Tony found himself preoccupied with demanding design projects. Laura rationalized his increasing absence from home as temporary and hoped with all her heart that the situation would change. She felt increasingly more vulnerable and anxious as she immersed herself in the art world. She expressed her need for support and understanding but discovered that Tony was too busy or tired to give her any form of nurturance. From time to time, he would hold her in his arms and reassure her of his support. As a gesture of goodwill, he would prepare a picnic basket and together they would escape to the country. The momentary sojourns away from home helped, but not much. Laura felt increasingly depressed, lonely, abandoned, angry, and resentful. She questioned her decision to give up her entrepreneurial life for as risky a proposition as becoming a sculptor. But, she had always fantasized that with the right man she could feel complete as a woman and as an artist. She may have been right. Unfortunately she was never to know. When Tony came home one day, Laura asked him to perform a household chore. He complained that he wasn't feeling well. She became furious. All the pent-up resentment and rage bubbled up to the surface. She accused him of being selfish, self-centered, insensitive, inadequate, uncaring—I think you get the idea. Then she went around the room and smashed all the clay statues she had made for her art class. She phoned the newly appointed CEO of her company and fired him. Then she called her lawyer and asked for a divorce. Tony tried to calm her down, but he failed. Nine months later they were divorced and Laura returned to her company with a greater resolve to never, never rely on a man for anything—not money, support, nurturance, understanding, or caring. Or, I might add, psychotherapy. After a few sessions, I pointed out to her how she had suppressed her needs as a way of sand-trapping Tony in the service of driving him away. She became angry with that interpretation and left therapy. She then entered psychotherapy with a woman analyst. Admittedly my pride was hurt. But there is no escaping one's own dynamics. She eventually left that analyst as well as two other psychotherapists.

SELF-RELIANCE: HOW TO AVOID TAKING CARE OF YOURSELF

A Successful Woman, like Janet, Lucille, or Anne, protects herself against her dependency needs by first denying that she has those needs; and, then, by entering, or more nefariously, creating, asymmetric relationships in which she caters to someone else's needs. Each of these women found themselves in a relationship where the son, husband, lover, or friend were making demands on their time, patience, and understanding. Each depleted her own emotional and physical resources in order to satisfy another's needs. Invariably, each entered into an avoidance behavior (sexaholic, alcoholic, workaholic) and drove herself into a state of physical and emotional exhaustion.

Nothing is wasted, however, in this world of emotional conundrums and avoidance behavior. This obsessive self-depletion serves a very important function. It allows the Successful Woman to avoid dealing with her own needs, her own Hidden Passions, and her hopes that one day she, too, will be nurtured and pampered. Instead, she defensively assumes the posture of being a superwoman, or what a prominent psychologist calls the Type E Woman: someone who has become everything to everybody.[4] This Successful Woman makes certain that she can create a relationship where she is primarily in the giving position so that she never has to confront the emptiness, pain, and frustration of not having her needs met. In order to maintain this asymmetrical relationship, this defense against having her own needs met, the Successful Woman has to develop and internalize a self-concept that never allows her to achieve a modicum of satisfaction with herself. Instead she is driven by a series of expectations, "erroneous expectations,"[5] that never allow her a moment's self-content. The idealized self-image, a childhood fantasy derived in part from parental expectations of her, forces the Successful Woman to push herself until she is physically and mentally exhausted. Perfection becomes an obsession. Irrespective of the fact that she might have a compulsive personality, the Successful Woman becomes demanding of herself to do more and better. No matter how successful Anne became at the accounting firm, she still felt she could do more . . . and better. There weren't enough hours in a day for her to accomplish what she wanted to complete. Anne conveyed an omnipotent sense that she could do it all, and still have time left over to cook a meal, take care of her adolescent sons, and maintain an exciting romantic relationship with Frank. She had even created a false expectation in Frank's mind that she was able to anticipate his needs and respond to them accordingly. It wasn't enough to simply take care of him. It was equally important to know what Frank was thinking and give it to him before he articulated his desires. If this sounds farfetched, think of the large number of women, who as secretaries, administrative assistants, office managers, lawyers, doctors, or accountants, see themselves as and perform the role of service provider. It is not an accident that teaching and social work have always provided women with satisfaction. Each of these professions fulfill the Successful Woman's basic need to nurture. The fact that women now become lawyers, social workers, or accountants can be very misleading. On the surface, these professions help the Successful Woman to meet her dependency needs by servicing clients, and also to derive gratification from the fact that she has mastered a new challenge (the new professional field). Together, this means autonomy and self-sufficiency. But what is equally important is the fact that these inherently busy service professions allow the Successful Woman an opportunity to deny her increasingly unmet dependency needs. These professions allow her to bury her emotions and passions in the "in-box," distilling and sublimating them in an incisive office memo or legal brief. Please don't get me wrong! I'm not advocating that women should only tend house. Or that they should not feel productive and committed. I'm simply pointing out that the professional life, if not properly evaluated and managed, can fit very comfortably into a Successful Woman's compulsion to deny her own needs for nurturance, dependency, attachment, connectedness, and self-definition. She learns to hide her emotions (much like men do) in the helter-skelter of a very busy professional life. And she isn't aware of it until it is too late! I am saying that women have learned to become workaholics or assumed other avoidance behaviors as a way of making certain that they don't have to come to terms with themselves and their needs. In many ways this is the best defense that they can mobilize against the feelings of hopelessness that they harbor, fearful that their Hidden Passions may never be fulfilled.

The Workaholic
When More Is Less

Work is simply one of the more acceptable (socially reinforced) addictions to which a woman can adhere in order to avoid dealing directly with her own needs and desires. Of course, not everyone who works has an addictive type of personality. The condition of workaholism is related far more to an excessive need to work, not to a monetary need, and almost always to the exclusion of any other activity in one's life. The Successful Woman who becomes a workaholic can be readily identified at the office. She is the one who is not only the executive in charge of the unit; she also acts as the secretary, the copier, and the support staff. She is a one-person office. She appears completely self-reliant, but she is headed for a major emotional and physical burndown (i.e., headaches, ulcers, increased irritability).

Evelyn is a twenty-nine-year-old child psychiatrist who works ten to twelve hours a day, frequently six days a week. Like all dedicated physicians she easily rationalizes why she has to work so hard and so long. Only two years out of her pediatric residency, and on her way to being "board certified" (a process that requires extensive preparation), she views her long hours as a necessary extension of her training program. She jokingly admitted during one therapy session, "I'm working a lot harder now than I was when I was in the hospital." Although said in jest, the truth was not too far. On her own in private practice, she felt that she had to work that hard in order to generate enough of an income to offset any potential emergency. Admittedly, part of her anxiety was "normal" and consistent with the behavior of anyone starting off a new business. However, when asked about the possibility of bringing a partner into the practice, she immediately responded defensively, "I can handle it. No one has to carry me along." When asked what that statement meant, she replied that she didn't want to appear weak and helpless, two adjectives that her father had used to describe her as she grew up. So she wanted to prove to her father that she was able to be independent just like her older brother, who, not surprisingly, had gone into pediatric oncology (tumors in young children). She had a good sense of humor and was able to deride herself as a complete product of sibling rivalry. She was "Larry's baby sister," and she was intent on showing Larry and her father that she didn't need their help. Not an unusual story.

Her patients enjoy working with her. They find her unusually empathetic. She sees forty hours of patients, teaches at the medical school, and does research on the psychological dynamics of the handicapped. Impressive? It makes me feel lazy and guilty. Why did she need me, if she's so self-sufficient and marvelous? Evelyn came to see me because she was feeling lonely. In the past she had gone on numerous dates, arranged by a church group to which she had belonged. But nothing much came of it. Recently she hadn't been attending the group or going out. She knew that something was wrong. In her usual offhanded, humorous fashion, she implored me to look into her eyes and tell her what I saw.

What I saw were the reflections of an isolated existence that she had created in order to protect herself from rejection. She would withdraw behind her intellectual defenses—sublimation, rationalization, humor, and compulsiveness. Working in her profession long and hard enough, she might have been able to totally obliterate the pain of feeling lonely. But by dealing directly with the pain in therapy, we were able to examine it, and I was able to teach her how to place it into perspective. After a few months, she hired a male social worker who helped her out. From that point onward, she stopped talking about herself as "Larry's baby sister."

Workaholics often have serious problems at work because they are unable to delegate their tasks. They try to do it all by themselves. But they miss deadlines and often are unable to set limits on their own time commitments. They become a slave to their job, and a slave to their fears. And, most frighteningly, their idealized self-image never gives them a respite: *more is not enough.*

The Sexaholic:
Separating Sex from . . . Everything Else

Bonnie was a forty-seven-year-old twice-divorced mother of a pre-adolescent daughter. She came to see me because she was unable to establish a meaningful relationship with a man, despite the fact that she pridefully admitted to having slept around *"beaucoup"* (her word). Her first marriage had been a complete disappointment. She felt sexually unfulfilled and entered into a series of *"liaisons dangereuses"* (again, her words). Eventually, as expected, her husband discovered her in bed with a lover and divorced her. A child was born out of wedlock and she decided to commit herself to becoming an exemplary mother. Bereft of any support, she went to work as a "gal Friday" in a manufacturing company, eventually married the boss, and took over the marketing division. The marriage dissolved in less than one year because of her infidelity. Now she was out both a husband and a job. But because of her excellent reputation as a marketer, she was able to find another job with a major competitor. She vowed never to mix pleasure and business again but decided to pursue both her professional and personal life with a vengeance. She was quickly promoted to vice president for marketing, while at the same time dating a "steady stream" (her words again!) of men, none of whom was able to relate to her on more than a sexual basis. She wanted more. But asked what she wanted, she replied, "I wanted a six-figure salary. I've made that. And now I want a man to whom I can come home and feel sexy and warm during the night and feel assured in the morning that he won't leave my bed. I'm tired of slam-bam-thank-you-ma'am."

In exploring her feelings about dating, Bonnie was confused. On the one hand she described herself as sexually liberated. On the other hand, the more liberated she became the more sad, lonely, and desperate she felt after sex. Instead of curbing her sexual appetites, the one-night stands made her want more. The irony was that she wanted an emotional commitment but felt that one of the ways men would feel comfortable with her was through sex first and "talking intimacy stuff" later. I asked her what she thought would happen if she reversed the order. That is, develop a relationship, then try to form some intimacy, and then have sex. Her response was to thank me and terminate therapy. Like the other men in her life, I, too, was simply a "one-night stand."

Not one of my great triumphs! But Bonnie's situation illustrates an important point. Even a professionally successful woman can be blindsided by her own vulnerabilities and continuously play out patterns of behavior that exacerbate her emotional needs. Because of low self-esteem and a strong yearning for emotional relatedness, Bonnie placed herself in a relationship that first stressed the importance of sex and then only lightly touched on emotions and intellect. In short, she was attracting the type of shallow men who were physically and emotionally disappointing because unconsciously *she* identified with being intellectually, emotionally, and spiritually hollow. Instead of trying to explore what she wanted and who she was, Bonnie took the quick way out—burning the candle at both work and play—hoping that the end result would be a man of compassion and intimacy. She used sex as a way of defending herself against her low self-esteem. A sure formula for disaster.

Alcoholism and Overeating: Drink, Eat, and Be Not Merry

Of all the avoidance behaviors (that is, avoidance of dealing directly with one's own needs) the most perfidious and difficult to treat is alcoholism. At least for me! Unlike Alcoholics Anonymous I haven't been as fortunate to claim their astounding cure rate of over 70 percent. My efforts in dealing with women alcoholics have been, at best, mixed. Some I have helped. Some I have not. But I hope I did nothing to make their already existing condition worse. Part of the problem, I suspect, is that the Successful Woman has a particularly difficult time accepting the fact that she may be an alcoholic. For her, the admission conjures up images of skid-row bums. Defensively, she retorts that I wouldn't make the same diagnosis of alcoholism in a male corporate executive who drinks a martini at lunch. My answer is always the same—that alcoholism, as I define it, is not dependent on the number of drinks but on the individual's need to take a drink.

Rosalynne was a fifty-three-year-old attractive career woman stationed overseas with a major New York City bank. She was a whiz at financial arbitrage (buying and selling currencies—a profession usually associated with men half her age). Her life was as she had wanted it to be—neat, predictable, orderly. But as one might expect, without any passion! She was a woman who had at different points in her life experienced a series of intense relationships, all of which she cherished as a distant memory. Although she wasn't actively seeking to rekindle that lost emotion, she was nevertheless trying to numb herself to the daily, almost dull routine of a responsible bank executive who found herself increasingly alone as she grew older. She, her cat, and her nightly glass of brandy fit into a neat pattern of a noneventful existence. From time to time, if the date were attractive, she would avail herself of his sexual advances. More often than not, her performance was wanting or her expectations were unrealistic. It was her habit to drink several glasses of champagne to prepare herself to be relaxed and sexually responsive. When I informed her that liquor had the exact opposite effect, she became angry. She felt like storming out of my office. But, with a twinkle in her eye, she remained seated and smugly announced that she didn't want me to think that I had the better of her. If she didn't confront the problem "like a man" (those were her exact words), she would never be able to lick it. Then she paused and added, *sotto voce*, "If indeed I have a problem." For a while she played along with me (or I should state, more correctly, that she played me along) by renouncing all drinking and repeating the catechism that alcohol was bad for her physical and mental health. She even pointed out to me what I had so self-righteously pointed out to her, that alcohol literally destroys the neurons in the brain. Evil stuff, she re-affirmed. But as one might expect, the conversion was neither genuine nor convincing. On her first date with a very "sexy number," she decided that she could afford a period of abstinence from her absti-nence and enjoy the evening without any feelings of guilt or inhibition. By her own admission, the evening was a "mild disaster" earmarked by a continuous struggle for control as to who would do what to whom. Then, when he had satisfied himself, she still felt unsatisfied, drank more, and became increasingly angry. When I asked her whether she was angry with *him*, she looked at me as if I totally missed the point of everything she had said. "Of course," she replied.

Rosalynne never came to terms with herself as a woman. Nor did she deal with an addictive problem that forced her to be dependent on both the bottle and on the kindness of strangers. She refused to attend Alcoholics Anonymous or a medical detoxification program, assuring me with full conviction that if she had a problem (of which she was still not convinced), it was certainly under control. She at-tended a few more sessions, left therapy, and also moved on to an-other job.

In treating the Successful Woman, I have found that alcoholism and eating disorders frequently go together. Drinking and eating excessively usually represent a problem of lack of nurturance and caring. Literally, the Successful Woman has not been sufficiently or properly cared for. There follows a strong oral hunger that has to be satiated. But what makes the problem particularly insidious is that the more she eats or drinks, the more she feels she has to eat or drink because the more she feels deprived and alone. By eating and drinking excessively the Successful Woman is avoiding the pain of loneliness and her own inability to confront herself directly and ask, "What am I feeling?" and "Why am I feeling that way?" From those two simple questions, a series of answers might spew forth that might one day help her feel complete and connected. She might discover that what is missing in her life is a slight modification of her career goals, away from achievement and self-aggrandizement to one of self-actualization. Or she may discover that she no longer fulfills the demands of her profession; and, therefore, must look within herself to uncover the Hidden Passion for a new career or a new life-style.

The sense of feeling complete and connected is related less to the final choice or outcome and more to the process of deciding to make that choice. The willingness to care about oneself and the desire for change will be the final arbiters for wanting to feel complete.

CHAPTER 3

Warning Signs: How to Recognize That Something Is Wrong

Hidden Passions are by definition difficult to find, evaluate, and liberate. It is a taxing process to unmask the frenzy of activity or complacency that have been put in place by the Successful Woman in order to cover over her real problems. It is an axiom of emotional bookkeeping that whatever is hidden on one side of the emotional ledger is acted out on the other side. What do I mean? Often the presenting complaint I hear may not be one of feeling dissatisfied with one's existence; it may be a problem which in itself seems to signify little other than a transient disturbance. There are certain behaviors and emotions that can be counted on to turn one's attention away from the main problem. For example, when a Successful Woman says that she is tired or upset, it can be readily explained away by her hectic schedule; it would be abnormal if she didn't get tired or upset . . . periodically. Yet many women (not only Successful Women) hide their Hidden Passions behind such an utterance. Please don't assume that I judge every woman who speaks of fatigue or discontent as a disguised proclamation of her dissatisfaction with life. That's not it at all! But I have found that there is a collection of feelings—fatigue, upset, boredom; feeling used or abused; jealous; envious; trapped; vulnerable; anxious; in a rut—that are warning signs that indicate something is occurring in addition to the immediate problem.

This concept of Hidden Passions is admittedly fraught with danger. One can either overread it or underread it. And so I have sought some guidance from the psychiatric literature that I would like to share with you.[1]

FEELING UPSET

Joan, a forty-eight-year-old married schoolteacher with two boys, found herself increasingly "upset over trivial matters." Neither Jonathan nor Matthew, her nine- and eleven-year-old boys, could do anything right. Their homework wasn't neatly prepared. They were increasingly disrespectful (so she thought) to her, and their father, a computer software salesman who traveled much of the time. Joan found solace from the increasing demands of her work, which included supervising a gifted children's program, by going out in the evening with friends whenever she had the chance.

Joan came to see me with a particular problem: she was unable to focus on preparing her lessons. The more she tried to concentrate, the more upset she became. In fact, she admitted, lots of ordinary things seemed to upset her. She frequently found herself spending time in the bathroom, gazing at herself in the mirror, wondering what had become of her young and carefree self. Very little had ever disturbed her. Now, any minor inconvenience seemed to "put her off" into activities marked by delays and distractions. It took her twice as long to do everything—dishes, laundry, grocery shopping, and preparing her teaching lessons.

When she first came to my office she quickly tried to establish both the ground rules of therapy and her own diagnosis. She insisted that she was not depressed. And, therefore, she would not require any "emotional boosters" (what she meant, of course, was antidepressant drugs). I asked her why she was so certain. She lowered her head and somberly replied, "I know. My mother was hospitalized for severe midlife depression."

"How is she?"

"She committed suicide."

Well, now I understood what I was up against. I was confronting a strong family history of depression, which she delineated for me without any hesitation. She then ticked off a list of her own clinical symptoms that would have clinched any psychiatrist's diagnosis of depression: weight loss, insomnia, feelings of hopelessness, helplessness. Yet what she thought she was describing was no more than an "unsettling feeling."

One day she opened up a diary that she always brought with her to therapy (a practice I often encourage, since a patient is not always able to express or recall all the feelings she might have had at a particular point in time) and read descriptions that she felt captured her sense of uneasiness. I elaborate on this because the feeling itself is so general, so widely recognized and accepted; and yet, at the same time, so incredibly difficult to elucidate. She began to read somewhat hesitantly, but certain of the point that she wanted to make:

> My daily routines are filled with anxiety and uncertainty, as if something terrible were to transpire. Something of major significance. Not cataclysmic, but significant. I can feel myself feeling upset as I move around the house, rearranging the boys' clothing or remaking their beds. And while I talk to them, I find myself interrupting the conversation with a need to comb their hair or press my hand against their shoulders. I feel uncertain about the purpose of my day. I find myself making nonsensical gestures in the middle of my sentences, which while doing so I consider them inappropriate. I hope I'm not schizophrenic. I doubt it. I should check with Dr. Pieczenik. I am very upset! But at whom? I think I know one answer. I am upset with me. But I don't know why.

Feeling upset is not the same as feeling depressed, sad, injured, angry. It is not an analogue of another emotion. Rather, it is a warning signal to the patient that she (or he) is particularly sensitive to whatever irritants are provoking them.[2] The emotion of feeling upset is also a signal to those around to tread lightly—to make certain that whatever demands or expectations are made, they are less than usual. For the purpose of understanding Joan and any other Successful Woman, feeling upset connotes a potentially combustible situation that arises from within oneself, particularly around the issues of self-esteem, self-definition, and the requisite entitlements. Feeling upset frequently means that some of the control mechanisms we use on a daily basis are not working.[3]

After several intense and heated sessions (the kind I like), Joan admitted that she had been brooding about several crucial decisions in her life: whether to divorce her husband, whether to start another career (because she found teaching emotionally debilitating), and what to do with her sons if she were to make any decisions that entailed a life change.

I asked her what she wanted most for herself. She was startled by the question: "I don't know. That's why I'm here."

FEELING TIRED

I categorize "tiredness" as a warning sign because in its chronic form it leads to the most painful of all psychological feelings—depression. In and of itself, feeling tired consistently affords us a premonition that something is wrong. And if we want that underlying condition to disappear, we must do something about it. It is in this quality of foreboding (perhaps a little too strong) or foretelling that I am most interested. Because often what appears on the surface to be a transitory physical condition, may be the harbinger of a downward spiral of change. Several strains of emotions weave through the complex fibers of so simple a statement as "I am tired."

To begin with, "feeling tired" has very little to do with physical fatigue. For example, when we are physically exhausted after a game of tennis, we rarely say that we are tired. Instead, we make some dramatic statement such as "I've had it!" or "I'm finished." Now, don't laugh or jump on me. It is true that one can be tired after a game of tennis, or even tired of playing the game. But in many instances feeling tired is a definite danger signal for the Successful Woman because it portends a sense of futility and exasperation with the present life situation.[4]

Paula, a thirty-six-year-old social worker and happily married mother of two children, came to see me about supervising her treatment of several difficult patients. Examining her cases, I noticed that each of the women she was treating was having a difficult time coming to terms with the routine demands of her life. Each wanted something more meaningful, something more intense in her life. I asked Paula whether there were any countertransference issues with which she could identify. She quickly, almost too quickly, assured me that she could find no issue that would hamper her progress as a therapist. I then asked her how she viewed the entire issue of women and change—whether it was their career, their husbands, their family, their life-styles. Paula said absolutely nothing. In fact, it would be fair to say that her silence was deafening. She simply went on discussing the next issue which, paradoxically, had to do with problems of termination and mourning. (No change is possible without first mourning the loss of something or someone in the past. One must give up part of one's past in order to proceed on to one's future. This may sound like old Confucius' advice; but, it, nevertheless, possesses the rudiments of psychic truth). Not surprisingly, Paula had as much trouble discussing the issues of termination (bearing sadness and loss while remembering the past) as she did talking about the whole concept of change. After several supervisory sessions, we decided together that Paula was, in fact, having serious problems treating these women "in transition" (as I called them) because she was in the process of dealing with personal and professional problems of her own.

One day I asked her what she thought about her patient process notes and her ongoing supervision with me. She smiled politely, and replied that "it was okay."

" 'Okay'?"

"No, better than okay."

"How much better?" (The purpose of this question was not to give me reassurance.)

"It's good. Really good."

"You don't sound as if you mean it."

"But I do. I think I'm getting a lot out of supervision."

"Like what?"

She lowered her writing pad and looked at me with a combination of incredulity, disappointment, and anger.

"What do you want me to say?"

"Only what you want to say. I just want you to tell me what feelings or thoughts you have." (This was one of the few times that even I realized how shrinklike I sounded.) She and I stared at each other for what seemed minutes. Clearly, there was some unresolved problem.

"Is this what you expect from your own clients?"

She looked at me and then at the door. And then she broke into a nervous laugh that ended in her burying her head in her hands. "I'm tired. Really tired. I'm tired of my job, my friends, and my family." This was the beginning of our turning point.

"Since you're so tired, what would you like to do about it?"

"I'm just tired. I just want to get through the daily grind, one day at a time. That's all."

"It sounds very ambitious."

"You're making fun of me."

"No. I think you're making fun of yourself."

"What do you mean?"

"By not taking your complaints seriously and doing something about them, you are making fun of yourself."

She tried desperately to hold back the tears.

"I'm feeling tired," Paula reiterated.

"What exactly is making you tired?"

"It's physical. But only in part. But I am really tired—of my work, my family." She explained that she had wanted to leave her husband some time ago. She had been feeling emotionally unfulfilled for years. Certainly she was lucky to be blessed with a good job, an absent but caring husband; and two obstreperous but wonderful boys. So she felt guilty about not feeling good about her life. She had been brought up to care for the needs and wants of others. Her mother now took care of Paula's bedridden father. Whereas her mother never complained overtly, Paula would always sense a feeling of helplessness and hopelessness, whenever her mother commented on how tired she felt after a day as a public health nurse at a clinic. Paula learned to associate that statement of tiredness with a feeling of resignation and futility. Her mother would often say that since there was very little that she could do to change her life, what was the point of complaining? Paula had acquired a similar attitude.

After working together for several sessions, we were able to focus on the one question she had not been able to answer in the beginning . . . "What do you want for yourself?"

As we explored that particular question, we uncovered an interesting insight. For a long time, Paula had been afraid to admit to herself that she felt tired because she automatically equated that statement with depression. In closer examination of her life and feelings, we (and I genuinely mean *we* since it was very much a collaborative effort) uncovered the fact that her feeling of depression was associated with the aura of helplessness and hopelessness that Paula had always detected in her mother. But that was not what Paula had been feeling. She wanted change! She did not want to give up or stagnate or withdraw. For her, there was a real sense of hope and potential. She wasn't certain how to bring about change—either in her career or personal life—but the need for a change in her life was of paramount consideration.

In a clinical depression, the individual's prevalent sense is one of confinement, of being held hostage to a situation she or he cannot change. In contrast, feeling tired denotes a physical debility while sparing a psychological viability. That is, at the expense of appearing physically impaired (that's a bit strong, but you get the idea), we are willing to sacrifice our psychological viability and potential for change by feeling tired rather than feeling depressed. Depression denotes the absence of a future. Feeling tired expresses the hidden hope for change.[5]

But, not all cases of feeling tired or emotionally unfulfilled result in the wife leaving the husband. As a matter of fact, Michele, the forty-nine-year-old mother of two grown children, the vice-president of personnel for a thirty-five-million-dollar corporation, and the wife of a senior diplomat, decided that she was no longer feeling fulfilled at her job. She came to see me about the possibility of changing her career, although she was not certain how she would do it or the direction in which this life change might take her. She was rightfully concerned that she might "throw the baby out with the bath water." She was afraid that in the process of changing herself (her goals, attitudes, and values), she might place herself in a situation where he no longer was a part of her life. When I asked her whether I should include her husband in some of the therapy sessions, particularly the ones related to mourning the past, she hesitated for only a brief second and then quickly responded that without his presence in the room to cheer her on, this life change would not be as significant or as much fun.

FEELING BORED

More than any other single emotion, boredom dominates the intellectual patina of the twentieth century. At its core, boredom is an emotion that connotes an absence of emotion or an inability to feel an emotion, let alone feel that emotion intensely. Boredom has become the shibboleth of the modern teenager cruising aimlessly through the streets. Boredom has acquired a status of intellectual chic, where angst and boredom are the twin repositories of deep insight.

Dr. Ralph Greenspan, a prominent American psychiatrist, studied the problems of boredom and categorized it as follows: "A state of dissatisfaction and a disinclination to action; a state of longing and an inability to designate what is longed for; a sense of emptiness; a passive expectant attitude with the hope that the external world will supply the satisfaction; a distorted sense of time in which time seems to stand still."[6]

For the Successful Woman, life is a struggle for survival.[7] It is not relevant that she may be driving a BMW or that she summers on Martha's Vineyard. What is most relevant to her perception of her work world is that there is very little margin for error. In periods of imagined or real threats to survival, she has little time for existential anxiety or boredom. The Successful Woman's continuous search for more and better leaves very little room for self-reflection or self-analysis. When she does obtain that moment, whether by choice or default, she finds she has a problem on her hands! Left without the emotions of self-fulfillment, the Successful Woman is susceptible to one of the most intolerable of all emotions—boredom. Not so ironically, like feeling tired, boredom is one of those danger signals that connote an imperative for change.[8]

Gustave Flaubert's *Madame Bovary* was a brilliant portrait of a bored physician's wife cast into the then-accepted dependent role of the middle-class lady-in-waiting. Waiting for life to happen. Waiting for excitement to arise. Waiting, of course, for Prince Charming to sweep her off her feet. In short, a literary and antique version of the Cinderella complex. But the present concept of boredom is far more complicated and sophisticated. The Successful Woman has difficulty verbalizing it. I recall an attractive corporate executive who told me that she was bored with her job, which entailed an extensive amount of traveling and dining out. In reality, she wasn't bored. She was actually exhausted from having to travel as much as she did, and she wanted a change of pace.

The case of Ilene, a twenty-eight-year-old college graduate, happily married to a successful auto mechanic, and content mother of two children, was more clear. Ilene worked part time in a department store analyzing credit applications, and she felt bored with her life. Sex with her husband was good, but not frequent. Taking care of her children was important. But she felt unfulfilled. She smiled during the day, but cried silently at night. There was a sense of emptiness within her that no amount of activity, reassurance, or involvement with her family could alleviate. What was needed was a change in *her* life and life-style. A disruption, if you will, from the constancy of contentment. A change that would engage her in something greater than herself or her family.

For Ilene, the change in her life came from a hobby that allowed her to transform monotony into moments of self-selected enjoyment. After repeated invitations by friends to go sailing, the idea of being on the open waters, tacking the sails (if that's the correct expression) and turning the wheel, suddenly seemed to contain all the elements of excitement, uncertainty, and danger that were missing from her life. A concentrated commitment to sailing was all that was required to make Ilene feel fulfilled and complete.

There are several reasons why so simple a solution as sailing could ameliorate as complicated a problem as boredom. For one, sailing afforded her a clear opportunity to master a task totally different from anything else she was doing. She had to be neither nurturant nor caring. She was engaged in an activity that addressed her principle need—as she defined it—to reach out to an activity larger than herself. The open skies and seas afforded her the transcendental sense of herself that she wanted from time to time. She had found the right medicine, in the right dose. She did not abandon her family and job for a life on the high seas. She did, however, entertain thoughts of supplementing her income by offering sailing excursions on the Chesapeake Bay. In any case, she terminated therapy after a brief six months and thanked me profusely.

Clearly, not all situations resolve themselves as simply. But the point is that boredom is a defense against incompleteness, and a physical activity can be a healthy defense against boredom. For Ilene, liberation from her own preoccupation was the essential element that reaffirmed the importance and pleasure of life. Sailing became an affirmation of her reinvolvement with life (as she defined it). Boredom is not only a psychological phenomena, but a sociological one as well. Terms such as *alienation* and *anomie* have been the ways political scientists and sociologists have described the problems arising from a mechanistic world that deprives us of feeling fulfilled. No matter how dramatic or worthwhile the professional activity, if continuously repeated on a daily basis, boredom and eventually a feeling of worthlessness set in. It is a phenomenon close to what I would consider inevitable.

Dr. James, a fifty-four-year-old orthopedic surgeon (and there are not many women orthopedic surgeons), came to see me about "feeling disgusted" with her marriage. Careful examination of both her marriage and her feelings toward her husband, however, revealed that after twenty-two years of marriage she was still very much in love with him, an English teacher who had helped her through medical school, internship, and some difficult years of residency. Although her children had not met up to her unrealistic expectations, she still enjoyed the parental role. So what was the problem? I watched her in silence as we approached the last few minutes of what I suspected might be our last therapy session if I didn't produce a rabbit out of the proverbial hat.

"You seem distracted," I noted.

"No, not at all. I'm thinking about what it would be like to be a psychiatrist."

"What do you mean?"

"Well, it must be fascinating to listen to problems of so many different people. I often wonder what it would be like to work with the soul of a person, rather than replace his hips. It's always the same—either it's a degenerative bone process, or a torn ligament, or fluid. How many times can I do the same thing?"

"Psychiatry has its repetitions as well."

"But not like surgery. There's nothing creative about what I do. I cut and sew. You listen, interpret, hopefully arrive at the correct solution. It's far more creative."

"Have you ever fantasized about being a psychiatrist?"

"No," she shot back. Then she paused and broke into a smile. "Yes. As a matter of fact, I spend a good part of my day fantasizing what it would be like if I had another husband, another life-style, another job."

"What stops you from changing what you're doing?"

"My husband is a high-school teacher who absolutely loves his work. But without my income, he can't do what he wants, nor can the children go to private school."

"So everyone in the family has the right to be happy but you."

"What do you mean?"

"You don't seem happy in what you're doing. You spend most of your time fantasizing about the things you might or could be." Then I paused. "What do *you* want?"

"I don't want to simply fantasize. I want to live out my fantasies."

"So why don't you do it?"

Over a two-year period I helped Dr. James assess her professional and emotional objectives, and then prepared her to take the necessary risks that would allow her a career change. Five years later she became a board-certified psychiatrist and claimed that her need to fantasize had diminished remarkably.

Because of her high degree of specialization, Dr. James had become victim to boredom. But no amount of fantasy could substitute for the underlying feelings of discontent and frustration she felt in her work world. Whether a plumber or surgeon, the problem of boredom seems to increase as specialization increases and creativity decreases. No matter how glamorous the profession. There is no natural way I know of avoiding it—believe me, I've tried. Boredom is the respite that allows life to be exciting. Without it, I am convinced that even an interesting life is not possible. But when it predominates, then there is a serious problem.

JEALOUSY AND ENVY

One of my best friends, a fellow psychiatrist with whom I trained at Harvard, warned me against the glow of success with the following admonition: "Beware the twin-headed monster: jealousy and envy." Over the last twenty years, I have found those words to be prophetic. Unlike anxiety, competition, and even boredom, envy and jealousy do not have strong redeeming features. They do not motivate us to obtain more. They do not alert us to impending dangers. These are emotions that feed upon themselves, gnawing at the fibers of health, until the only residue left is venom and bitterness.

Jealousy

Underlying the emotion of jealousy is a hidden fear that there is a limited supply of whatever is desired—money, power, glamour, prestige. And the most important commodity of all for the Successful Woman—success.[9] In the workplace, the jealous Successful Woman desires another person's position, prestige, competence, or earning power. No different from men. But I've encountered an inordinate amount of jealousy among Successful Women, indicating to me that there are major problems in their self-esteem and in their ability to feel complete. Whatever other passions (the more constructive ones —love, creativity, sense of vitality) are hidden, they are often hidden quite deeply in these women. And the presence of sustained jealousy indicates that there is serious trouble.

A few months ago a beautiful woman in her mid-forties, Mary, walked (no, better yet, sauntered) into my office. She was striking— tall, svelte, with a mane of black hair through which she nervously ran her long, tapered fingers. She exuded a quiet sensuousness. And she knew it! I must admit to a mild infatuation. I would have assumed that she would have been the object of every woman's jealousy. Yet she came to me because she couldn't explain her sudden outbreaks of jealousy toward other women. I was completely befuddled. How could this attractive, Successful Woman be so jealous of other women? From what she initially told me, she had everything. She had recently become a partner in a prestigious law firm and claimed she was extremely happy at her work. She was involved in international law and civil arbitration. On occasion she would fly to The Hague and argue before the World Court. More often than not she was involved in transnational-corporation disputes over commercial interests. She had two teenage girls who were doing exceedingly well in an exclusive private school. She was married to a neurologist who had an active, busy practice. She went out of her way to assure me that her marriage was fine. But when asked how often she had sex, she remained silent. She denied any desire to leave her husband; but then she admitted that on occasion she had thoughts of leaving him because he was boring. When I asked what made him boring, she flared her nostrils and gave me a dirty look, as if I should have known better. By her own admission, he was a very active man who loved to play tennis, entertain friends, and attend gourmet cooking classes. Hardly boring! And yet she claimed that he was indeed boring. When I asked her what her hobbies or outside activities were, she replied abruptly, almost acerbically, "living." When asked to expand upon that, she repeated herself, but this time more emphatically, "living." And, here, my dear readers, lay the clue to the mystery. After extensive questioning, she did admit to resenting the fact that her boss, a slightly older woman, was earning significantly more money and working fewer hours. In pursuing the matter further, she admitted that her "boss" was a senior partner in the firm and a "rainmaker," someone who brought in the large corporate accounts. "It is patently unfair," my client said.

"Why?" I asked, undaunted. I had treated enough lawyers to know that the "rainmakers" were an invaluable part of the firm. Without them there was no "rain" or business. And for the intangible measure of their services, they received a certain undefined percentage of the business they brought in.

"Women can be very unfair. They use their guile and sexuality to elicit favors and business, while men have to slug it out."

I bit my tongue to contain my surprise. I responded in my smooth, mellifluous "shrink" voice, "What do you mean?"

"I mean they often take what is not theirs. What does not rightfully belong to them."

"Do you mean, like men?"

"Yes. Like men."

"Like your lover who won't leave his wife?"

This time it was her turn to be dumbfounded. "How did you know?"

"It's not relevant how I know. It's far more important to try to understand why you are here and what I can do to help you out."

She suddenly became very sullen and withdrawn.

"What's the matter?" I asked.

"Nothing."

At that moment, she looked like a spoiled child who was throwing an emotional temper tantrum.

"How did you know about my lover?"

Her question showed her jealously of my ability to formulate an insight about her without her having admitted to an adulterous relationship.

"I'm an intelligent guesser."

"Maybe I'm not as difficult to understand as I think."

"No, no, I can assure you that you are. That's your way of manipulating people, by keeping them off guard and at a distance. When you mentioned that 'living' was your hobby, but wouldn't answer my question about your sexual relations with your husband, I put two and two together. That makes for a lover. Your intense feelings about your boss are displaced from some other source—another bothersome female. Who's more annoying than the wife of a lover."

"He won't leave her. He claims he can't leave his son because he is too young. Well, what does he think I have? I have two little girls."

"Are you upset because he won't leave his wife, or are you upset because you can't have what she has—him?"

Mary became calm. I talked about jealousy and how normal a part it is of our lives. There could not be a world without jealousy. It was part of a competitive world. I pointed out to her that she had a strong competitive nature, which probably arose from the fact that her oldest and only brother invariably forced her into a position of fending for herself, whether it was for the attention of her striking, domineering mother, or the love of her aloof, distant father. We went on to examine how throughout her life she maintained that competitive edge in order to ensure her survival (so she thought) at the expense of sacrificing her dependency and nurturing needs. In the beginning she resisted the notion that she could be competitive with her husband, measuring her success (number of billable hours) against his accomplishments (total number of patients seen per week). As a result, she no longer perceived him as either a romantic partner or a supportive husband. Instead, he was a "rival" with whom she had to contend, albeit a friendly one. She tolerated him because of the children. But her jealousy of his professional success was costing her marriage and the expression of her passions. She admitted, somewhat reluctantly, that she still found her husband physically attractive, and that her present lover both physically and emotionally resembled her husband. She also acknowledged that she found herself making increasingly more snide comments about her boss. Needless to say, the jealousy she felt toward her lover's wife was debilitating. In short, Mary was a possessed woman—filled with a desire to have those things and people she could not have. The therapy sessions uncovered that she continuously placed herself in a triangular relationship to recapitulate the oedipal struggles wherein she would compete with her father for the love of her mother. Later on she had to compete with her older brother (sibling rivalry) for the love of her mother. Some readers might be surprised that in her particular situation, she was not struggling for the love and affection of her father, which would have been the normal course of events. Because her mother was so domineering, so powerful, so central, *she* was, in fact, both the source of creativity and the psychological irritant for Mary.

The work of therapy consisted of first allowing her to recognize how much her personal and professional life was dominated by competition and jealousy. Then I gently demonstrated to her how those two emotions were evident in her therapeutic relationship with me. Once she was able to laugh at the moments when she would try to compete with me about interpretations regarding her need to interpret her behavior before I did, we were able to analyze the nature of jealousy itself and how it had the potential to destroy many good qualities (passion for creativity, fulfillment, sense of being alive, vitality) which were submerged for fear she might become too vulnerable and, subsequently, too dependent.

Mary was ultimately fortunate. Her competitive and jealous feelings began to subside as she began to understand them. She started to have sex with her husband again and, not surprisingly, enjoyed it. She terminated with her lover, and, not long after, terminated with me. A few months later she sent me an article she had written for a law journal on the importance of understanding the human element in transnational law and thanked me for my professional assistance.

Envy

Envy is the evil extension of jealousy. Envy is far more pervasive than jealousy and far more invidious. Unlike jealousy, which can flourish only in the sunlight of human activities, envy lies dormant, to arise in the shadows of any mundane activity. Every aspect of our life could be filled with envy. We envy someone even though he or she may have absolutely no connection to us. We can envy an attitude. We can envy a possession. We can envy someone's existence. Envy is a divisive, lethal emotion that can devastate one's own life. And it is by its very nature seemingly illogical.

Just as competition and sibling rivalry are the core of jealousy, the feeling of personal deprivation lies at the center of envy. As one of my patients described it: "I not only feel deprived of money and power; I feel that some fate has denied me the ability to have what I want." It is not sufficient that a person feel deprived of something. It is crucial that he feels as if he has been denied the opportunity to acquire it.[10]

Marianne was a twice-divorced Hollywood producer whose preoccupations appeared to be, in retrospect, producing movies (of which she did only three in a period of fifteen years) and possessing whatever anyone else may have had. If another producer hinted at the possibility of acquiring a storyline or screenplay about a particular topic, Marianne would hire a writer to research a similar project. Unfortunately she was so busy trying to catch up with all the other producers in Hollywood that she was never able to do what was really required of a good producer—anticipating the trends, not following them.

When she came to see me she complained of extreme fatigue. She had been referred to me for stress management by an internist. She had been seeing the internist off and on for years, always beset by one or another chronic disease. Often she worked so hard to get a project off the ground that she became physically too ill to see it through. When I asked her why she was continuously in motion, she replied that it would be irresponsible to do anything less.

"What would happen if you reduced your activity level?"

She replied that she would be in a complete frenzy because she had nothing to do while everyone around her was developing projects.

"And if you stopped completely?"

Her face blanched. "It would be like death," she replied. "I would feel completely empty."

We began to explore this feeling of emptiness—how it had pervaded her entire childhood and life. Her mother was an alcoholic who spent most of her time away from home with lovers. Her father was an insecure, unsuccessful businessman who was always in a complete frenzy trying to make ends meet. When I tried to describe the similarity between her behavior and that of her father, she refused to recognize it. Instead of insights, she wanted quick, easy exercises to follow so that she could learn to relax when developing a movie project. I reassured her that I could teach her some desensitization techniques, but that there was no easy solution to her complicated problems, except to try to work as hard on herself as she had on her projects.

I should have know better. She was polite for the remainder of the session, thanked me for my advice, and, as we say in Hollywood, walked off the set. I subsequently heard from several other therapists that she had done the same thing to them.

Clearly, not all of my patients walk off the "set" (therapy) so brusquely. For the most part, I like to leave them (and you) with the thought or hope that if you can't accept what I have to say in total —don't! Just take those parts of what I have said or written and use them in any way that you believe is beneficial to you. If only to buy you some breathing space, I ask you to put down the book and try to reflect on those insights that you may have found to be partially useful to you. Remember, help can appear in different-shaped packages. Don't be particular! Take what you can from wherever!

The problem of uncovering and correcting pathological envy (I add the word *pathological* because we all feel a certain degree of envy) is that the feelings of deprivation and emptiness are literally projected outward, away from the Successful Woman onto everybody but herself for her own misfortunes or deprivations (either real or perceived).[11] Envious Successful Women, like Marianne, become fault-finders and grievance collectors who involve themselves and, indeed, re-create situations that reaffirm their feelings of deprivation and abuse. Eventually they become paranoid, always blaming others for their misfortunes. The envious Successful Woman becomes so engrossed in her own grievances that she isn't willing to entertain the fact that she may be responsible for her situation.

The envious Successful Woman finds satisfaction in only one thing—finding fault with other Successful Women. She has lost the grace of compassion, the gift of charity. In order for her to feel victorious and in control of her life, others must be deprived of their respective successes.

FEELING USED

As the Successful Woman becomes increasingly pressured in the course of business, she also feels increasingly vulnerable to abuse. As one high-powered executive of a Fortune 500 company explained to me, "The more I advance up the corporate ladder, the less important I feel as a person, and the more significant I become as an object to be used, manipulated, and taken advantage of." This disingenuous comment came on the trail of a litany of facts on how important work had become. Although she could tick off the costs she felt she had incurred in order to achieve her professional success—two divorces, absentee motherhood, two children living with her ex-husbands—she now found herself conflicted about what she really wanted. When asked specifically what she felt like when she was being "taken advantage of," she replied vehemently that she didn't like it.

"Why? Isn't that the recognized price for success—use and be used?"

"The least I could expect from my shrink was that he could understand what I was feeling." She was indignant.

"I'm trying to understand, but you seem to be fighting me rather than helping me."

"Help you? Ha! How can I help you? You're the doctor. I'm just a patient."

I pointed out that she was doing the same thing with me that she was accusing the system of—placing her in a position where she could be manipulated, dominated, or used. With a sense of relief she admitted that this was the same feeling she used to have with her father, who would first have to deprecate her worth before he would spend any time with her. How incompetent and stupid he made her feel before he helped her build her rabbit's cage. Afterward she would feel pleased that he had spent the hours with her alone and not with her brother. When we delved a little deeper into her feelings of being taken advantage of, she admitted that she was beginning to feel increasingly hurt, humiliated, angry, vulnerable, and threatened at work. She was thinking of changing her job; the one she liked so much. Perhaps changing her profession as a corporate finance officer. When I asked her what she wanted to do, she didn't know. She had never seriously thought about it, except for having always wanted to obtain an MBA (like her father's). Other than that, she had no other particular desires. Husbands were out. Being a mother didn't titillate her. What was left? For the first time in three months she looked frightened. Wasn't there anything she had wanted when she was younger? Something different? Something unusual? Something that had appealed to her heart and not her mind? She thought and then smiled. As a child she had loved to travel—bus, train, plane—anywhere and everywhere. When she was a teenager, she took off the year after she graduated from high school and went to Australia, and Papua, New Guinea. She blurted out the fact that she "wouldn't mind" doing something in the travel business.

"Like what?"

"I don't know—something where I can be directly involved with people and in a situation where I am in control so that no one can take advantage of me."

"Can you think of anything?"

"My own little travel agency. I'd like that." She paused and smiled. "I think I would!"

Within months of having quit her corporate job, and two months of intensive course work, she opened up her own travel agency—Advantage Travel—after the emotional issue that had brought her into therapy.

I use this case to illustrate what happened to one Successful Woman who came into my office to discuss an emotion that I would have suspected was de rigueur for the corporate jungle in which she lived. But despite the reality that being taken advantage of is part of the business world, it signaled to me that there was a deeper pool of discontent of which this particular emotion was only one part. Happily, because of her willingness to go into therapy she was able to use her discontent to mobilize in a healthy way certain Hidden Passions. Every emotion leads one way or another into the soul. It's simply a matter of which road you take.

ANXIETY

We have all experienced anxiety. We recognize its uncomfortable telltale signs of sweaty palms, a racing pulse, and a dry throat. The causes vary, as one might imagine. For the most part, anxiety serves as an alerting mechanism that helps us react to real or impending danger. In the life of the Successful Woman, there are certain psychological realities that can precipitate acute anxiety attacks and that have been well documented in the literature. Some of these insights I will pass on to you with the postscript that anxiety can often be used quite constructively to mobilize some of the other Hidden Passions.

One of the most common anxieties in the Successful Woman is the fear of success. Women's need to succeed can be seriously compromised by an unconscious competing dynamic called *the fear of success.* Anxiety is often the first sign that a Successful Woman may fear achievement. Ironic, isn't it?

Nena was a twenty-eight-year-old scientist who had been born, bred, and dedicated to the concept of achievement. Her father and mother were both college professors, and since early childhood she had been destined to achieve something great. One would have thought that after having attended Andover Academy, Harvard, and Cambridge University in England she would have been comfortable with the feelings associated with achieving a high goal. Although she was able to set her own personal goals (with some help from her somewhat intrusive parents), she found herself increasingly more anxious as she approached the attainment of any given goal. Why? In part, the answer goes back to some of the issues I mentioned earlier—the way women have been socialized to associate femininity with such traits as dependency, passivity, submissiveness, or learned helplessness. It was all right for a woman to appear sweet, tender, loving, and nurturing, as long as she didn't compromise a feminine image. But once she became aggressive, assertive, or independent, she was seen as somewhat masculine. Nena had often been accused of being a "ball-busting" scientist, while her male colleagues who manifested the same aggressive behavior were praised for their "forthright manner." For Nena, this conflict between feminine and masculine appearances created tension and stress that were manifested in backaches and tension headaches. She began to notice that whenever she came closer to the successful resolution of a project, she became extremely nervous, anxious, depressed, and unhappy. Not surprisingly, she would commit some major error that would throw the project into jeopardy. She wasn't sure of the reason for these "stupid mistakes" but realized that there was enough negative behavior that she needed to seek out professional help to break the pattern. What I uncovered in therapy was that despite the fact that both her parents were high-powered, hard-driving professionals, her mother would take her aside and confide in her that all those years of studying and working made her feel less feminine, less wanted as a woman. She confided to her daughter that she had always suspected that her husband had a mistress. Quite frankly, her mother added, she didn't blame him. If she had to do it all over again, she would have taken the more feminine route and not that of a hard-nosed scientist.

You can imagine Nena's reaction. She was, at best, confused. Here was her personal and professional role model giving her mixed messages—living the life of the hard-driving scientist while regretting the cost it incurred. No wonder Nena was anxious whenever she approached a moment of success. After several heated sessions, Nena was able to admit that what she feared most if she were to succeed in her projects was a feeling of rejection, abandonment. And a marked loss of femininity and sexual desirability.

Nena's fear of success is quite typical of the Successful Woman who exhibits a disproportionate amount of anxiety usually centered around issues related to performance, achievement, and success. Nena was able to work through her anxiety and fear by reality-testing the fact that as she successfully completed a project she didn't become less feminine or attractive. Eventually she met a man who reinforced her new self image as a compassionate, sexy woman. In time she completed several major experiments, became the director of her laboratory, and married.

Another reason for a Successful Woman's anxiety is her uncertainty about achievement. Unlike men, Successful Women are unable to evaluate their performance against others. Women, in general, have a *process orientation* while men have an *impact orientation*.[12] Women are more concerned with their internal standard of measurement than with comparing themselves against some rival or competitor. A Successful Woman measures her performance against herself. Against how well she *should* be doing. Not how well she is doing relative to Sally or Harry. If a Successful Woman fails she tends to blame herself. And if she succeeds, she attributes it to hard work and good luck. Men, on the other hand, tend to measure their achievements by their impact on the environment or by how much power they are able to amass as a result of their achievement. Men tend to see their success as resulting directly from their own ability. Their failure is attributed to the inherent difficulty of the task.

To make matters worse, the Successful Woman accentuates her failures and discounts her accomplishments. She diminishes her full impact even when she gets to a position of dominance. Critical remarks are often interpreted as a direct attack against her self-esteem. She may make the premature decision that she is "on the skids."

In conclusion, there are many reasons why a Successful Woman may feel anxiety or guilt. But the most common ones are those related to her obtaining success. Achievement for her means an inherent conflict between the feminine traits of dependency, nurturance, and caring and those newly acquired masculine traits of achievement, competition, and autonomy. Not so ironically, the Successful Woman fears her very raison d'être—success.

CHAPTER 4

Discovering the Different Types of Hidden Passions

Most people recognize passion as a rush of emotion. A high. An intense bodily sensation. The rush of adrenaline created by the moment or memory. When I speak of passion, however, I am really speaking of compelling, intense emotions that, when combined with the routine activities of daily life, make the Successful Woman feel whole, complete, and alive. Love. Desire. Exhilaration. As well as the less intense emotions. Feeling good about a sunny day. Feeling moved over a young daughter's first endeavors at ballet. Feeling tender walking in the rain with your husband. A moment's humor from a comedian's joke. You get the idea. Feelings. Intense feelings and sensations.

Passion can exist between two people. Passion can exist between an individual and a work of art. Passion can exist within ourselves through the creative process. I want to use passion as an emotion which empowers us to live life as it should be lived—to its fullest. The essential ingredient of my notion of passion is a positive one. A creative life force. A feeling that leads to a change, whether it is simply a change in sensibility or a more dramatic one like a change in lifestyle.

PASSION FOR LIVING

Let's start with the most basic passion, a passion for living,[1] which by definition must precede all other passions. Unlike depression, pain, masochism, and a dictionary filled with negative emotions, very little has been written in the fields of psychiatry or psychology about pleasure, passion, or joy of living. The psychiatric movement, which fifty years ago was really the psychoanalytic movement, emphasized the study of unconscious motives and purposes, ideas and thoughts, the interpretation of dreams, and the bestowal of insight. The conflict of ideas, impulses, and feelings were the underlying issue with respect to most problems. Feelings were viewed as simply a manifestation of those conflicts. Presently the concept of feelings is viewed as a positive manifestation of an ongoing life process. The most primordial passion is the passion for living. It is basic. It pervades everything we do. It is a feeling akin to the feeling one has when the doctor informs us that the spot on the lungs in the x-ray is not cancer. It is a feeling of lightness and joy, combined with a sense that you want to become more fully engaged with life in all its facets—from the physical to the intellectual and emotional. The essential ingredient of a passion for living is a positive, creative one.

Passion empowers you to live life with spontaneity and joy, bemused by the simplest element and challenged by the most complex. Defeat becomes simply another opportunity to try all over again—and the promise of tomorrow becomes as intoxicating as the achievements of the past.

Sally was a forty-year-old, twice-married, attractive woman who after ten extremely successful years at a large manufacturing corporation was in the process of being fired. When she entered my office she was trying desperately to ward off a severe depression by being busy—buying a home and adopting a baby. In the midst of all this activity she had been hospitalized for severe abdominal distress (ulcerative colitis, a gastrointestinal ailment due to stress) which gave her some relief from all her immediate problems. I told her that given her circumstances it would be abnormal if she weren't depressed. At which point she started to cry.

For nearly half the first session she cried, while at the same time reaffirming how grateful she was that she could at last relieve the tension that had been building up within her for so long. Was she having a nervous breakdown, she asked? I assured her that it was all right for her to experience sadness and hurt. We talked about her inability to prioritize her problems, which had led to a vicious cycle. As a result of her inability to decide which issues were most important to her she became more flooded with emotion, more out of control, and more desperate. Through therapy, she was able to identify those aspects of her life that were causing major problems: being overly self-reliant; an inability to accept her limitations; unwillingness to come to terms with the fact that she no longer wanted to work in a corporate structure; fear of change. Once she could see how much she had buried her life in process and busywork as a way of avoiding the pain of having to answer the question *What do I want?*, she was able to come to the realization that, indeed, her major priorities were not work, status, and power, but a return to life's simple pleasures: a walk in the woods; a new interesting date; and a job that allowed her to be her own master. She wanted to reengage life without illness or excuses. Soon after, the veil of despair disappeared and she began to see a semblance of hope and order. She felt "rejuvenated" (her word).

PHYSICAL PASSION

The most basic, and perhaps most primitive passion, is physical passion. It is exactly what the words state—a passion for the physical senses. If the Successful Woman does not have time to smell the roses, or walk in the grass, or notice a gurgling brook, then her life is too busy, too crowded with routine activity. Taking time out to enjoy the sensual pleasures of life—the smells, the sounds, the tastes—reaffirms the Successful Woman's physical presence in the world. It reassures her that she has not lost touch with her basic senses. That there is beyond us a physical reality of great import and beauty. It allows her to forget herself and, for even a brief moment, transcend her immediate limitations and concerns. It is the most immediate and simplest form of physical gratification.

Renee, a thirty-two-year-old systems analyst, used to jog three miles a day through the woods near her house and swim a half mile a day at a university pool, always making certain that she "felt the day." What she meant by that was that she wanted the smell of a flower, the feel of a wet field of grass, the cool aroma of pine trees, to sustain her through the day at the office. She came to see me when she realized that she was no longer in touch with these senses. Without realizing it, her entire life had become her computer terminal. Eventually the absence of tactile physical pleasure and her insight into how important it was for her, played a major catalyzing influence on her life. She left the desktop computer and the office behind her and joined a corporation that sold outdoor recreational equipment. This new job allowed her to spend the majority of her day "in the field." And she loved it! Her future plan was to develop her own company, vowing never to return to an office or computer again.

PASSION FOR DISCOVERY

When we take overseas vacations, most of us design it so that we can discover new and different situations. In part, it breaks the monotonous pattern of our regular life. In part, we are genuinely interested in losing ourselves in a situation so different from our own that we can, for a period of time, surpass our own limitations. To discover a new event, place, or idea calls for not only the heightening and exercise of our basic senses (the physical passion and the passion for living), but it invites our intellect and faculty for creativity to participate in a voyage of discovery.[2] Personally, this passion is the one with which I can most easily identify. In some ways, it is the passion to which I have (without sounding too dramatic) dedicated my life. Each day I sit down in front of an empty yellow pad and begin to write. Sometimes it's very difficult, laborious, and unproductive. Most often it is enriching. I am challenged to think, create, and write. To me, this is an essential part of my life.

Hillary was a fifty-year-old widow who was in a rut. Her husband, the founder of their fifty-million-dollar company, had died and left her with a complicated organization. As the new CEO, she had questioned all the old assumptions about how business should be done. When I saw her in therapy, a few years after starting, her business seemed to be running itself. But she, in turn, did not feel she was running her own life. Something was missing. Something was incomplete. She no longer felt challenged. She felt that she had lost her purpose in life. She felt aimless, uncertain. She didn't want to date or meet new men because one was just like another. There was nothing new to uncover. In part she was depressed. But in greater part she was frightened to risk the possibility of a new disappointment. Frightened to make the effort and discover that there might be nothing new after all.

Was all of her time and effort wasted, as she suggested? I told her that she had lost her passion for discovery—her old desire to see the world in a slightly different light. Not black. Not white. Simple chiaroscuro—a series of black-and-white shadings. It was well worth the effort. How did I know? she asked. Because my personal and professional experiences taught me to continuously challenge life, otherwise, life had a way of becoming boring and oppressive. Unless she tried, she wouldn't really know. She agreed to try a few small exercises (discussed in chapter 12) that would allow her to regain her confidence in uncovering new experiences as well as give her an opportunity to rekindle the smoldering embers of her Hidden Passion for discovery. I asked her to imagine those aspects of her life that she would like to have expanded. She had mentioned that she always liked politics and sailing. So I encouraged her through small, graded initiatives—starting with sailing lessons as well as organizing an informal fund-raising party—to engage herself more actively in those two activities.

Needless to say, there is a happy ending. She also found a new companion. He was a handsome, interesting, retired businessman who helped her rekindle her interest in politics, sailing, and not so surprisingly, expanding her business.

What makes the passion for discovery particularly unique is the fact that it broadens the Successful Woman's intellectual horizons. It liberates her from her sense of self and extends that self into new areas of endeavor. Like acting, the passion of discovery allows her to be someone else—in another time and place. The very basis of a passion for uncovering the new and different arises from our ability as infants to separate from the protective, nurturing environment of our mothers. As an infant she crawled away from her mother's arms to uncover the exact nature of the table leg. At a very young age, she began to question, evaluate, pioneer, and explore—poking, touching, probing, trying to make sense of where she was and where she had to go. These initial feelings were not lost as she became older and less prone to exploration. They simply were buried in a morass of caution and avoidance, awaiting the day they would be rekindled and used again to enjoy the world in a productive embrace. And truthfully, I have seen the greatest change in those women who were willing to probe, explore, and dare to enter into the unknown and *take a chance on themselves*. Not necessarily on the prescriptions of the system around them.

There is a prevalent misconception among many Successful Women and, I must admit, among many of my own colleagues, that as we grow older our ability to experience pleasure or even passion must attenuate. There are those who argue that it is intolerable for us to even think about carrying into our seventies the feelings and passions we experienced when we were in our twenties and thirties. I say, nonsense! Einstein lived to quite a ripe old age, all the time producing unique, brilliant scientific formulas and discoveries. He had retained the one essential ingredient—a childlike wonder to explore and discover, always asking the simplest and most basic of questions about his surrounding universe. Questions that you and I would have felt foolish to ask. What is time? What is speed?

Admittedly, very few of us are like Einstein, nor do we necessarily want to be like him. But we must highlight the importance of a passion that at best we take for granted.

PASSION FOR GROWTH

A passion very clearly related to the passion for discovery is a passion for growth and mastery. In some ways, we also encounter a paradox. The very essence of the Successful Woman has been her ability to master a body of knowledge, integrate it, and then use it effectively. For the Successful Woman, the concept of expanding through the acquisition and mastery of new information has usually been used to further her career goals. Many women are surprised when I suggest that it might be enlightening if they turned those very same skills and desires inward. To uncover their underlying desires and passions that would allow them to answer the three basic questions: What do I want? How do I get it? What will it cost me?

Georgette, a thirty-eight-year-old mother of three children and proprietor of a small retail store, came in to see me because her husband was having an affair. She didn't know what to do about it. Should she leave him? Should she confront him? Should she discuss it? All three questions highlighted a problem that she had with him. She was afraid to talk to him about problems in their relationship for fear that any mention of discord between them would precipitate his derisive comments about her, her intellect, and her clearly apparent lack of self-esteem.

I decided to do something quite unorthodox. Instead of concentrating on the dynamics of the interpersonal relationship or his sadistic nature, I decided to focus on building up her self-esteem. In a few months she felt strong enough to confront her husband on her own terms. And it worked! I was not surprised, because much of the therapeutic technique I favor concentrates on converting helpless, hopeless feelings into a self-centered feeling of confidence, mastery, and growth. Although Georgette had been a successful proprietor of a million-dollar retail store, she knew that she lacked an intellectual body of knowledge that might give her the self-confidence for which she was desperately looking. On the surface she appeared cool, calm, collected, and self-assured. But with many Successful Women, appearances can be deceiving. When confronted with personal choices or issues relating to their own sense of self-worth, their apparent self-confidence dissolves very quickly. In large part it is because the issue of who they really are and what they really want for themselves has never been addressed. And if it had been addressed, it received less attention than any of the other issues pertaining to achievement in a male-dominated world.

Once Georgette decided that she wanted to study political science and invest herself (for the first time) in a political campaign, she felt confident enough to confront her husband with a simple question. (Can you guess?) Who do you want? Me or her? He was flustered with her sudden boldness, and his answer suggested that he wanted her. I say suggested, because until the very last moment of her subsequent ultimatum, he was still unable to respond to her in a definitive manner. She then very politely told him to leave the house. One year later, she met and married a coworker in the campaign and lives happily with her children and her new husband. She is now what she had always dreamed she would become one day—a professional political organizer. She dared to hope, risk, and discipline herself to master a new body of knowledge. A lot of hidden moxie (guts). All I did was to uncover her passion and redirect it toward her.

An important part of a passion for expansion is the ability to immerse yourself completely in the task at hand. What? You kidding? Isn't that the very problem we had with the Successful Woman originally? Wasn't she too busy, too preoccupied, worrying about things other than herself? A valid point. But what I am talking about now has nothing to do with achievement for others, or acquiring power, money, and prestige. As I have stated previously, there is no real problem with these male-oriented values. I am not speaking of the Successful Woman who feels completely fulfilled by her current roles (although, quite truthfully, if she picks up this book and begins to read it, I would hope that she would be affected by its contents). I am talking to the Successful Woman who feels incomplete or unfulfilled. The woman who is willing to first recognize her problem and then commit herself to a course of action that will unleash passions that are directed solely to finding out what she wants and how she goes about getting it. The answer may be a short bout of passion; a long-term emotional relationship with a new man or woman; or simply a new hobby.

Immersion in pursuing the Successful Woman's self-definition is a necessary part of the passion to discover, expand, and master. When immersed in an activity (like writing, for example) the senses of time and personal discomfort dissolve into an exhilarating voyage. On the surface it may appear paradoxical that committing herself fully to uncovering "the self" is antithetical to the principle of expansion. But in order to expand her horizon, she must immerse herself in herself. It is really quite simple—*an important critical mass of self-adoration is required in order to proceed on to a joyous journey of self-discovery.*

Charlotte, a twenty-six-year-old pharmacist, left home when she was barely sixteen. From then on, she spent most of her time studying and working so that she could provide for herself and remain independent. She needed men only occasionally for companionship; more often for a sexual release. Over the years she had been so successful in becoming self-reliant that she was astonished to one day discover how isolated from her social self she had become. She began to experience a profound sense of emptiness, but at first she didn't know where it came from or what it meant. When I asked her what she wanted for herself she replied in a choking voice how she wanted to feel something very deeply; to reach inside herself and throw out her sense of emptiness. I asked her whether she was willing to immerse herself in herself. She replied that she would do whatever was required.

Over several months we examined her fear of dependency and the fact that she never again wanted to repeat the traumatic confrontations that she had experienced with both her mother and father. She was willing to sacrifice the possibility of a long-term relationship with a man, to obviate the problem of confrontation. But we were only scratching the surface of her problems. When confronted with her choice of profession, she admitted that it wasn't what she had really wanted. She had always dreamed of being a veterinarian. After making certain that dealing with animals was not another way of escaping the responsibility of dealing with people, we worked on a strategy for her future. She saved enough money to enter vet school, got into one, and four years later, she and a fellow classmate opened a clinic a few blocks from my office.

This case also illustrates what I have found to be a vital element in self-discovery—the need to be with others. Although the passions we have been discussing are largely self-directed, more often than not they will include a "significant other," whether an individual or a group. Including these significant others in the process of discovery saves the undertaking from being completely narcissistic or self-indulgent. There is, without getting too high-minded, a transcendental quality to this aspect of the need for another that Charlotte demonstrated. As much as she desired self-reliance, she quietly yearned for the companionship of another person, but she could only admit it when she felt good enough about herself to admit her own dependency needs. It is that need for others—whether individually, in a group, or in a group of groups—that allows us to have an identity within a meaningful context. "No man is an island," said John Donne, and right he was.

PASSION FOR FUSION

One of the most complicated and severe problems that I had encountered in therapy with the Successful Woman is a fear of being alone. Many women who have embarked on a professional career have paid a very heavy price for it. They have given up a marriage, a family, and in many cases a clear identity of themselves. I'm not saying that most professional women have made a mistake, or now regret their choice. But unlike most men, whom I believe have both a false sense of themselves and therefore a false sense of security, the Successful Woman is terribly frightened of being alone. She is continuously searching, consciously but more commonly unconsciously, for someone with whom she can share her anxieties, fears, hopes, and disappointments. In short, she desires someone to love. In reality, the Successful Woman is no different from anyone else, including yours truly. We all desire to be with someone. To share life's experiences. To discuss our hopes. To commiserate in our disappointments. To exchange points of view. Love! Simple, ordinary, unadulterated love. But there ain't no such thing. Just because we may want it. And because we may know what it looks, feels, and tastes like does not necessarily mean that we are entitled to it, deserve it, or, worse yet, will be the fortunate recipient of it. On the contrary, songwriters wouldn't be so rich if love weren't such a complicated, disappointing, and frustrating emotion. I don't have to tell you what a ripe area "love" is for analysis. One simply needs to look at the self-help corner of any bookstore to find rows and rows of books on how to identify true love; how to make a man or woman fall in love with you; how to make yourself more attractive; more understanding; more this or more that. The more books, the more titles, and the more confusing the titles are getting: men who want women; women who can't have men; woman who hate men; women who want men. You get the idea. My bottom-line message is a bit different and really quite simple. Despite all the trappings of success and power, the apparently Successful Woman may not be happy because she has never really addressed the fundamental issue of what she really wants for herself. In part, because she never trusted those underlying emotions that were brewing inside of her for so long. Unless the Successful Woman can address certain basic needs or emotions she will continue to feel frustrated, incomplete, uncertain, ambivalent.

So why am I talking about love when this section of the book is about a passion for fusion? Because several prominent psychotherapists[3] have correctly identified three unconscious wishes that accompany love but have nothing to do with love per se. They are the desire for fusion, validation, and aliveness. My own observations and conclusions are not too dissimilar from theirs, except that I have found these three unconscious wishes (Hidden Passions) to be extremely strong driving forces that in and of themselves have become a separate entity (or passion), divorced (so to speak) from love. Yet still very much a part of love. And so I have decided to treat fusion as an entity unto itself. By definition, there is a consensus that love is an emotion that denotes a sharing of feelings. Reciprocity is central to love. However, unlike those psychotherapists, I find that the passion for fusion is also a give-and-take emotion. Like love, fusion implies a feeling of mutuality. But love also includes elements of romance, infatuation, maturation, strife. Fusion is only one part of love, and love requires fusion and then some. So what exactly am I talking about? What is fusion? Am I saying that the Successful Woman wants to submerge her own newly acquired identity into someone else's?

Many practitioners feel that fusion, or the need to feel complete by identifying with another person, is unilateral, unhealthy, and probably immature. I disagree—but only with this caveat: the desire for fusion can be both a healthy or unhealthy emotion, a mature or immature reaction, depending on a therapist's bias. The preponderance of my patients who have described their need to feel fusion were neither schizophrenic, borderline, or in any other way psychologically impaired. They were, as I have already described, extremely successful women who had discovered that they wanted something more to their lives than billable hours, clients, customers, a new Mercedes, or a household with contented children and spouse. They felt that there was something more for them. They just didn't know what it could be or how to get it. And they were dissatisfied enough to take the courageous step of trying to identify, and hopefully rectify, the problem.

Erika was thirty-one years old and single. She enjoyed her profession as a grade-school teacher and, in total defiance of the Peter Principle, proved that an excellent teacher could be promoted to the highest levels of competency (not incompetency). She was slated to be a principal. In the evenings she attended night school to acquire the prerequisite credits for an administrative position. She had dated frequently but felt that there was more to life than a series of short relationships. She wanted to have children when she found the right man.

Erika came to see me because she felt that "something was missing" in her life. By her own description, she felt "incomplete." And after several sessions she pinned that feeling down to the fact that she had never had an intimate relationship with a man. Heeding the words of her mother, who throughout Erika's life had warned her never to rely on any man, she chose a profession that could make her self-sufficient while at the same time provide her with an outlet for her nurturing feelings. In therapy we explored the dilemma she had successfully created for herself. On the one hand, she had become independent, autonomous, and felt good about herself and her professional skills. On the other hand, she wanted to be intimate with a man on a long-term basis. In particular, there was one colleague to whom she was very attracted, but whom she purposefully kept at a distance. She felt inside, however, the yearning to be close to him. She described her frequent conversations with him and how she found him tender, caring, and warm; and her fear of having to rely on those emotions from a man. She was afraid. The clue to her dilemma lay in the man's apparent warmth and in her childhood bereft of nurturance. Her mother, a cold, demanding, manipulative woman, had made certain that her daughter carried forth the seeds of her discontent. Erika protected herself the best way she knew how—by erecting a shield of professional competence and busywork. In every relationship she made certain that there was an emotional distance between her and a man. Now, I explained to her, she was no longer satisfied with that emotional distance and wanted to become closer, more intimate. But to do so she would have to lower her defenses, which, I am pleased to say, she did. Once her defenses were down, and she began to trust her colleague, she was pleased to discover that he was everything she had imagined—warm, tender, caring, supportive. He was, in effect, everything her mother was not. She learned to express what she needed and wanted, to articulate her needs, and to have a relationship in which she could be dependent. Six months later she married him. A two-year routine follow-up visit revealed that although they had the usual marital problems (such as a clarification of role definitions—who does what around the house) she was extremely happy and fulfilled.

Erika is a good example of what can happen when the Successful Woman trusts her feelings, is willing to explore these feelings and their roots, and then takes the next step to give up the past and move forward.

The desire for fusion that most psychotherapists talk about arises from a childhood dynamic not too unlike Erika's; a neglectful, uncaring, nonnurturing mother who in effect creates a child who has a distorted sense of herself—usually fragmented and immature. Because the child does not possess the ego strength to comfort herself internally, she resorts to looking for external cures and gratifications—a series of lovers, dependence on alcohol, work, or drugs. The woman-child is always in search of the emotions or stimuli that will block out the painful feelings of self-doubt and incompleteness. For many women, fusion can be an unhealthy, unrealistic solution to feelings of negative self-worth. By fusing or merging with a man (or a woman, for that matter), she hopes to recapture the secure feelings she fantasized having had with her unnurturing, uncaring mother.

Given similar dynamics, Erika used fusion to become, for the first time in her life, a Complete Woman.

PASSION FOR REAFFIRMATION OF SELF

This sounds a lot more complicated than it really is. Remember when you were young and ran back from school to show your parents your terrific report card? Great feeling wasn't it? The card didn't mean anything until you received that smile, or pat, or hug from one or both of your parents. It was a wonderful feeling when one or both were able to reaffirm what you already suspected—that you were a great kid! But what if you were the girl whose dad said nonchalantly, "That's nice; but what about the one B you received in history?" That was something that made you cringe a little inside, wasn't it? Not only did it spoil your accomplishment; your dad was also able to denigrate your efforts. Despite the fact that you received almost straight A's, you were no longer certain of your own academic accomplishments. So in seeking affirmation of your self-worth (or validation of your self-esteem) you discovered that you were really not as good as you thought. Furthermore, it left you feeling that you would probably never be as good as you hoped, no matter how hard you tried.

Many a Successful Woman I have treated has had to spend the majority of her professional and personal life seeking validation of her self-worth from teachers, lovers, bosses, peer-group friends, and, last but not least, "shrinks." Many a patient has come into my office to simply get an assessment of whether I liked her or not. When I explain that I am not there to like or dislike, but to help her with her problem of having to be liked, such a patient often leaves the session in a huff. The sad fact is that the Successful Woman spends a considerable amount of her time and energy trying to find out whether somebody out there really likes her for what she is. I call this search a passion because it has all the intensity and obsessive determination that one might expect from a passion. I call it a Hidden Passion because many Successful Women do not want to admit that this is what they are doing. Presumably, such an admission would minimize their autonomy.

Sabrina was a twenty-year-old receptionist who found herself on a continuous merry-go-round of dates. She was an extremely bright, erudite, self-taught young woman. But all she could see was that she had only finished high school and this led to a series of male friends, each of whom was smarter, brighter, or better looking than the last one. Each boyfriend lasted approximately four months. Sabrina couldn't understand why. I pointed out to her that she placed the men in an untenable position. She had them meet her friends and parents, prior to the development of any significant relationship, so that everyone could see that "special someone" in her life. When I asked why she had to show them off as if they were prize bulls at a fair, she asked why it was wrong. "I'm proud of them."

"And what about you? Were you proud of what you were doing? Were you proud of yourself?"

"What do you mean?"

"Are you sure that you weren't trying to show yourself off, trying to show everyone how good you must be in order to bag a great catch like this guy. Weren't you were using those guys to inflate your own ego?"

Sabrina needed to inflate her self-worth through association with men who were attractive and accomplished. Her unconscious reasoning went as follows: If these men are accomplished and attractive and they want to go out with me, I, too, must be accomplished and attractive. Ironically, or should I say perversely, there may be some truth to that reasoning. But where it falls down is in the fact that Sabrina in no way feels any better about herself once her friends are gone. Which once again places her on the prowl to hunt up another "self-esteem booster."

In this case, I agree with most therapists who feel that reaffirmation of the self through another person's love rarely works. However, here is my escape clause: a certain amount of validation is required in order to maintain one's self-esteem. We all have to know that people out there like us, but we can't use that impression as the bedrock of our self-esteem.

The Successful Woman must learn to identify this Hidden Passion for reaffirmation of self and determine how much is really required to support her self-worth, and how much is too much.

PASSION FOR ROMANCE

Find me a woman in love, and I'll find you a woman falling out of love. Cynical? Hardly. What is unfortunate about those of us looking for romance is that it entails a very high risk/reward ratio. That is, as high as one may feel when one is in love, is as low as one might fall once out of it. Having said that, I return to my original premise. Successful Women feel incomplete and wanting. What they want or miss is contained within their Hidden Passions. One of those passions is the passion for feeling alive, or its most immediate cousin—romance. One of the quickest ways to feel vibrant is to fall in love—have an affair—be romantically involved. The rush of adrenaline coursing through the arteries. The flushed face. The dry throat. The sweaty palms. The moment of contact—when you are ready to release physically, emotionally. Incredible. Rather than the rapid ascent and descent of infatuation and immature love, the Successful Woman's primary desire is for a sustained feeling of aliveness.

Once again, I trace the root causes of this passion for romance back to childhood. And who is to blame? Once again, mother ranks on top. The need to feel alive is often attributed to an underlying melancholia that arose from a childhood loss of warmth, love, and security of a nurturing mother.[4] In short, mother either didn't show love or gave it erratically. The child grew up with a sense of inner emptiness. In order to cover over that feeling, the child, and then the adult, engages in all sorts of activity that gives a "rush." We've become all too familiar with stories of addictions to various substances and lifestyles, which lead inevitably to self-destruction.

Not every Successful Woman who is in search of romance is on the road to self-destruction. On the contrary, many are not aware, despite numerous affairs or a long-term marriage, that it was really passion that they needed.

Mona was a forty-two-year-old married accountant who took her two children and moved out of their very affluent home so that she could have what she knew was missing in her life—romance. Her husband was an attractive professional who had provided her with all the comforts she needed—except passion. Not transitory passion or infatuation but a clear sense that he was emotionally connected to her inner core. That feeling that "I got you under my skin." She came to see me in order to reality-test the validity of her feelings. She wanted to make sure that she wasn't engaged in self-destructive behavior. I listened to her. We went over her past. It had a lot of the dynamics that could lead to an addictive personality who would always need a rush or a high. But Mona was incredibly astute about her own short-comings. She had a clear sense of what she wanted—and what she didn't want ("a quick fling or fix"). I told her that she seemed to be doing the right thing for herself. She eventually met a man who made her feel intellectually, emotionally, and physically very special. His primary concern was how he could enhance the pleasure of giving to her. He became to her what she had been to other men—nurturant, caring, and exciting. She found him to be the truly romantic man. They got married, and three years later they were still very much in love.

PASSION FOR MATURE LOVE

When I speak of love I am talking about a gamut of emotions that includes infatuation, sex, fusion, and romance as well as a sustained, mature relationship characterized by cycles of occasional discord and friction. There are many Successful Women who have enjoyed the excitement of infatuation and romance. Few of those I see in therapy, unfortunately, have experienced the sustained warmth of a mature love.[5]

As one of my clients blurted out, "Romance, I got. But love is what I want." So why can't she get it? In her particular case, the problem lay in the fact that her need for a quick rush from romance never abated. She went from one romantic interlude to another. The prospects for her ever sustaining a mature relationship were, and are, not great. For my client nothing could go wrong during her period of romance. She was totally smitten with the man she was dating. He could do no wrong. And if he did do wrong, it was perceived as a factor enhancing his "character." If the man was imperious and demanding, he was perceived by my client as being decisive and self-assured. If he acted crude and boorish, she interpreted his behavior as an indication that he was "down to earth." You get the idea. Love, or at least infatuation (read romance), is blind.

Mature love can recognize faults right away, but incorporate them into a total picture or judgment. The man may be a boor, but he is gentle, kind, and considerate. He may be demanding, but he is also giving. The mature relationship thrives on an integrated picture—warts and all. She wants a mature, vibrant relationship based on the hard-won precepts of power sharing. She wants to be involved in a relationship that is earmarked by an emotional, physical, and intellectual give and take. In the spirit of the Soviet *glasnost*, it is no longer a question of *kto-kovo*: who is on top of whom. It is rather an issue of whose turn is it right now—mine or yours? Fair. Reasonable. But not so easy to achieve.

The basic difference between the woman who wants romance and one who wants a mature relationship is measured by the degree of reality-testing (evaluating the *true* facts about a situation) that the Successful Woman is willing to accept.

Vera was a thirty-three-year-old divorced beautician who derived an immense satisfaction and self-esteem from running her own beauty salon. But she realized that something important was missing in her life. On the surface, it appeared as if she needed a man. Once Mr. Right arrived, her friends told her, all problems would be resolved. She, however, sensed that this wasn't the case. When I saw her she was in a relationship with a married man thirteen years her senior. Despite the disparity in age, and the fact that he was married, she entertained the notion that "given the right circumstances" (God, how many times we have heard that), he might be the man with whom she would like to spend the rest of her life. I brought up the fact that she might feel comfortable with him because he was already married, and that she knew that the likelihood of his leaving his wife of fifteen years was minimal. Was she romanticizing a relationship that could never be? She retorted that she wasn't stupid; but their relationship had such a comfortable, relaxed quality that neither one was trying to prove anything to the other. Perhaps, I pointed out, neither one feared the loss of the other because neither one would be available to the other on a long-term basis. She then switched approaches. She could not live without him. He was the man for her. I explained to her that at some point down the line in the foreseeable future, there would be an accounting for her free spending of emotions. Characteristically, the romantic period is the initial period of love when nothing can go wrong. All is right with the world and with each other. Often one partner wants to feel one with the other partner—fused in an interminable bond of love and fidelity. We all recognize the phrase "How did I live before I met you?" Everything is one breath; one motion; one immense overwhelming feeling of togetherness.

Vera nodded her head in agreement. Without her realizing it, I was setting her up. For Vera was placing herself in the same trap she had with her previous marriage, when she had also felt that she could not live without her husband, only to discover sometime later that living with him was far more intolerable. What Vera was really talking about was dependency, not love. One of the great mistakes that most people who are in love make, particularly on the romantic/infatuation end of the scale, is to confuse dependency and love. On the surface this may not be too serious a mistake. Yet in reality it may be the difference between pathology and health. In its most dramatic manifestation, a dependent person would attempt to commit suicide or enter into a severe depression when rejected by his or her lover. Although Vera did not recognize it at the time, she was extremely depressed when her first husband left her. (I might note at this point that it is always difficult to assess who left whom. Therapists must always rely on their instincts and intuition to assess the degree of distortion that characterizes a patient's perception of the world and her relationship to it.) But Vera was having problems accepting my insights regarding her problem with dependency. I told her that a dependent person perceives herself as someone who has very few options or choices with respect to relationships. Love becomes a necessity, an addiction. She must have more and more love. More is never enough. So love is no longer a free choice but a compulsive need. A dependent person needs the other out of necessity, not choice.

Vera recoiled in disgust. "You make me sound like a parasite."

"Perhaps *parasite* is too strong a word."

"Then what would you call someone who sounds like an emotional leech?"

"I think you're a bit too harsh on yourself."

"Me? It's you who brought up the subject. I was perfectly content to live with my 'elder statesman' [as she called him] when you just popped all my illusions. I didn't pay you for that."

"What did you pay me to do?"

She looked down, somewhat chagrined. "To make me feel better."

"How can I do that without examining or interpreting your feelings and behavior?"

I was able to therapeutically provoke Vera because I knew from both her history and our relationship in psychotherapy that she was someone who could tolerate a lot of frustration and was, above all else, eager to learn. In fact, over a period of four months, Vera began to understand the difference between having healthy dependency needs and being a passive-dependent personality. She learned that she could depend on others as well as others could depend on her without having to negate her own personality or needs. This realization helped her to make critical choices in her life.

I define dependency as the inability to function, either emotionally or physically, without the feeling that someone is actually taking care of you. As a baseline, you must understand that we all have dependency needs. It is both natural and healthy to want to be taken care of, nurtured by people whom we care about and whom we know have our interests at heart. If we're tired, we love a backrub. If we're hungry, we appreciate a dinner that says we're special. Without sounding too Freudian, I would say that one way or another we all are looking for a mother or father surrogate to take care of us. Fortunately, for the greater part of our lives, this feeling of having to be taken care of does not rule our existence. Not so for the passive-dependent person for whom dependency becomes the sine qua non of her existence.

Unlike the Successful Woman who feels that there is something missing in her, the passive-dependent personality is not able to mobilize herself to achieve anything without the help of a surrogate father or mother. The Successful Woman likes to be with people but doesn't need them to reaffirm her self-esteem. In contrast, the passive-dependent woman can't live without the presence of someone who can fulfill her physical and emotional needs on a constant basis. She invariably defines herself in terms of her relationships.

Amy was a single, twenty-eight-year-old printing-press operator who came into my office sobbing. Her fiancé of five years had decided to leave her and marry someone else (for reasons unknown to her). He had complained about her neediness. She didn't know what he meant, and he would never explain it to her. She asked to be placed on medications that would make her stop having suicidal feelings. She felt humiliated, depressed, anxious, and told me that she was unable to sleep or eat. I seriously contemplated hospitalizing her but she convinced me it wouldn't be necessary if she could see me the next morning. So I overlooked her manipulative style, determined to deal with it at a later time, and set up an appointment to see her early the next morning. I worried all night whether I had made the right decision. I had images of her lying in a water-filled, red-stained bathtub—her wrists slashed open.

The next day Amy came sauntering into my office twenty minutes late wearing a broad smile and whistling. She announced that she was terminating therapy. Why? She had met someone the night before who was even more wonderful than her ex-fiancé. And she was certain that this relationship would work out. So she was no longer in need of my good services. The man gave her a whole new sense of herself—who she was and who she could be. He was going to help her carve out her new identity.

This rapid change in attitude and emotion is characteristic of the passive-dependent personality. In reality it doesn't matter on whom they are dependent as long as there is someone there to service their emotional needs. You can always recognize the passive-dependent person by the simple things that she cannot do: buy a car, engage in a hobby, leave a disappointing job or relationship, intellectually or emotionally separate from her parents. His or her primary goal is to be in the completely passive state of receiving care and love.

One of my training supervisors in psychiatry once said that "love or romance is a quasi-psychotic state." What he meant was that the exhilarating feeling of love overcomes whatever other considerations might have taken precedence, like the need for compatibility, respect, commitment. So when reality intrudes, such as everyday concerns, both lovers find themselves out of love. Perhaps the only way that love can endure between two people is when they each accept their own individuality and separateness. This is the basis of a mature love—the very thing for which the Successful Woman has been searching. It is a relationship characterized not by selfish, self-gratifying needs but by a mutual give-and-take. By mutual sharing and caring. A key element of this mature love is the ability to be both tender and gentle—in and out of bed. You would be amazed to learn how many men have no idea about the need for patience, tenderness, and empathy during lovemaking. And an equal number of women are afraid to let their needs (particularly in bed) be known. Often the Successful Woman is not aware of her own needs. She would rather remain silent than incur the wrath or silent withdrawal of her partner. A martyr in the making. But in mature love we are talking about the union of two strong egos, each with a clear sense of itself, where neither fears the loss of one's identity in the relationship. It is not a game of power or control. The Successful Woman no longer invests her energy in the search for love but in the relationship itself. In mature love, the Successful Woman is aware of the specific dangers inherent in the first stages of romantic infatuation as well as the subsequent stages of adjustment in which reality impinges upon illusion or self-deception. The relationship is characterized by a mutual sensitivity, caring, accommodation, and acceptance. The Successful Woman does not need it to reaffirm her identity. She simply wants to feel complete and fulfilled.

CHAPTER 5

*What Prevents the
Successful Woman from
Feeling Complete?*

FEAR OF CHANGE

Of all the issues the Successful Woman must confront directly to feel complete the most *compelling* is the problem of change. Ironically we would have assumed from her level of success that change was a natural state of living. She had made a series of choices in her life that entailed change in some major way: to enter the work world, to study, to get married, to raise a family. She had chosen one or all four and had changed her life accordingly. She had to risk. Right? Wrong! She simply went the way of the lesser of the evils. In most cases it took neither effort nor courage.

Most of the women who come to see me have two features in common: an inability to identify what is missing in their lives and the fear of change. The truth is that these two elements are intertwined and I will address them as "fear of change." A complaint that I frequently hear from the Successful Woman is "I want to change but I don't know how."

Janet, a successful, industrious entrepreneur, was tired of running her small computer software company. She was happy with her three-year-old marriage and two children. But she felt there was something definitely missing in her life. Something that would make her feel bright-eyed and alert every day. Operating the company was old hat. She needed a new challenge. Without her having to tell me in so many words, she wanted to uncover the passion of expansion and self-discovery. When I asked her what she thought she wanted she looked at me sternly and then broke out laughing. "I really don't know! Funny, isn't it? I have a B.S. in computer science and an M.B.A. in financing. I'm as educated as one might hope to be, at the finest schools. I've started up my own company and in seven years I have terrific net profits. My health is good. I'm not bad to look at. So why am I complaining? Believe me, I'm not that kind of person. Once I set my mind on a goal, I pursue it, and then, usually, I get it. But I'm having a terribly hard time deciding what I want."

"I'll put it another way. If you sold your business tomorrow, what would you do the day after?"

She started to smile.

"Well . . . it's there, isn't it?"

"Photography. And documentaries. I like shooting pictures. I'd love to go around the world on assignment from some magazine or journal."

"What about it?"

"What do you mean?" She was totally flustered.

"What about taking a chance on something about which you really care?"

"Oh, come on, be serious!"

"Writing used to be a closet hobby of mine. While I was in med school I took a special course in the evening on playwriting and then over the years switched to poetry and prose."

"Yeah, but that's you."

"Why couldn't you do it?"

"It just can't work. I have too many responsibilities. I can't spend my time on something so selfish."

"First of all, what's wrong with being selfish? And if you can't be selfish for yourself, then for whom?"

"Come on, Dr. Pieczenik, be serious. It's impossible! I have a multimillion-dollar business."

"Sell it!"

"Even if I could sell it, there's my husband. And then there are my children. What about them?"

"What about them? They'll love to see animal pictures from around the world."

Over the next few weeks we continued to talk about the issue of change. One day she entered my office totally disheartened. Her business had taken a turn for the worse. She explained that the results of poor decisions had put her third-quarter earnings in the red.

My feeling was that our discussions over the previous months were too threatening. Unconsciously she had made business decisions that would force her to focus on her business more intensively. That way she wouldn't be threatened by the risks and the problems she would inherit if she changed her life dramatically.

The list of excuses for fear of changing anything—whether it is one's life-style, job, spouse, location—is infinite. Believe me, I've heard all kinds of excuses. They are intended solely to mask the fear of change.

> —I can't do it.
> —It's impossible to change.
> —Who will care for my children?
> —I don't have the time.
> —My husband isn't going to like this.
> —How am I going to support myself?
> —I don't have it in me.
> —I'm too frightened.
> —I want to have children before I do something like that.
> —I'm too lackadaisical.
> —I'm too sensitive.
> —Maybe it's not the right choice.
> —I hate rejection.
> —I'm too old.
> —I don't have the experience.

Excuses! Excuses! Excuses! They are the most important tip-offs that the Successful Woman in front of me is frightened of change!

The fear of disappointment and failure inhibits the Successful Woman's desire to risk change. We are by nature afraid of the unknown. Some less so than others. For most, the unknown represents a black hole into which she projects her grimmest expectations, her self-doubts, her uncertainties. For the Successful Woman any connotation of failure can be quite disconcerting. She is not used to failure. If anything she has proven herself to be a person marked by success. Once Janet was able to identify those fears that made her unable to change—fear of the unknown, fear of failure, and, most important, fear of making herself look foolish—she went on to take photography lessons. Then in a concerted effort to overcome her fear of appearing foolish, she purposefully committed every conceivable photographic error from overexposure to uncorrected lens length and shutter speed—all in an effort to desensitize her to the travail of becoming a serious photographer. In this case, "committing mistakes" makes perfect.

HABIT

People are for the most part creatures of habit, and the Successful Woman may even personify this more than others. It's what made her successful. There is something extremely comfortable about knowing what the next day will be like. A calendar, a watch, a phone book, and a scheduling pad are essential components of a daily life earmarked by habit and punctuality. Take any of that paraphernalia away and you may precipitate an acute anxiety reaction because the pattern of regularity and consistency is directly challenged. Twelve years ago I decided to abandon my watch. I wanted my activities to mark the passage of time and not the other way around. So I decided to break the habit of time. And I was successful. Most Successful Women, however, are not able to use time for their personal advantage, and instead make themselves slaves of habit by orchestrating meetings, deadlines, and appointments.

It takes a lot of courage and energy to break a pattern of behavior that has long been ingrained. An old job, like an old shoe, is comforting. It's easy. It's controllable. The boss you hate may be a lot more tolerable than the boss you've never met. But everyone needs change. And so should habits.

Elissa worked as a waitress in a luncheonette. Her husband was a successful plumber who drank away his weekly profits. He would also beat her when he was drunk. After each beating she would run away to her mother's house. When he sobered up, she would return to him. When I asked her why she was always willing to return for more of his punishment, she replied, "I know him, I need him, I want him."

Such masochism is disturbing. There was very little that I could do for her. She left therapy after eight weeks and I haven't any information on what became of her. I only use Elissa as an illustration of the force of a habit—a masochistic habit. Nevertheless, a habit. The perversity of allowing herself to be beaten was the only way Elissa could communicate with her husband. His beatings were Elissa's only proof that he cared about her.

Imagine the wife who has led a comfortable life for twenty years with her professional husband and is contemplating leaving him for another man. Perhaps she was missing passion in their marriage; she had indeed grown "accustomed to his face." It is certainly understandable if she pauses before she crosses over the threshold before meeting her lover. She stands to lose a great deal. Most of all, she knows she may lose the security of predictability that she has built with this man over twenty years.

But, not all habits are destructive. With a little bit of insight and a lot of humor, one can often break the pattern of a particular habit—if the desire is there.

Victoria, a thirty-three-year-old academician, wanted to "expand her horizons" to include "something more than school books and committee meetings." She had toyed with the idea of starting her own consulting firm but was afraid that no businessman would take her seriously. Every time I asked her why she postponed writing her business plan or initiating some business contracts, she proceeded with a litany of excuses that would preclude her from such a venture (including the fact that she knew next to nothing about the business of consulting). I then replied by singing the refrain of a popular Simon/Garfunkel song, in which the song says that the closer you get to your destination, the more the goal seems to slip-slide away. She broke into laughter. The following week she went to see a lawyer about incorporating her new consulting firm—S.S.A, Inc.

Habits afford us a convenient way of avoiding asking the hard questions. "What do I want?" "What am I willing to pay?" By concentrating on the daily routines—the meetings, the schedules, the appointments—the Successful Woman has very little time to think about what is really happening to *her*. Habits allow her to concentrate on everything but herself. On the past. On the future. She can ruminate over the meetings she has just attended as well as worry about the meeting she is about to attend. But she rarely confronts her unhappiness and uneasiness as both the cause and result of meetings that are dreadful and boring. For the most part, the Successful Woman enjoys being controlled by her habits and routines. But no matter what she does, or how well she does it, it's never good enough.

Whenever the occasion arises, she will criticize herself. She's relentless. Almost abusive. She never lets up on her faults and deficiencies. At this point in her life I have discovered that she has very little appreciation for her own strengths. And less appreciation as to how to use them. She may appear content, but she seethes with discontent from within. She knows in her heart of hearts that she is dissatisfied with herself, but she will not come to terms with it. So the resentment builds up. Until she needs more new habits and routines to cover over the discontent. By keeping busy and holding on to the past, she never has to worry about the present—the here and now. And what she will do for herself.

INABILITY TO FORMULATE PERSONAL GOALS

Incredible, isn't it! The Successful Woman is successful despite the fact that she has *not* learned to formulate career goals early on in life. Very few of the Successful Women whom I treated were ever encouraged to ask themselves "What do I want?" Instead they slipped into a male-dominated socialization pattern that was effortless because it was there, and, on the surface, secure. So what's wrong with becoming an accountant or a doctor or a social worker? Nothing! The professions have always been an excellent way to enter the mainstream of upper-middle-class American life. And "a girl's gotta make a livin'," doesn't she? And why should a Successful Woman be any different from a successful man? Did he sit down at some crucial part of his life and list his goals in order of their priority? Is it fair to expect women to accomplish a task that no man has ever undertaken? My answer is "Yes, and for that very reason." A woman's childhood socialization usually revolved around the fact that she should be a nurturing, caring figure. Her primary socialization agent was a mother who, irrespective of professional accomplishments, taught her daughter to respond to the need for nurturing that her future husbands, lovers, and sons would require. She was rarely asked what she might want. She was not taught how to determine what was right for her, what she should require from the world around her, and how to put that information into a concrete, goal-oriented plan.

Fran is a thirty-eight-year-old successful entrepreneur who is married to her second husband, a lawyer. She had three children with her first husband, who was also a lawyer, and three children with her current husband. Her life reeked with men whom she abetted, supported, and nurtured. Her father was a prominent neurosurgeon who she always admired. Since childhood she had immersed herself in medicine, eventually earning a masters of public health. Always a bridesmaid and never a bride. In her heart of hearts she had wanted to be a surgeon. When asked why she never pursued her dream she replied with the one hundred and one answers I might have expected. She was too busy, too lazy, too frightened. The truth of the matter was that she *was* all of them, and why shouldn't she be? Other than myself, no man in her life had taken her emotions seriously. None had supported her goal. As a matter of fact, no man had ever asked her what she wanted for herself. She, in turn, never pursued it. Eventually her frustration made her easy prey for a chronic dissatisfaction with herself and with everyone else around her. She deprecated both her husbands as being "weak jerks," but "lovable jerks." Her present husband, a pleasant but unambitious man, simply shrugged it off good-naturedly.

In couples therapy one evening I asked her husband whether he had ever encouraged her dream of becoming a doctor. "Of course," he replied defensively. He paused and added the clinker: "Only after she's finished raising the children. Then she'll have all the time in the world." He chuckled. She was trapped. But she was no innocent victim. She had designed, manufactured, and placed in proper position the psychological trap that would not allow her to take herself seriously. I pointed out to her that others treated her the way she treated herself. No better. No worse.

Fran's is the tragic story of a Successful Woman who early on in her life entertained the hope of becoming a doctor. But she had a dream, not a formal declaration or strategy to guide her through life's vagaries. So Fran was caught in the daily flow of business meetings, car pools, appointments with the pediatrician, PTA luncheons. All worthy undertakings. None, however, that would further her goal of becoming a doctor.

I wish I could report that Fran was able to pursue her Hidden Passion in a serious, meaningful way. Unfortunately that was not the case. Instead of trying to take herself and her Hidden Passion seriously, she decided to terminate therapy and resume it at a more convenient time.

The ability to formulate early personal goals depends on the support the Successful Woman receives from her parents and the personal conviction that she is worthy and able to obtain that goal. And if personal convictions aren't strong enough, then the demands of a predetermined socialization process will be set in motion. For many a Successful Woman, the absence of a carefully planned personal objective is de rigueur. For those who seek to unleash their Hidden Passions, this haphazard approach to life is less than a satisfactory solution.

FEAR OF RISK

To risk herself in a relationship, or for the process of change, requires two fundamental steps for the Successful Woman: 1) overcoming the inertia of laziness; and 2) having the courage to overcome both the fear of loss and the fear of the unknown. "Risk" is *the* essential ingredient of change and the natural lubricant that allows the Successful Woman to overcome her reliance on habit, routine, and certainty.[1] Risk is the shibboleth of all self-help books, the ostensible key to personal growth, and the much-touted keystone for entrepreneurial expansion. It is a word used loosely and, often, flippantly. "Don't be afraid to risk your present security for . . ."

For the Successful Woman, risk is a carefully measured and recognizable commodity, for there is only so much risk that can be handled. Should she grant a new customer a major loan? Should she speak out in a group meeting when she is the only woman? Should she marry again (when, in fact, she has learned very little from her previous marriage and divorce). Should she trust her instincts in all of these decisions, or "go by the book"? And what about her children? Every day she must balance their needs against hers. Is she spending enough time with them? Is the time really quality time? Or is she simply rationalizing to herself? When it comes to her, the need for risk is less apparent, less pressing. Answers to important questions seem obvious. Why should she risk her job, or her relationship with her boyfriend, because she feels incomplete? Who the hell is she, anyway, to take such incredible chances with her family and friends? She stands to lose everything around her simply because she doesn't feel fulfilled. Isn't that type of thinking self-centered, narcissistic, and self-indulgent?

Lonnie is a thirty-one-year-old married woman with a loving husband who is supportive of her. They both adore their seven-year-old child. About six years ago Lonnie finished law school in the top 5 percent of her class. As a result of her outstanding academic record she was accepted by the seven most prestigious law firms in New York City. But after having worked for a summer in the firm of her choice she decided that working full time as a lawyer on Wall Street was not for her. After a great deal of soul-searching and with her husband's support, Lonnie took an incredible risk and applied to become an executive at a major talent agency. Since early childhood she had been fascinated with show business. She knew that she herself was not talented or ambitious enough or tough-skinned enough to withstand the constant rejection of a life in the fast lane of entertainment. But she didn't want to give up her childhood fantasy of somehow being around creative people. This meant being part of the structure that supports creativity. Like all good talent agents she started out in the mail room earning less than minimum wage. What in God's name was she doing to herself, to her newly born infant, and to her husband? Her parents exploded. When she replied that she had to go through this mailroom ritual in order to achieve the position she had wanted, her parents were dumbfounded. Only her husband understood. Her parents, who had paid for both her college and law school tuition, refused to talk to her for several months. But she was willing to accept the obvious incredulity of her law school classmates, and to risk losing the love of her parents and the support of her husband in order to fulfill a dream that had kept gnawing at her since childhood. In short, she had uncovered her Hidden Passion and dared to risk almost everything to obtain it. She calls me from time to time to tell me how well her life is going. She *loves* her work. She was sure she made the right decision. Someday she hopes to be the first female president of the talent agency. In the meantime, she has fulfilled her childhood dream and every day is a challenge to her intellect and emotion.

A hell of a success story, isn't it? Lonnie dared, she risked, and she gained. She could have lived a very lucrative, interesting, if not exciting life if she had remained on the anointed legal track. But something inside of her told her that she would never be happy. So she mustered all the courage she could collect to go with her passion. As Lonnie once explained it to me, "The courage to take that kind of risk didn't come from waiting around until I could talk myself out of that fear. I just plunged head first into what I wanted. Feeling nauseous and uncertain all the time. To this day I have some gnawing doubts about whether I did the right thing. But when I see how happy I am, how happy my husband and child are, then I know that I've done the right thing."

Inherent in the fear of taking a risk is the fear of loss.[2] Loss of prestige. Loss of self-esteem. Loss of support. Loss of nurturance. Loss of a significant relationship. Loss of love. In order to change, you must give up or lose the old habits, rituals, and routines. Change also entails the pain of that loss. There is no such thing as a personal loss without pain or suffering because change cannot occur without the giving up of the past. In therapy, I try to help the patient relinquish the old values, attitudes, and behaviors that contributed to her feeling incomplete or lonely. The crux of that "letting go" is the willingness to endure the pain and suffering that accompanies it. From a psychiatric point of view, I would say that teaching the patient to work through the loss of an old love, an old hurt, or an old belief system is one of the hardest demands made on my own intellect, patience, and emotions. No one knowingly enters a situation where he or she would be in pain. The average person is not masochistic. But therapists are in the business of encouraging a patient to tolerate the pain of loss. We force the patient to confront their sufferings. Without that suffering there can be no change, and, without change there can be no psychological health. A pretty drastic and gloomy message? Not really. The sooner the Successful Woman understands the imperative of enduring the pain and suffering required for her to give up her parts of her past, the better off she will be. Like many women, the Successful Woman, like all of us, must confront certain universal transitions and learn to endure the sufferings of eventual loss. What do I mean? The list of major transitions that *must* be mourned include the crucial developmental milestones in our lives that we must all learn to give up at some point or another.[3] And if we haven't learned to tolerate the pain and suffering of their loss then we will never be able to proceed with our normal development and growth. So change entails an acceptance of our limitations and our finiteness.

Developmental Milestones

1. The self-contained infancy state when the baby seeks and receives immediate gratification for which she must do nothing in return. If the Successful Woman doesn't mourn this period of immediate gratification, she then stands to become an addictive personality.

2. The common fantasy of omnipotence when the child feels that she can do anything and everything. In her mind there are no limitations to what the Successful Woman can do if she refuses to give up this fantasy of doing everything for everybody.

3. Desire to control, dominate, or possess one's parents. This fantasy is part of the classical oedipal conflict, in which the son is in competition with his father for the love of his mother. When translated in terms of the woman this means that if the Successful Woman has not yet resolved her oedipal feelings toward her mother in competing for her father, she will become anxious and frightened when confronting success or achievement.

4. Childhood dependency, fear of letting go of such childhood needs as nurturance, warmth, and approval, leads to the passive-dependent condition that I discussed in the last chapter. The Successful Woman attains her sense of self-worth from the people with whom she works. Her peer group and job achievements determine who she is. And so she becomes dependent on or addicted to receiving approval and acceptance from her job setting if she refuses to mourn this normal stage of development.

5. Distorted images of a mother or father. The Successful Woman may find herself consciously or unconsciously identifying with an idealized image of her father—a successful investment banker or physician—or the unspoken expectations of a frustrated mother. Or the Successful Woman may try to identify with the exaggerated image of a powerful and omnipotent mother who has been, in effect, the role model for the Successful Woman.

6. Adolescent omnipotence. Adolescence affords us a legitimate opportunity to act and seem crazy without completely worrying about the consequence of our behavior (to a certain degree, of course). The Successful Woman has not often mourned the loss of that sense of omnipotence; the feeling (not too dissimilar from the childhood omnipotence) that the gods are riding alongside. The consequence of this attitude is that the Successful Woman burns the candle at both ends

—at work and at play. She's wheeling and dealing in the boardroom while she's making love all night. Life becomes one frantic, frenetic sorority party to be savored.

7. The desire to remain uncommitted. This attitude is a strong holdover from the omnipotence of the adolescent period. In effect, the only thing that the Successful Woman can commit herself to is her job and her ambition. The rest becomes secondary—her emotions, her passions, her relationships—all of which will be played out and discarded as they serve their purpose. Commitment is the glue that stabilizes the Successful Woman. And commitment to uncovering her Hidden Passions and changing her life accordingly is what makes the Successful Woman complete and well integrated. For the first time, she makes a commitment to her own needs and her own growth.

8. The potency of youth. The Successful Woman carries with her the fantasy that she has the energy, agility, and potency of youth. This attitude is clearly analogous to the omnipotence of adolescence. But it is never more sadly true than in the aging Successful Woman who feels that her time has not yet come.

Along these same lines I might add as a small postscript that the Successful Woman must learn to mourn her fading looks and sexual attraction. Eventually the time comes when the Successful Woman feels threatened by years of physical and sexual deterioration and the inevitable self-delusions with which she must live. There is no sadder sight than an aging movie star who will not recognize that her time has long gone. Simply recall Bette Davis in that wonderful movie *Mr. Skeffington*, and I need say no more.

9. Physical health. As we become older, our health starts to wane no matter how many decathlons or marathons we may run. Physical deterioration is a natural process of growth, and sooner rather than later, we must in one or another way come to terms with it.

10. The termination of life. This, of course, is the last, and hardest of all terminations—mourning one's own existence. As my mother so shrewdly asked me as I stupidly suggested to her that she might want to end all the pain she was enduring through the last years of her life: "What do you think is out there, my son? A sweet dessert?"

The passage of time can be used in a very constructive way. By recognizing the fact that time is a limited commodity, the Successful Woman can, if she is realistic, bring some focus and clarity to her choices about the changes she may want to make. Death becomes a compelling ally, forewarning the Successful Woman that there are only a finite number of choices she can make within a given period of time. And if she avoids confronting the problem of her own mortality, then she will fritter away the most valuable of all commodities—her life.

FEAR OF CREATIVITY

Creativity is a fragile psychological process which, if not properly developed, can be easily crushed. For the most Successful Woman creativity is something that is discussed "after (work) hours" and behind closed doors.

Robin, a forty-eight-year-old ex–English major with the first draft of the great American novel tucked away in the right upper drawer of her desk, is still embarrassed some twenty-six years later that she has not fulfilled her college dreams to become a novelist. Sitting in her carpeted office facing the Capitol, she took some comfort in her accomplishments. By age forty-eight, she was a senior partner in one of Washington's prestigious law firms. She supervised twenty junior partners and drew a salary well over three hundred thousand dollars. She was considered an expert in communications law; and she may in the not too distant future leave the firm to become a judge. On one level, she congratulated herself for even entertaining the idea that one day (or year) she would change her present status. She knew she was ready for a change—"a creative change." While her conscious thoughts turned toward images of herself in a black robe, her restless fingers tapped nervously over her desktop, down to the right upper drawer. According to Robin, her fingers had been meandering there for well over the twenty-six years since she first entertained thoughts of becoming a novelist. Like several housewives she had known, what better way to leave the roost than through law school. She had convinced herself that if she really had been "all that creative," she would have been writing all along like her good friend Jack, who was both a novelist and lawyer. He wrote for two hours every morning before he came to the office.

It was clear to both me and Robin that despite her words of contentment, she felt that she had betrayed herself by not having pursued her original creative impulses. Each day she perseverated over the same few questions:

"How can I know if I have any talent?"

"You can't," I replied.

"But . . ." she stammered desperately trying to wrest some guarantee from me that I could assuage her fears.

"There is only one way to know. . . ."

"How?"

"Write and then submit it."

"But this manuscript is twenty-six years old. It's no longer timely."

"I'm sure Homer would like to know that his *Iliad* is out of date."

"Don't be smart! I'm no Homer!"

"Then be content to be what you are—a very successful lawyer."

"Damn it! I want to be a writer."

"Actions speak louder than words."

"For this I pay you money?"

"If I can bully, intimidate, implore, cajole, and threaten you into writing would it have been worth the money?"

"Absolutely."

"Too bad. Because I'm not going to do it."

You get the idea. We went around and around. It turned out that her fear of putting pencil to paper became so great that at one point she refused to draft her own legal briefs and passed them on to her junior associates. Unfortunately she never completed writing her first novel and terminated therapy with her now famous punchline: "I'm having an affair with Jack. If I can't write, I can at least fuck a writer." She left therapy the way she came in—angry and disgruntled with herself.

To risk one's life on the notion that one is creative is, at best, a tricky proposition. Herman Melville wrote *Moby Dick* in nine months and for the remaining forty years of his life published only a few other novels. What happened to his creativity? I know an author who at the age of fifty-three looks back at his creative life and admits to me that the most creative period occurred in his early thirties when he was desperately trying to make a name for himself. He wrote three novels within thirty-six months, each of which became a national and international bestseller. Since then he has not written a book worth publishing. What happened to his creativity?

An old wives' tale has it that the creative person must have a touch of madness. Recent evidence suggest that this hypothesis is not totally incorrect. Individuals who are most creative are the family members of individuals with manic-depressive illness, but who themselves do not have the illness. The successful creator has the ability to execute his ideas in a systematic, disciplined, and professional manner. Exposure to new ideas, new places and experiences creates a fertile medium for the creative mind. But the need to be creative is an essential ingredient in wanting to change one's life to a personally more rewarding and enriching one. To discard her fear of creativity, the Successful Woman must first be able to take a risk. And the only reward in the process may be creating, itself. Not much consolation, is it?

FEAR OF SELF-CONFRONTATION

How does a Successful Woman acquire a relatively accurate reading of herself? The ability to scrutinize her own assets and liabilities is no easy matter. Even the best-trained psychiatrist is unlikely to be able to dissect out her component parts and tell you what she is feeling about them, or how those different aspects of her personality will contribute to a potential change in her life.

When I was a first-year psychiatric resident at Harvard, twelve analysts were assigned to supervise my therapeutic techniques and treatment modalities. I decided that only fifty percent of my supervisors were any good. So I freed up the other six hours to study international relations at MIT. Intellectually I had always felt that psychology was a necessary component for analyzing international relations. Personally, treating patients was not sufficiently challenging. The process of self-examination that eventually led me to become a deputy assistant secretary of state and an international trouble shooter for four different administrations began with the same fears and doubts that the Successful Women I have treated were experiencing.

My own sense of incompleteness began to surface while I was still at Cornell University Medical College in New York City. While examining the in-patients at the Paine Whitney Psychiatric Hospital, I realized that the role of full-time clinician would not satisfy my intellectual and emotional needs. Something in me told me that it wouldn't be—complete. Where would I find growth, expansion, discovery, creativity, if I spent all of my hours focusing on the problems of my patients? But what was I looking for? What did I really want? I talked to my clinical supervisors, but, as well meaning as they were, they were definitely at a loss to help me. It wasn't really till my military service in the Public Health Service at St. Elizabeth's Hospital, during the peak years of the Vietnam War, that I realized what I wanted to do—combine psychiatry and foreign affairs; become involved in the foreign-policy community in such a way that I could have an impact on the course of national policy so that we could never again become involved in another Vietnam War. Slightly idealistic and naïve. But certainly a goal worth holding up for myself. The reality of my immersion in foreign affairs was far more difficult, and through an undefined path. But I was lucky. Two events reinforced my intuitive sense that I had to pursue this route of endeavor. One was the death of my father. A wonderful, kind man who had dedicated his whole life to medicine. From him, I had learned the importance of defining your goals and applying yourself through self-discipline to the almost herculean task. The second major influence (in an unexpected way) were my supervisors at Harvard who were always talking about their future plans and goals in the conditional sense. Although they were at the time in their middle and late forties, they were always talking about what they would do when they would retire at sixty-five. Imagine these wise men who were supervising me and counseling patients having a definite problem in realizing their own personal aspirations. They had done the requisite self-analysis. They just couldn't take a risk on themselves. They were too busy; too involved with their psychiatric practice; too fearful of losing a comfortable life-style. In my opinion they were frightened men who found it easier to talk about living their lives and other people's lives, than in actually living life on its own terms. Don't get me wrong. I am not faulting them. But what I realized through them was that there are no real experts on how to live life. Even a psychiatrist, whose professional obligation it is to gently guide and steer the client into self-awareness, may be no better equipped than the client in answering the one fundamental question—What do I want?

The Successful Woman's ability to analyze herself and confront difficult choices is neither God-given nor learned. It is simply the ability to look in the mirror and swallow whatever pride or fear that holds you back from taking that first giant step to making a change in your life. I know, it's easier said than done. Later on I will try to show you how you can do it without making it too painful.

When the Successful Woman asks herself the hard question, *"What do I want?"* there is an immediate inclination to assume that by asking this question she is denigrating her past achievements. That couldn't be further from the truth. On the contrary, by confronting herself, alone or with the help of a therapist, she is reaffirming those parts of her life that have been enjoyable, worthwhile, productive. She is simply pushing them one step further. How can she feel richer, more complete, more fulfilled? If organizational skills have been an important part of your professional life then when you ask yourself what it is that you want, you must remember those aspects of your organizational skills that you happened to like or appreciate (e.g., interacting with people, setting up an agenda of priorities). From there, try to figure out how you can transfer those skills into an as yet undefined life-style.

Alice was a successful social worker in her early fifties whose husband had died a few years before she came into therapy. She had a thriving practice specializing in the treatment of psychosomatic diseases (that is, physical disorders that originate in or are aggravated by an individual's emotional state, such as ulcers or asthma). Not so ironically Alice was beginning to develop backaches secondary to stress. She refused to acknowledge that the backaches might be due to her overscheduled, hectic practice. When she came to see me she was in tears. But she didn't know why. She admitted that she was beginning to question whether she wanted to continue as a social worker. But every time she thought about the possibility of leaving her secure, profitable profession she became emotionally distraught. She was confused. Why should she be thinking about leaving her profession?

Although Alice could still help her patients, she was burnt out. But she was unable to see that. As much as she might want to continue as a social worker, she had very few emotional assets left upon which she could draw. When I asked her about her feelings about herself as a woman and wife, she broke down crying again. What became evident in this process of personal confrontation was that she was slowly beginning to realize that she felt that she had done a less than adequate job taking care of her husband, whom she called a "cardiac cripple." She had very little patience for his demanding ways, and she had hired a full-time private nurse to be his caretaker. Further probing revealed that she resented the fact that he needed her after all those years when she needed him and he wasn't there. But the gnawing guilt lingered on. To her credit, Alice was able to convert a basically negative, destructive emotion into a positive, constructive one. She decided, through the course of therapy, that what she felt toward her husband and how she had dealt with it was in the past. She would learn to mourn the loss of a functional husband and recognize the angry feelings she possessed toward him. Although they remained married until his death, she gradually gave up her patient load. Only after his death had she resumed painting oil canvases, a Hidden Passion she had since graduate school. She is now busily preparing for her first art exhibition.

The need to confront yourself is essential for change. Asking yourself the questions that no one else will ask you or, more sadly, care to ask you is, at best, extremely difficult. But without even attempting to ask oneself the question "Who am I?" and the equally important question "Whom do I want to be?" then the status quo becomes the modus operandi of your life.

FEAR OF DISCIPLINE AND COMMITMENT

The Need for Discipline

Why would a Successful Woman who has achieved success through years of hard work, self-sacrifice, and perseverance require self-discipline regarding her Hidden Passions? Haven't I just turned my basic approach in this book around one hundred and eighty degrees, by beginning to extol the virtues of self-restraint and self-discipline? No. The Hidden Passions that the Successful Woman seeks to uncover are deep, complex, and by their very nature turbulent. If unleashed by conscious effort, through therapy or the use of this book, those unbridled passions can become extremely destructive, forcing the Successful Woman to ride the vagaries of her emotions. It is important that those Hidden Passions be directed toward a specific goal of self-fulfillment or personal growth. Think of those Hidden Passions as wild broncos. Once unleashed from the corral they buck and jump, indiscriminately trampling anyone or anything in front of them.

In and of itself the wild bronco has no redeeming value other than a thirty-second point of amusement for a July Fourth crowd. Without any intended offense to rodeo lovers, once the bronco is spent, he is of no use to anyone.

If we continue this fanciful analogy, we can safely say that a Hidden Passion that is released acquires a life of its own. It will take the

Successful Woman rapidly up to the peaks of euphoria (if that passion happens to be romance or infatuation) and bring her just as quickly down. Along the way the Successful Woman may feel the intended exhilaration as she's flooded with norepinephrine (an adrenaline analogue); but then, afterward, it is sheer, demented hell. And the only impression that both the woman and the observer can extricate from the experience is that it is far better to be in control than out of control. Before you know it, the Successful Woman will clamp down the brakes of control, forcing herself to an abrupt stop.

The answer, as you can surmise, lies somewhere in the Aristotelian middle—passions burning gently and firmly, constrained by careful judgment, temperance, and adjustment. In short, self-discipline. Without discipline there can be no constructive use of passion.[4] Passion in and of itself leads to either self-destruction or burn-out.

The Hidden Passions, once released, must be nurtured, developed for their creative energy, and for the drive that energy provides the Successful Woman once she has decided to commit to its growth and her own. If left unbridled the result can be personal chaos and non-productivity. It is particularly interesting that the Successful Woman is intuitively judicious about the danger of unleashing her passions. She has often expressed great fear that if she does release her passions then they will be on a course of destruction. At this point I caution her that true growth evolves from a combination of creativity, passion, risk—and self-discipline.

Martha was a recently divorced fifty-eight-year-old wife of a senior government official. For eight years she and her husband had little sex. This in itself didn't seem to bother Martha too much. She never felt properly stimulated, and consequently she felt she had no obligation to be passionate. Whatever passions she had were directed to the rearing of her two children and her profession as a high-school history teacher. She had discovered a modicum of contentment in her well-structured, highly ordered life. Until, of course, the day of reckoning. Her husband came home one day, and without too much fanfare he packed up and left the house to move in with the proverbial secretary.

When Martha came into therapy she conveniently used the dictates of the Catholic Church as an excuse for having suppressed her own sexual desires as well as the long-delayed recognition of her marital problems. I pointed out that the Church can only be blamed for offering her a spiritual sanctuary; how she decided to use that sanctuary was totally up to her. The archbishop neither derived the pleasures of her infrequent orgasms nor could he be equally blamed for her anorgasmic states. I knew then that both I and the Catholic Church would be blamed for whatever happened to Martha. We were both in for a pretty rough ride. Before anyone (namely me) realized it, Martha began to make up for lost time. She started to date not one, not two . . . but three men at the same time. Needless to say she had sex with a vengeance. I felt like a man from the temperance movement shouting the evils of liquor in the middle of a liquor store. To no avail. I explained to Martha that she was depleting her reserve of passionate energy simply to satisfy her need for revenge. And it wouldn't work. Without reigning in her acting-out behavior she would quickly find herself acutely depressed. She rebuked me for my Calvinist approach. Discipline! she laughed. Her whole life had been nothing but discipline. First, the Church demanded discipline. And now me! And look where it had gotten her—one ex-husband, one broken family, and an insatiable appetite for sex with strangers. Soon afterward she left therapy, committed to a life of hedonistic revenge. I subsequently heard from two other therapists that she had become addicted to drugs and alcohol.

Not a pleasant story. What makes it particularly unpleasant is the fact that she was highly insightful about her own condition and equally conversant with the potential consequences of her behavior. But all the knowledge and insights in the world are of little value if there is no willpower or determination to change in a constructive, disciplined fashion. The reason for discipline over unbridled passion is really quite simple—everyone has a limited amount of passion. To disseminate it indiscriminately is both self-defeating and debilitating. The end result is depression, frustration, disappointment, and physical and emotional debilitation.

On a more positive side, Mirit, a twenty-five-year-old secretary who had been taking night courses in accounting but was uncertain as to what she would do with them (always denying that she had the discipline to be an accountant full-time), spent several sessions with me concentrating on nothing but the issue of discipline—what to do in order to acquire it. We started with simple assignments. First, she took on the analysis of a financial balance sheet and reported to me in writing what she thought the financial health of a fictitious company was. Then she worked her way through a cash flow analysis until she was able to present me with a complete financial package (i.e.: a business plan) of a new company that she would have started up if she had a certain amount of money. Soon afterward, she gained the necessary confidence to admit to herself that she had the self-discipline required to pursue a serious career as a full-time accountant. Five years later she sent me a card announcing that she was joining one of the big eight accounting firms.

The Need for Commitment

Once the Successful Woman has ventured into the realm of her Hidden Passions she is often unaware of the magnitude of the risk and commitment required to make herself feel complete. How could she be? There are no accurate measurements for what lies beneath the surface. From the point of view of a therapist, I rely completely on the patient's past pattern of behavior; her unspoken words or feelings; her non-verbal cues; and most important, on my own intuition. There is an indescribable feeling that I get in the pit of my stomach that tells me whether the woman who is walking through my door is serious about changing her life, or whether she is someone who is simply flirting with self-indulgence. Commitment is an emotional attachment that often rides in the wake of an initial euphoria or hypomania. One rarely becomes committed to an idea or a person unless one has first felt the rush of adrenaline. In part the notion of commitment has an illusory aspect. What one is attempting to do in a commitment is to sustain, on a lower level of intensity, the overwhelming sense of euphoria and infatuation one had initially experienced with the person. In other words, romantic love or infatuation is an important lubricant that helps slide commitment into place. By making an emotional commitment to another person or to pursuing one's own goals one becomes vulnerable to rejection, failure, disappointment, and, worst of all, success. Yes, success. I have known many people who have made commitments to people and projects and have succeeded in achieving their initial goals. But to their complete dismay they discover that they really don't want what they have obtained. The great German philosopher Nietzsche once said that when the gods want to be cruel they grant you your wishes. But what if you no longer want those wishes to come true?

Fortunately, for most of us the real problem in developing ourselves or in entering a long-term relationship is the problem of commitment, which is directly tied to the fear of placing oneself in a position (whether it is a marriage or a job) that will, by its very definition, curtail our maneuverability and options. In other words, once we have made a commitment to changing our life-style we are no longer as free to complain about our choices or envy others. Whatever may arise from our commitment is a direct result of our boldly and openly declared intention to remain with that particular course of action. However, human nature is not so rational or controlled. Most of us enter the world of commitments with great trepidation and uncertainty. Only after we've accepted the marriage vow do we really understand what we have gotten ourselves into. Until death do us part. For better or worse. My God, one couldn't have devised a more frightening series of words to have scared away a prospective suitor. I often wonder if we as a society didn't select those words as a way of weeding out the faint-hearted.

Without commitment—an emotional/intellectual bonding—no serious growth can occur. In psychiatry we have a whole series of diagnostic categories for people who have varying degrees of problems in forming commitments. A sociopath, for example, is someone who has very little capacity to accept guilt or responsibility, and has almost no capacity to honor a commitment. Fortunately for me, I have treated very few Successful Women whom I could categorize as sociopathic. Some, however, had what I would diagnose as characterological problems that allowed them to form only very shallow relationships.[5]

Rebecca was a twenty-five-year-old dress designer who found herself, over a five-year period, hopping from man to man and job to job. In the beginning she thought this was cute. She was part of the yuppie generation interested only in "me" and making money. Loyalty and commitment were, at best, alien if not repugnant notions. However after her third lover she was becoming increasingly more anxious about her future, and she seriously began to question her life-style. She entered therapy, so she said, because she was having a problem forming a meaningful long-term relationship. When I asked her why, she became silent. As I probed further I discovered that she had been very close to her father, who was an internist. And at the age of forty-two (when she was fourteen years old and at the peak of her attachment to him) he died unexpectedly from a heart attack. Naturally she felt abandoned, hurt, alone. Her mother, a warm, caring woman, recognized the problem immediately and tried to rectify it by remarrying within a year of her husband's death. But Rebecca rebelled and swore to herself that she would never again fall in love with someone who could leave her so unexpectedly. Without fully realizing what she had done psychologically to herself, she became an itinerant student who came to classes whenever she felt like it. Eight years later, and living on her own, quite independently, she was still wandering from job to job, man to man, and therapist to therapist. Needless to say, she was just as unable to commit herself to the process of therapy as she was to anything else in her life. She left just at the time she was beginning to form a therapeutic alliance with me.

On the more positive side, Muriel, a forty-three-year-old French professor of literature, was tired of teaching college students; but she didn't know what else to do. As we explored the possible alternatives, we uncovered her passion for politics, foreign cultures, and travel. The choice was obvious—join the U.S. foreign service. The idea appealed to her, but immediately she gave me five good reasons why it couldn't be possible: She was a newly naturalized American citizen born in France; the State Department didn't take very many women; so on and so forth. You get the idea. I gave her various assignments that required progressively more effort, discipline, and commitment until she eventually finished spending three months preparing for the written part of the foreign service exam. Then she froze. She felt that she was doomed to fail. No matter how much she learned it would never be enough. I told her that she was probably right. Then I taught her some simple relaxation exercises and helped her to focus and concentrate her energy and imagine herself in an overseas consular post in the U.S. Embassy. One year later, she sent me a postcard from Bangkok, Thailand, in which she thanked me for helping her become a junior consular officer in Ching Mai.

Commitment is the emotional glue that allows changing one's life to have two distinct and necessary characteristics: "durability" and "irreversibility." Like the recent _perestroika_ in the Soviet Union, one never knows whether the patterns of change are simply a fad or a permanent feature. Only through discipline and commitment to the implementation of change can one achieve permanence and consistency.

CHAPTER 6

The Un-*Successful Woman: A Hostage to Herself*

What happens to the Successful Woman who refuses or is unable to change? Or what I call the *Un*-Successful Woman? A fair percentage remain just as they began—dissatisfied, restless, and aimless. They are unable to clearly define their identity or needs. They cannot assert the three basic tenets of their existence: *I am. I need. I want.* How do I know? By monitoring my "failures" and "successes." It has always been a standard practice of mine to routinely follow up patients after they have left therapy. I do this for two reasons. First, I am genuinely interested in what happens to anyone I have evaluated or treated. By doing my own follow-up, I can provide an informal monitoring system for my ex-patients. Second, this allows me to assess my own clinical acumen and skills. Was my clinical judgment of Ms. XYZ correct? If not, why not? In a way, I've created my own self-evaluation mechanism.

Having maintained an effective follow-up on 80 percent of the women I have either treated or evaluated, what have I found happens to those women who have not "gotten better"? For these *Un*-Successful Women, unfortunately, the news is not good. No amount of achievement, connectedness, busywork, sex, or food seems to alleviate their disturbing sense of incompleteness. The *Un*-Successful Woman is sentenced to what I call a "crisis of ambivalence," doomed to play out the mandates of her contradictory realities. She remains hostage to the façade of success she has adopted. She becomes the emotional victim of the eternal triangle—seeking peace of mind with or through a man she knows can never be hers. She is frustrated by the fact that she can commit herself to the rigorous demands of her profession while she accepts inertia, fear, and laziness in her personal life. Ambivalence results from the presence of two contradictory emotions at the same time. Normally the Successful Woman is ambivalent about making a choice. That's natural. But she enters a crisis of ambivalence whenever she is unable or unwilling to make that decision. She is continuously torn by the façade of success that she has acquired and her basic underlying feelings of insecurity. She is unable to find her psychological center because she is unwilling to confront her own needs and desires. Instead of asking herself What do I want? she puts herself down by parroting the concerns of others: What should they do? Who should they be? Let us examine these contradictory realities that lead to the *Un*-Successful Woman's crisis of ambivalence. Clearly, not all *Un*-Successful Women exhibit all of these traits. But most demonstrate a majority of them.

SELF-ASSURED OR SCARED?

She looks good! Confident. Self-assured. Self-possessed. She's got it made! But she feels frightened, torn between the image of success she must maintain and the feelings of vulnerability she is trying to protect against. The Successful Woman resents the fact that she bought into the feminist rhetoric of the 1970s (assertiveness, autonomy) only to be trapped in the male-dominated achievement-oriented world of the 1980s. Where did she lose herself? As she enters the 1990s, she's looking better but feeling worse. Despite her veneer of success, she has become fearful of life—the continuous, unending process of self-examination: assessing the need for change; the cost of risk; and the problems of uncertainty. She feels trapped by her accomplishments— a hostage to her success. And she is unable to derive any inner peace. As her image of success becomes more visible to the outside world, the Successful Woman finds herself feeling more and more like a fraud.

She alone realizes that there is a marked discrepancy between her outer self and her inner self. Those warning signs of feeling incomplete become more frequent—distraction, feeling upset, boredom, anxiety. She spends proportionately more time and energy propping up her façade than addressing those Hidden Passions that don't want to disappear (no matter how much she wills it).

Alexandra was a thirty-five-year-old senior executive of a major Hispanic food distribution company. She had come into therapy because she was not happy in her marriage. Her husband was, as she described him, "a typical Hispanic with all that macho bullshit." They had no children. She wanted out. But she also wanted more. What more, she really didn't know. All she knew was that the more she tried to succeed, the less worthy she felt.

In trying to work with her, I opened up the issue of what she wanted for herself. She replied with all the standard platitudes—autonomy, self-reliance, money, security, and a man to love her for what she was. But when I asked her to define who she was she became silent. It was clear that she was torn by her ambivalence. On the one hand, she wanted to hold on to her well-earned image of success. On the other, she was frightened of dealing with the real issues in her life: her desire for a mature relationship, and a desire to break out of the corporate structure and go it on her own (she had always wanted to open a boutique specializing in Hispanic art).

Why didn't she do either? Her answer: I'm too busy; I'm making too much money. Her real concern: fear. Rather than deal with her fear—of risk and commitment—she left therapy, saw two other therapists, and moved one more rung up on the corporate ladder. She had become a captive to success. I have had other patients who have refused to deal with the relevant issues in their lives and ultimately remain in an emotional rut.

GOAL-ORIENTED OR UNDIRECTED?

After leaving therapy the *Un*-Successful Woman often immerses herself in her work with a complete vengeance. She takes on more projects, hires more personnel, and networks like crazy. When she feels totally exhausted from her ten- to fourteen-hour work day she leans back in her desk chair, gazes up at the ceiling, and reaffirms with an air of distraught contentment that she is very busy. That is good. In fact, that is very good. She does not notice the emotional bruises that brought her into therapy in the first place. She forgets about her desire to feel whole with someone who can appreciate her humor, sexiness, and love of the theater. For a moment, ever so brief a moment, she wistfully recalls the fleeting dream of becoming a theatrical producer. For what other reason is she saving all those hundreds of thousands of dollars, waiting to be placed in the "Amanda Production Company." She has made up the company name—but she has placed it on "hold"—as a way of enticing her into the theater. The same way she has done with most of her thirty-five years of professional life. Amanda feels trapped. There is nowhere to go. She doesn't want to go home. Her relationship had been on a low burner for quite a few years. Her children are long grown and gone from home. She sits at her desk, reluctant to go home. She wants to pick up the telephone to call a business associate with whom she has had a pleasant flirtatious relationship. But what's the point? She doesn't want the headache of the entanglement. So she hangs up the phone. But she wants to talk to someone to tell him how she feels—her doubts, her successes, her hopes, her disappointments. For that, she needs intimacy.

In every part of her office she sees a part of herself. Amanda the administrator, the problem-solver, the executive. But, where is Amanda the person? How does this all fit into her future? She breaks out into low laughter. What future? What she sees is what she gets. The present is her past and future. She moved into this office ten years before and if she's lucky she'll remain here another ten years. A corporate nursing home.

My follow-up interviews revealed that Amanda was quite a typical *Un*-Successful Woman. Having mustered the courage to enter my office, she felt that if beneficial results didn't accrue immediately there was no point in waiting. Her life was too hectic. She couldn't afford one or two hours each week spent on herself. How could she give up a six-figure salary with all those wonderful perks? A life of creativity and personal growth could be very frustrating, unrewarding, uncertain, and lonely.

As you can see, rationalizations came in hot and heavy. But despite the fact that the *Un*-Successful Woman may possess an impressive title and job description, she still feels undirected. Whatever her accomplishments, whatever her successes, she feels none of it really belongs to *her*. She belongs to the company. Therefore the company defines the parameters of her self-worth: gross income, net profits, earnings per share.

Like an alcoholic who understands that drinking may be bad for his or her health, the *Un*-Successful Woman is torn between her ability to achieve specific business goals and her inability to attain personal goals. At one and the same time, she feels pride and shame, fulfillment and emptiness, direction and aimlessness. She is torn by her crisis of ambivalence but feels she can do nothing about it.

IN CONTROL OR POWERLESS?

Rhonda was a twenty-eight-year-old insurance broker. She worked in a medium-size firm. After talking about problems she was having with sex, and with developing a lasting relationship with a man, I asked her how she was doing. "About the same," she answered. "Maybe a little worse. At work I feel comfortable. I know who I am, and, I know how to relate to all kinds of men. But place me in a social situation and I clam up. I freeze. I don't know what to say or how to say it. I can't really believe that a man could be interested in me for more than sex. It really bothers me. Eventually I sleep with the guy because he's been aggressive and forthright—traits that I can identify with. But then I feel angry with myself, and with him, for allowing him to act the part of the intimidating male. At work I have no qualms about acting the way he did. I enjoy intimidating. No, that's not the right word. I enjoy persuading my customers to buy insurance. But I feel guilty if I don't sleep with a guy after all his effort."

Rhonda was having a hard time dealing with her own sexuality. The male values that she could incorporate at work were in conflict with her needs for tenderness, understanding, and patience in her social life. So Rhonda learned to "fake it"—to make the man feel potent, experienced, and sexy. Instead of coming to terms with her own needs, she learned the "tricks of the trade" (as she called them). She learned how to maneuver the entire evening, holding out the promise of sex. She learned how to fake an orgasm so that she could keep the man interested in her. In fact, this helped her feel in control of the situation. Somewhat powerful. Rhonda had gone from a woman who was afraid to explore her Hidden Passions to a self-described "strumpet." She had entered a world of self-delusion, debasement, and impotence. What she had mistakenly identified as giving her control and power (faking pleasure and orgasms) was, in fact, a sign that she was out of control and powerless.

Control is a central issue for the *Un*-Successful Woman. Both her professional and personal life is centered around the expectation that she is very much in control of her feelings and behavior. At work she is a professional. At home she is a warm, caring caretaker. In both settings she is controlled and controlling. Truth or fiction? Let us simply call it faction—half truth, half fiction.

I have an axiom to share with you that has passed the test of time: *The more control you need, the more powerless you have become.* The *Un*-Successful Woman enjoys being in control of her own life. She likes paying for her own clothes, food, and entertainment. She enjoys relying on her own wits, as well as directing her life plans. If she has children, she finds pleasure in determining what schools they will go to, what outside activities they will engage in, and planning for their future. In short, the *Un*-Successful Woman wears, and enjoys wearing the mantle of chief executive officer both at work and at home.

For her, the issues of power and control are inextricably tied. She feels that the more control she can exert over an event, problem, or individual, the more power she exhibits. That just ain't my experience! Power is very definitely a subjective phenomenon where the individual perceives him or herself in a position where she can influence, persuade, or have an impact on the course of events—including people's lives. In and of itself, neither control nor power are bad. Each of us uses power and control to order our lives, and to make an impact on others. Yet there is a fine line between helping a loved one by empowering him with certain attributes (love, admiration, caring) and controlling him with that love. With her husband or lover, however, the situation is more precarious. By self-admission, the *Un*-Successful Woman feels less in control of her relationship with men than she does her work. In general, the more insecure the *Un*-Successful Woman feels, the more she gives love and the more controlling she appears to her "significant other." So instead of instilling a mutual love or respect for the help and love that she has given the other person, she discovers hostility, resentment, and, in some cases, actual disgust. Through power and control (disguised as nurturance and caring) she has created the opposite emotions she had intended. Baffled and confused, she withdraws, wondering how this phenomenon could have occurred. All the *Un*-Successful Woman had intended to give to her lover was warmth, caring, attention, and advice. And how does that ingrate repay her? With anger, resentment, and recriminations. She, in turn, has turned from a woman who had felt very much in control of her life into a dish rag of confused emotions and helpless pleas. Power disappeared with the last kind act. What happened?

Eleanor, a thirty-seven-year-old businesswoman, came to see me about a problem she was having with Henry, the boyfriend she had been seeing for over three years. Eleanor was a cofounder of a successful furniture-manufacturing company. She had gone through "trial by fire," as she put it, in creating and building the company. Henry had been in the venture capital business, providing money for new start-up companies. They had met through mutual business acquaintances. After they started to date, Eleanor found out that Henry really wanted to break away from his firm and start one of his own. She was extremely helpful, giving him advice on all aspects of starting a business; things that she had "learned the hard way." When she was in her helping mode their relationship went along smoothly. He even started talking about living together and getting married. But as Henry's new business started to become successful, he started canceling appointments, forgetting "meaningful anniversaries," and in general acting angry and peevish. Eleanor didn't understand what was happening.

I pointed out to her that although Henry was genuinely grateful for her help, his resentment and anger at feeling manipulated and controlled was the price that she was paying for it. "What!" she blurted out. "How dare he feel manipulated and controlled. I was the one who was manipulated into giving him help. Without me he would have fallen flat on his face." Now it was her turn to become enraged. It didn't make sense. She had given freely of herself because she felt that he needed her help. I tried to explain again that although he was very grateful to her, he was also feeling controlled and suffocated. What was happening, I added, was that she had gone from a helping to a managerial role—a fine but important distinction in the reactions each approach generates. The relationship had disintegrated into a power struggle over who was on top of whom.

"That's nonsense. If anything, I feel I have absolutely no power over him. He does what he wants when he wants to. He never even asks me for advice anymore. But I still monitor his cash flow!" She said that with glee, and I pointed out to her that even now, after their intimate relationship had ended, she still relished the fact that she had some control over him—if only over his cash flow (which is equivalent to holding your opponent by the throat). I told her one of the ways she coped with feeling insecure about a relationship was to make herself invaluable to the man and then controlling him. "Nonsense," she responded. "It's his problem, not mine."

I told her that she was right. And I was right. It was, in fact, both of their problems. If he didn't feel as insecure as he did, he would have focused on the positive aspects of her assistance and not viewed it as simply negative. However I was more interested in her problems of power and control and what she would do about them.

As a cofounder of her company, she had transformed her working relationship with her partner, originally supportive, caring, and nurturing of each other, into one that was manipulative, controlling, and argumentative. Eventually she had bought him out.

I am constantly amazed at the number of women in therapy who do not want to hear what their therapist has to say. Eleanor left therapy with me, and I understand from her third therapist that she has taken a leave of absence from her company to travel around the world. I hope she'll use the year to come to terms with herself.

JOB STATUS OR
PERSONAL FULFILLMENT

The ambivalence between appearing in control while at the same time feeling powerless has become an increasingly important issue for the _Un_-Successful Woman both in her personal relationships and in the workplace. More and more women are talking to me about the increased turbulence they feel between their job titles and responsibilities, and their personal gratification. As they rise, deservedly, through the ranks of their firm, they feel increasingly more alienated from their job. What the old respected sociologist Max Weber and his gang used to call "anomie." But rather than becloud this discussion with sociology or Marxist dialectics, we can consider the problem to be control over one's work life. As the nature of work becomes increasingly more specialized, the *Un*-Successful Women is deriving less satisfaction with the piecemeal nature of her involvement. Several *Un*-Successful Women lawyers have complained to me that as younger associates they were assigned bits and pieces from different cases, never once feeling that they could identify with the finished product (which might take years to achieve) or with the firm itself. They looked as if they were in control of their jobs, but they felt powerless to affect any significant change, particularly in their work setting. When asked what they would like to do, the responses ranged from quitting their job in order to concentrate on themselves, to going into solo practice, or staying at home with their children. For many *Un*-Successful Women, working in a high-powered law firm means that their time, work, and product are not theirs. The only thing that conceivably belongs to them is their vacation time, maternity leave, and possibly their bonus at the end of the year (and even this is questionable). Unfortunately, law schools and law firms can become the new repository for the going-to-be-Successful Woman who really doesn't know what to do with her own life but wants to learn some marketable skills that will allow her to make a living. In principle, there is nothing wrong with that. In reality, however, the situation is far more serious. Having treated women along the entire spectrum of the legal profession—from students to law professors to managing partners of mid-size firms to solo practitioners—nowhere among these women have I found a sense of deep satisfaction with the legal profession itself. My conclusion is that the law apes the male values of aggressiveness, assertiveness, and competition and leaves many *Un*-Successful Woman lawyers feeling empty and incomplete. This phenomenon seems to be less true in the helping professions, like medicine, social work, nursing, or teaching. Although I certainly don't want to incur the wrath of feminist groups, these professions still seem to afford women a desired opportunity to be emotional and giving in the work world. The legal jobs that many *Un*-Successful Women have chosen, by their very male-oriented nature, will leave many of these women feeling incomplete.

OUTWARDLY DEMANDING OR INWARDLY LAZY?

In an earlier chapter I pointed out that the Successful Woman has totally unrealistic expectations of herself. She needs to accomplish more, to do things perfectly, to prove herself to everyone, to make herself indispensible, and, worst of all, to please others without feeling stressed or tired. She makes things happen. She insists. She coordinates demands. She facilitates. But usually for someone else. When asked why she doesn't use the same amount of energy and focus for pursuing her own life goals and ambitions, she retorts defensively that her job saps most of her energy. She has no time left for herself. When asked why she couldn't work a little less vehemently on the job and reallocate some of her energies to herself, she simply nods her head and reassures me it's not possible. She can't. Then I become more insistent. "You mean you *won't*." At that point, if the Successful Woman is in touch with her feelings, she'll start to resent me. She will simply sit in silence, stewing in anger.

The bottom line is really quite simple. The *Un*-Successful Woman would rather continue to invest her time and energy into projects that are given to her, as opposed to those she might initiate on her own behalf, directed solely by her own requirements for self-fulfillment. In that sense, the *Un*-Successful Woman is lazy. She won't help herself. In her mind, however, she has rationalized her laziness as a function of her busy schedule.

Guess what happened when Adele, a senior executive at an investment banking house, decided in therapy that it was too costly, in both time and money, to pursue the well-deserved answer to "*What do I want?*" You're correct. She returned to her office and began to schedule feverishly, making certain that she didn't have one free moment for herself. One year later I received a call from her telling me that she had been hospitalized for a bleeding ulcer. But even then she wasn't certain that she had the willpower to pursue her Hidden Passion.

"Too lazy to start up your own day-care centers?"

"Perhaps," she replied. She thought for a moment. "Maybe you've got a point. Just maybe you have a point."

INVOLVED IN LIFE OR
EMOTIONALLY NUMB?

Rose inherited a small chain of dry-cleaning stores from her father and built it into a large business. By all outward measures, she was successful. She earned a good living, enjoyed the satisfaction of having developed a strong business, and as a recently divorced mother of four she made sure that she spent a great deal of "quality time" with her children. But something was wrong. By her own admission she felt that she wasn't involved in life. When I asked her what she meant, she said that the business was draining her of all her vitality. She felt conflict that in business she needed to be mistrustful, while in her private life she was asked to be open and trusting. She preferred the latter but didn't know if she could keep "switching." She wanted to spend more time with her children. She wanted to attend PTA meetings and become involved in community-oriented work. But from her point of view the risks were very great. Perhaps she couldn't maintain the style of life to which they were all accustomed. Private schools. Expensive vacations. A large house. Wouldn't that be selfish of her? As she said the word *selfish* her face flushed red.

On the contrary, I said. If she thought only of others, and not of herself, she was headed into a life filled with resentment, frustration, and self-hatred. Eventually her children would grow up and leave the house. Then what excuses would she have for not having involved herself in life as she had wanted? I told her that her work had served a very misguided function of numbing her desires to be engaged on a multitude of levels with life. It was easier to think about her involvement with her work and children than with her expressed desire to feel and experience new sensations and new events.

Rose had a choice: either numb her own life by caring only for others or begin to involve herself in living. She opted out to continue to expand her chain of dry-cleaning stores. Her children remained in private school. And on checking up with her recently, she has not yet attended an evening concert or a PTA meeting. And she infrequently dates.

Other *Un*-Successful Women who have decided to numb themselves emotionally have taken up a variety of "numbing activities": binge eating followed by excruciating diets; drinking; sex; and drugs. Next time you visit your local hospital, notice how many units cater to the treatment of substance abuse. Women are becoming increasingly more addicted to hard drugs as a way of dealing with empty lives. The sudden high that the drugs provide represent a futile attempt at trying to feel complete and fulfilled.

COMPETENT TO LOVE OR FEARFUL OF REJECTION

The *Un*-Successful Woman who is not able to resolve her problem of feeling complete often enters into situations that are marked by masochism (inflicting undue physical or psychological pain on oneself), addiction to love (the need to hold on to the idea of love rather than assess the reality of a relationship), impassioned love (a sense that you cannot live life without him), and a desperate need to cover over feelings of emptiness or depression. This woman is continuously drawn to men who are, for one reason or another, emotionally unavailable. She is drawn to situations that are precarious, fraught with emotional bombshells, uncertainty, and general Sturm und Drang. She finds the nice, stable, obtainable man quite boring. And if she can't invest herself fully in an exciting relationship, then she doesn't want to love at all. Recall the words of that "oldie but goody," "It's now or never." That sense of dramatic finality characterizes her attitude toward the man she can really have. Because if she were to have a steady, stable relationship with him, as she professes to want, she would withdraw in an attempt to reject him before he rejected her.

Marie was a thirty-two-year-old daughter of a lieutenant colonel in the Air Force. She was, by her own description, an Air Force brat who spent most of her time alone while both her parents worked to make ends meet. Marie worked as a personnel counselor in an electronics firm, setting up alcohol- and drug-prevention programs for company employees. Occasionally she would run one or two of the group's counseling sessions in order to get a feel for the type of problems the employees had. She met Roger in one such group. He was a twice-divorced ex-alcoholic who worked in the marketing department of the company. They were immediately attracted to one another. His aloof, distant manner was very exciting to her and she admired the fact that he could admit that he had a problem. To her, this demonstrated both his emotional sensitivity and vulnerability. By being open, he appeared strong.

Unfortunately the next few months showed that her initial impressions were a projection of her own deprived childhood. Like her father, Roger was a moody alcoholic who went into jealous tirades whenever he felt personally threatened, either by her leaving him or becoming too intimate with him. Also like her father, even when he wasn't drunk, he was rarely available to her, either physically or emotionally. But the more abusive Roger became, the more understanding and patient Marie became.

Up to a point! As the newness of the program wore off, Roger attended the sessions less frequently. He became obnoxious at work. She finally broke off their relationship when he became verbally abusive to her during one of her group counseling sessions. After work, he was apologetic and swore that he could change. Marie took him back. But as he became more intimate and loving she began to withdraw. The tumultuous cycle started all over again. Eventually Marie left Roger for good. She transferred to another firm in the Midwest where I understand she has met an ex–drug addict. Any bets? The cycle of masochism and addiction to love remains as an unbroken pattern of behavior that acts as an ineffective cover over feelings of emptiness or depression.

For the most part the *Un*-Successful Woman who is unwilling to change is on a psychological treadmill and can't afford to get off. Unless, I repeat, she starts to focus on the one person from whom she has been running—herself. But to address her needs she has to overcome inertia, laziness, the fear of risk, and the fear of commitment. She has to be courageous enough to say to herself that she cares too much for herself to allow anyone to abuse her or devalue her—no matter how successful she may think she is. One can only begin to love someone else by first loving oneself. And one can only love oneself if the core issues of self-esteem and self-respect have been properly resolved.

ADDICTIVE LOVE

What happens when the *Un*-Successful Woman lives continuously
with chronic dissatisfaction and disillusionment? Does she remain a
success? The answer is more complicated than one might expect. Certain negative traits within her personality become unduly accentuated
(the medical term is *hypertrophied*), and she discovers that she feels
increasingly more desperate and anxious. The initial goals that seemed
so alluring and attractive (power, status, achievement) are no longer
as compelling. As their inherent value is questioned, she becomes
increasingly less self-confident and self-assured. What was once a well-
defined ego with a sense of direction and purpose begins to dissolve
into an amorphous, ambiguous sense of self. It is no longer clear that
she feels connected to anything or anyone. So there is a horrifying,
panicky sensation that she is floating, unattached. Her sense of self is
less strongly defined by her own accomplishments and more by how
others see her. And the pride of success that was once a function of
looking at specific accomplishments now becomes a need to attach
onto someone else (usually of the opposite sex) in order to derive
sustenance, nurturance, a feeling of reality, and a personal sense of
completion. The *Un*-Successful Woman no longer defines herself in
terms of what she may have wanted, but of how well she fulfills the
needs of the man to whom she has attached herself. She becomes, in
the words of the song, *addicted to love*. She needs the presence of a
man (no matter how bad he may be for her) as a way of reassuring
herself of her own presence. The woman who is physically and emotionally beaten clings to her man because in his own perverted way
he is still relating to her; and, she in turn reaffirms her sense of self.
She becomes addicted to a love relationship that affords her two
essential ingredients: 1) an analgesic effect that relieves the pain and
anxiety that she is presently feeling and arose from her sense of being
unconnected, and 2) the other person's reassuring presence as a way
of distracting her from the painful choices and decisions in her own
life. In effect, the *Un*-Successful Woman becomes addicted to "bad"
men and "bad" feelings, all in the service of making certain that she
does not have to confront the real problems in her life.

The *Un*-Successful Woman becomes addicted to men whom she
knows are not good for her as a way of avoiding emptiness, fear,
anxiety, anger, and pain. The greater the fights and turbulence between

the *Un*-Successful Woman and her man, the greater the distraction that preoccupies her time and lessens her need or desire to look at her own problems. So the greater the addiction to love, the greater the distraction.

Like all addictions, there is a definite price to pay. If you've ever been addicted to cigarettes, alcohol, or drugs, you will know exactly what I mean. When the addictive substance is removed you experience a painful physiological and emotional withdrawal. And so it is with the *Un*-Successful Woman who is unable to come to terms with her own Hidden Passions and must attach herself to another person as a way of relieving her own anxiety and pain. Take away that other person and what happens? The *Un*-Successful Woman literally goes into a cold-turkey reaction: chills, nausea, vomiting, sweating, shaking, cramps, anxiety attacks, insomnia. And what does the *Un*-Successful Woman do to relieve these feelings of withdrawal? She frequently turns to another man, possibly a past relationship that never worked out, or to drugs.[1]

Hard to believe, isn't it, that three simple questions, if never asked—*"What do I want?" "How do I get it?"* and *"What will I risk for it?"*—can lead to so much misery and pain. Perhaps I am dramatizing the pain. Rest assured, if anything I am underemphasizing it. But the situation becomes even more entangled. Where once the *Un*-Successful Woman spent most of her time focusing on her career, family, or friends, she now spends more of her time invested in other people's problems, which are chaotic, confusing, disturbing, and emotionally painful. She involves herself in relationships that need fixing. Why? Why should someone who is rapidly falling into her own personal disarray involve herself with someone else's problems? For one, misery loves company. But even more important is the fact that as long as she does not have to focus on her need to take responsibility for herself, she is doing fine (or at least that's the way she thinks).

Remember, the *Un*-Successful Woman has always been good at figuring out how to solve problems. What easier task is there, if she can't solve her own problems, than to try to solve other people's problems. And believe me, she will do well by them. For herself it's a complete strikeout. But for others she may hit a home run. She will gladly help her friend Sandy, who's breaking up with Lewis, because she can avoid having to make any decisions that might resolve her own pain. At this point in her life, the *Un*-Successful Woman does not really know who she is. Being involved in other people's lives keeps her from having to stand still and confront herself with the questions she must ask of herself, and with the decisions she must make. All this to avoid her own pain, anxiety, indecision, confusion, fear, and depression. Yes, depression.

Many therapists consider what I am talking about—the need to feel whole or complete—as the first step to depression because they feel that the Successful Woman is engaged in a futile effort to recover the loss of a mother's love that in fact she may never have had. As I stated in earlier chapters, I don't think that the Successful Woman is inherently depressed. She may become depressed. Initially there is no evidence of anger, loss, disappointment. Instead, I hear talk of a yearning, a sense of wanting, not of loss. So when the *Un*-Successful Woman has the opportunity to explore her own needs, but refuses or is unable to (for whatever reason), she has lost the chance to evolve and grow. And that loss of a chance or a dream transforms itself into a narcissistic injury, as damage to the self-esteem that is then internalized as anger or rage or, more commonly, depression. To avoid dealing with her pain, the *Un*-Successful Woman forces herself into a position of hyperactivity and irresponsibility.

Susan was a fifty-three-year-old corporate executive whose first husband died from a heart attack at the age of thirty-nine. They had no children and had been an extremely close couple. When he died, she became very depressed, fearful that the world around her had been taken away. Just prior to the time of his death, they had been talking about adopting children. She had felt that although they led a very rich life, it wasn't complete without the presence of children. He had been hesitant. In retrospect, she admitted that she had been angry with him over that hesistancy, but had never had the opportunity to articulate her feelings. Susan came in to see me two years after her husband's death. She had been dating an old boyfriend who was abusive. Although he kept her emotionally strung out, she was having a problem breaking off the relationship.

Of course I asked her what she wanted for herself. She replied with a weak smile that she wanted to be happily married again and adopt a child. What prevented her from having what she wanted? She shrugged her shoulders sheepishly. "I can't let go. I'm afraid of being abandoned again. I know he's not good for me. But I need him now." I pointed out to her that she was acting like a woman who had no self-esteem and who didn't believe that she deserved to be happy. She was living in a fantasy world of what it would be like *if* she and her boyfriend were able to live together. But whenever I pointed out to her that her fantasies were not realistic she became angry and questioned my competence. Although this was the first session, and we had only met an hour before, I figured that my training and experience gave me the right to judge her present situation.

When I suggested we take a short break, she became more enraged. Why was she so angry?

"All you men are alike—either criticizing me and putting me down—or raising my expectations and then abandoning me. Just like my husband."

I added, "When he died inconveniently and left you alone and stranded."

She wanted to cry, but she wouldn't give me the satisfaction that I was right. The anger and depression she had felt after her husband's death was still with her. Unless she decided that it was in her own interest to mourn the loss of her husband and proceed with her life in the way she had outlined it—continue with her profession, find another mature man, and adopt a child—she would soon find herself bouncing from one turbulent relationship to another until there was nothing left of either her emotional or professional life. In an attempt to shake her out of her self-righteous anger, I told her that the outcome was grave if she did not attend to her own needs now, instead of worrying about her boyfriend and the disruptive nature of their relationship.

I didn't see her again for two months. When she made an appointment to see me, she announced in a voice filled with righteous indignation that per my instructions she had left her boyfriend. She was now dating an accountant in his early fifties whom she felt could be protective. From her description he was a passive-dependent fellow who offered her the respite she needed (running away from herself). Well, no sooner had she started dating him than she also found a married man with two children who could not in his wildest imagination consider leaving his family. The last I heard of her she was on to her third married man, living in some variant of a *ménage à trois*. Her need to be attached had become more pronounced and, as she became more desperate, she had also become more depressed.

Many of the unfulfilled *Un*-Successful Women who come into my office tell me how much trouble they are having with their boyfriend or husband, but swear that the only thing that keeps the relationship together is the incredibly wonderful sex life they have. Most if not all of the women have been instructed in one way or another to believe that good sex means "real love" and that sex couldn't be "that good" unless the rest of the relationship was really "that good." So much for popular psychology. For the *Un*-Successful Woman addicted to love, nothing could be farther from the truth. In fact, as a result of the different psychological dynamics working on many different levels, a bad relationship can be a necessary ingredient for making sex piquant and exciting. How this phenomenon comes about is largely a testimony to the ability of the mind to rationalize difficult situations in a way that make others seem most pleasurable! *Un*-Successful Women who are unfulfilled and become addicted to love are projecting their own frustrated needs (feeling incomplete; sleepwalking through life) onto their less than deserving lover. What the *Un*-Successful Woman needs to believe in order to sustain an untenable relationship is a fantasy of her lover as a dormant flower awaiting her tender love and care in order to blossom. She feels that she is the only one who can awaken her lover to *his* Hidden Passions. In one of the cleverest tricks of the mind, she is able to rationalize his anger, depression, sadism, and moodiness as something that she alone can understand and change. Perhaps, she decides, he has never *really* been loved before. In effect, the *Un*-Successful Woman is pitting her love against his shortcomings. Her love can overcome whatever real or imagined pathology he might have. And one way she can awaken him to her love is through the sex act. So we return to where we began, with an intensely passionate sexual relationship that the *Un*-Successful Woman is able to use to awaken her lover to the passion of love he long deserved. At the same time, both parties discover that sex is a good way to break up the tension that exists between them. Sex becomes the one area of her personal life in which the *Un*-Successful Woman feels competent and appreciated. If the *Un*-Successful Woman is truly mismatched with her partner, sex can become the most reasonable, interesting, and legitimate way of relating to one another.

Lucinda was a twenty-one-year-old college senior who had been dating one of her professors of political science. You've seen this scene in scores of films. Neither the scene nor the outcome are likely to change. He, as you can imagine, was married, with two children. Lucinda wanted to get a master's degree in international relations, so she felt particularly honored when he asked her if she would be his teaching assistant. Soon it happened: The respected professor and the impressionable graduate student found themselves in her in-town apartment most afternoons and sometimes all day Saturday. Over a six-month period she became indispensible to him—grading his papers, writing his exams, scheduling his lectures. She felt warm and wanted. In that way he was very much unlike her father, an aloof physician who rarely showed her any affection or spent time with her.

Lucinda and her professor soon began to talk about marriage, with the professor saying all the words Lucinda wanted to hear. He would leave his wife and children and move in with her; six months later they would be married. That afternoon she gave of herself, in a way she had never done before. It was rapturous bliss for both of them. Six weeks later she announced that she was pregnant. He said nothing. Their subsequent relationship became rocky. The only thing she had to hold on to was the "incredible sex" they had between them. He broke appointments. He grew tense. The day of reckoning finally came. Should she deliver his baby or abort? Would he come with her to see the obstetrician? He promised that he would. She ended up going for her abortion alone. She became depressed, but she quickly reconstituted herself, determining never again to allow herself to be taken advantage of like this. But after several weeks and a handful of excuses, the professor returned to her bed.

Lucinda came to see me because she wanted to break off the relationship and pursue her master's degree without distractions. A few months into her therapy I received a call from a therapist at an abortion clinic who wanted to know some relevant information about Lucinda. Without speaking directly to me, Lucinda was notifying me that she had failed in her noble endeavor. She was, as I had prophesied, an addict to love.

Like so many other *Un*-Successful Women, Lucinda grew up too quickly, and in the process had not received her share of nurturance, affection, and attention. In Lucinda's case her father had had prostate cancer and was in and out of hospitals for various treatments. She was always in the hospital to either help her mother or visit her father. While her mother worked in a bank to support the family, Lucinda acted as the surrogate mother, taking care of her younger sister as well as doing all the shopping and cooking. Her mother would come home exhausted, complaining that she no longer had a family life or a husband. At one point, her mother confided in her that she was having an affair with the regional bank vice president. Instead of being shocked, Lucinda replied that she understood what her mother was saying. While her mother was very appreciative that Lucinda didn't judge her harshly, in fact, Lucinda admitted to me that she had felt that she had no choice. She was totally overwhelmed by the role of confidante her mother was putting her in. But at the same time she felt extremely guilty that she was now an accomplice to her mother's betrayal. Lucinda listened to her because she was afraid of the repercussions if she didn't. She stood to lose her mother's love and precipitate a medical and family crisis with her father. So she was both protective of her mother's secret and her father's health. But in the meantime she felt extremely vulnerable and anxious. Exposed.

Despite her youth there wasn't anyone out there to protect her. Her own needs for warmth and caring went unmet. While she was pretending to be strong and healthy, she became emotionally more needy. At school she hung around the older boys, in the hopes that one of them might notice her. She wanted advice from the older girls in the high school, but none was forthcoming. She was alone. And her need for affection, attention, and love grew exponentially. Having learned to deny her own yearnings she looked around for situations that would give her the opportunity to help others (so that she could forget her own needs). When the professor came along she had an opportunity to express love through both sex (at which she had become extremely proficient) and her intellect (she helped the professor in his academic tasks). All the while she hoped that he would one day help her and give her the long-awaited love.

Two basic ego defense mechanisms were operating during this deteriorating period of the *Un*-Successful Woman's life—denial and control. Denial is a psychological mechanism that allows the *Un*-Successful Woman to be out of touch with the reality of her own circumstances and the feelings that those circumstances engender. Control is a personality modality which allows her to delineate and measure her environment. An *Un*-Successful Woman uses control as a way of relating to herself and to others. She can attempt to control her emotions. She can attempt to control the person whose presence and activity might activate that emotion. Both denial and control are tools of self-protection. Each feeds into the other. Denial supports control, and the absence of control invigorates denial. Using both control and denial the *Un*-Successful Woman takes her addiction for love into someone else's relationship in order to replay the oedipal strivings, recreating what I call the Eternal Triangle.

THE ETERNAL TRIANGLE

Unable to attain an inner core of wholeness, the *Un*-Successful Woman wanders through her life in a desperate search for people and relationships she can introject to make herself feel complete. In simpler terms, the *Un*-Successful Woman tries to complete her personal jigsaw puzzle with relationships that are frequently destined to self-destruct. A love triangle may become (at least on the surface) a convenient escape from feelings of insecurity, uncertainty, and nonconnectedness.[2] The *Un*-Successful Woman will invariably form an attachment to someone who is unattainable, based on her compulsion to recapitulate and master the childhood task of winning the love and attention of someone who is not going to give it to her (e.g., the aloof father). But underlying this compulsion is a basic fear of forming a meaningful relationship with a man (or woman) of one's own choosing. By holding on to a love triangle (e.g., having an affair with a married man), the *Un*-Successful Woman assures herself of not having to go through the pain and loneliness of a potential abandonment; she cannot lose what she cannot have. In her heart of hearts she feels safe in her extramarital relationship because she knows no matter how strongly he may protest otherwise, her lover will never be available to her. She knows she is safe. She feels exactly the same way she felt when her father stood by her and held her little hand in his big palm. But a love triangle is usually destructive—often causing the *Un*-Successful Woman to feel humiliation, jealousy, rage, and rejection.

Helene, a thirty-nine-year-old single corporate lawyer, had an ongoing five-year affair with Alan, a senior principal at an investment banking firm. They spent an inordinate amount of time together. But she, rightfully, wouldn't feel complete until he divorced his wife and married her, which he claimed he had every intention of doing. Alan promised to do this when three of his daughters graduated from high school, which was only four years away. Over that four-year period of time I saw Helene on a monthly basis, helping her deal with her anger, jealousy, and humiliation. She felt ashamed that she was forced to walk the "back streets" of life in order for them to maintain their love affair. Although she professed to understand Alan's difficult situation, she nevertheless felt as if she were the sacrificial lamb on this triangular altar of love. However, true to his word, he divorced his wife of twenty years and married Helene as soon as his three girls graduated from high school.

Helene left therapy and sent me letters that kept me informed of her not surprising progress. As one might imagine, she was immensely happy. Within a short period of time she gave birth to their daughter, whom she not so sarcastically named Patience. Then it started to happen! Her underlying feelings of humilation, anger, and hurt, buried all those years of having to wait, began to crystallize. Previously, Helene had been angry at her rival—Alan's ex-wife. But now his ex-wife was no longer there. So as logic would dictate she became angry at him. Where once he stood as the pinnacle of honesty and virtue, now he stood denigrated as naïve and simple. Where once he was frugal and wise, now she saw him as cheap and petty. Her rage started to escalate noticeably. She returned to therapy during this period of time and gave me a tongue lashing that I abruptly stopped. I was not the object of her rage, I reminded her, I was simply there to try to help her with her problem. I asked her what she wanted to do for herself, and she replied that it was none of my business. So the anger turned to revenge. Within a short period of time she began an affair with another married man and left Alan. She took Patience with her. In a letter postmarked from halfway around the world she wrote to me (I'm paraphrasing) that revenge was sweet and worth waiting for. Her revenge for having felt humiliated in the love triangle was to place Alan in her former position. Taking Patience away from him was her way of paying him back for having placed his three daughters' welfare ahead of hers. After that letter, I never heard from her again.

The *Un*-Successful Woman who refuses to confront her own needs and is unwilling to change accordingly becomes chronically dissatisfied and disillusioned. She also discovers that she feels increasingly more anxious, desperate, and insecure. In order to cover up these feelings of disorientation, alienation, and unconnectedness she finds herself compelled to attach herself to someone else (usually a man) in order to derive sustenance, nurturance, and a personal sense of reality. She becomes addicted to love and enters a love triangle (eternal triangle) as a way of numbing her pain and to avoid dealing with the difficult choices and decisions in her life. She seeks out love and the impossible triangular relationship as an imperfect solution to her interminable problem of not ascertaining *who she is* and *what she wants*.

PART
II

HOW TO BECOME
THE COMPLETE
WOMAN

CHAPTER 7

How to Make Yourself Number One

The road to self-discovery is probably the most exciting, fascinating voyage you will ever make. Despite the intense loneliness that may be involved in learning to put yourself first in your own life, I guarantee the following: you will experience immense satisfaction in probing your inner thoughts and feelings, examining them carefully, weighing their relative importance, and making some life-altering decisions. All for you! And not for a selfish you. Quite the opposite. For an individual who has finally realized that you deserve the respect, caring, loving, and commitment of all of the significant others in your life on whom you currently focus your attention. There *is* enough of you to go around. But the circle starts with you, not ends with you. While less than that seems to suffice for the short term, you *are* reading this book. You do know you are feeling imcomplete. You are not happy. And I am saying that all this can change for the better over the long term, if you will make a commitment to yourself—and make yourself number one.

TIME OUT FOR YOU

I want you to take five minutes a day out of your busy schedule to think about yourself. I don't care if it comes from your jogging time, your morning sleep, your car-pool lineups, your lunch hour. The time just has to be there and it has to be spent focused on you!

Sit down or lie down in a quiet place, where you won't be interrupted. Be alone with yourself. Imagine that there is no one "out there" except you. You are the only one to whom you can confide your thoughts, doubts, uncertainties, fears. You are the only one who must listen to your inner voice, *the best part of you*, which usually gets repressed. That inner voice will be an important companion to you on your journey toward self-change. But before you start you will have to make your first commitment. An easy one, but a commitment nevertheless: *You are the one and only person about whom you must think during this time.* Not anyone else! Not your parents, your sister, your brother, your kids, your husband, your job. Not nobody! Get the point? For the first time in your life you will have no one else to think about. You will be resting in silence, thinking only about "me," "I," "myself."

Let me just add a few words before you proceed. This will be your first exercise coming up. For many of you this exercise will appear familiar or childish. If you feel that it may not be relevant to you then simply move on to another section of the chapter. However, try to bear with me for a little while longer. An exercise is not the Gospel or the Ten Commandments (at least not the way I write it). It is simply intended as an opportunity for you to develop those skills (focus, patience, analysis, relaxation) that are required if you want to learn and grow. Many of these are exercises that have been used by a wide variety of psychiatrists, psychologists, and psychotherapists and are adapted for specific use in this book. Remember, the basic intent of these exercises is to allow you a method of acquiring some degree of control and comfort over the process of self-analysis and personal growth. The exercises are broken down into different components (steps, questions, reflections) in order to ease you gently into a graduated attempt at helping yourself.

Again, take it easy on yourself and try to enjoy this exciting adventure.

Step 1: *Relax with Yourself*

1. Rest in a quiet place—your home, your office, your car. Close the door. Close your eyes. Relax. Let all the tension of the day flow down your body, down your tight neck, down your arms, legs. Visualize the large muscle groups in your arms, shoulders, back, stomach, thighs, legs. Now verbally instruct those muscle groups to release their tension and relax. For those of you who have taken TM (transcendental meditation) or Behavioral Desensitization, you will immediately recognize what I am doing. Feel and visualize that tension disappear.

Now begin to see a physical image of yourself as a person who is a friend. A person who looks like a best friend. A person who looks affectionately at you. Remember, no one in this world could ever be as good a friend to you as you can be to yourself. Feel embarrassed? Awkward? That's okay. We all are when we begin to encounter a new person.

2. Feel a warm sensation permeate your body. Your body is flushed with kindness and compassion. How do these emotions feel? Warm. Relaxing. Secure. A soothing, almost caressing feeling will move over your entire body. There is a real warmth inside of you that is all yours. It's from you and by you and for you. If you don't feel this right away, don't worry! You can start up again in a few minutes or sometime later. Remember, you are in no hurry. You've waited this long. You can wait a little longer.

If you are relaxed and want to continue, I want you to talk to yourself. I want you to tell this new person that she is your best friend! Silly? Not really! I'm always amazed how hard it is for the Successful Woman to accept herself as someone she should care for or love. So talk to this new person, this new you. Tell yourself about all those wonderful traits you've always been proud of. Your intelligence. Your sensitivity. Your helpfulness. Your diligence. Your self-sacrifices. Enumerate all of these wonderful parts of you—for your own benefit. Congratulate yourself. You've done enough if you are able to do this for three or four days.

Step 2: *Accentuate the Positive*

Now that you are able to sit down with yourself for five minutes a day, I want you to take ten minutes to entertain a very scary question:

If I have only twenty-four hours to live, what should I write for my eulogy? While a depressing question, it's one that quickly helps you focus on the good parts of what you've accomplished. And after you've investigated them in your mind, and reached a tentative list of good things about yourself that you would include in your eulogy, you've no doubt started thinking about those things you are sorry you did not get to accomplish. This is an exercise that is meant to help you like yourself; at least, to appreciate your own positive attributes. So the longer the list the better. I'm sure that you can easily come up with ten accomplishments—as *you* see them.

Now put yourself in the role of your husband. Your children. Your parents. Your colleagues. Your friends. What ten items would each of those groups include in a eulogy for you? Don't they make you feel good about yourself?

Yes, you are a deserving person. You've accomplished a lot in the eyes of many people. You have the right to think about *new* things. New accomplishments. *Changes* that will suit the person you *now* want to become. Remember, change doesn't have to mean that you are now going to disappoint everyone who currently admires and loves you. Undoubtedly, some people will get more of you; some people will get less of you. But no deals were ever struck early on in the game of life that said that apportionment can't change. The only thing that really counts—and that you have to keep foremost in your mind—is that you have to come out a winner.

Step 3: *Taking Inventory*

When I was in medical school, slaving over my textbooks, absorbing an inordinate amount of information in a compressed time span, I used to ask myself the question "If I only had twenty-four hours to live, how would I spend the remaining day of my life?" Would I really sit at a desk in a sparse dormitory room trying to memorize the twelve cranial nerves? The answer was "Certainly not." Clearly I didn't want to spend the last day of my life studying. But what that question really did was force me to pry open the other crevices of my life—the doubts, the uncertainties, the hopes, the dreams, the disappointments—to expose them to the light of day. That type of questioning forced me some twenty years ago to ask myself some basic questions about what I really wanted. As a result, I realized that clinical medicine was not going to be my full-time vocation. But neither would I abandon it. What I did was to incorporate its relevant parts into the "me" I wanted to become—and this involved everything from understanding international relations from a psychological perspective to using my knowledge of people and personalities in my fiction and nonfiction books.

I may have come to grips with "me" earlier in life than most. Now it's time to come to grips with you. Now that you know the many reasons why you like yourself, you're ready to ask some more difficult questions. You may want to use a pad and paper. And assume that you will now be spending fifteen to twenty minutes with yourself, trying to answer the following questions:

> **1.** How satisfied are you with the way that you have lived your life thus far (on a scale of 1 to 10)?
>
> **2.** Are there goals you had wanted to obtain but were not able to for whatever reasons? What were they?
>
> **3.** Are you satisfied that your specific talents (be they in the arts, sciences, business, or professions) were ever explored? Developed? What are they?
>
> **4.** If you had another chance to live your life, what goals and talents would you try to achieve and master?
>
> **5.** How satisfied with your life would you be if you could achieve these goals (on a scale of 1 to 10)?

Compare your response to the "currently satisfied" scale in question 1 (above) with your response to the "future achievements" scale in question 5 (above). If they are different—if future possibilities would be more satisfactory than current reality—it is time to seriously consider change.

The really difficult questions about risk and commitment come next.

> **6.** What prevents you from changing your life?
> **7.** What do you risk by making changes in your life?
> **8.** What do you gain by making changes in your life?
> **9.** Do the gains outweigh the risks?

A short parenthetical note. No matter how long one lives with someone, one never, never really knows him or her. Believe me! I'll tell you a funny (perhaps not so funny) thing that happened when I completed this section. My wife of twenty years, who proofreads all of my manuscripts, started penciling in her own responses. And I was quite surprised by them. She is an accomplished ex-academician (Ph.D. in sociology) cum-businesswoman who now owns and operates a chain of bed-and-breakfast inns across the country. She is also a mother of two and a wife. She had several very interesting answers that opened up a series of discussions between us about where she was at this particular point in her life, and what things in her life she might want to change.

In response to question 1, on being currently satisfied, she replied "For the most part. But I would like to be connected to a larger community and concerned about people other than myself and my immediate family." When I asked her what she meant, she reminded me that prior to our marriage she had always been involved in social causes. Now that she was in business for herself, she disliked the absence of altruism and concern for the larger community. She really couldn't get excited about the financial "bottom line." She answered question 4, about future achievements, in a way that I found refreshing and typical of the Successful Women I have been talking about. "I would do something with more creativity. But at present I don't know exactly what it is. Also, I would not have as many routines. I want more spontaneity in my life." Her last response should become the motto of the Successful Woman (and I didn't even coach her): "If I had a chance to do it over again, *I would become more selfish, more goal directed, and more outwardly emotional.*"

Fascinating! After several weeks of discussion, my wife decided to sell her business and start a new professional life, returning to her socially conscious roots. She eventually wants to join a nonprofit organization that deals with civil rights. For the present, she has made a small start in expanding herself by agreeing to join the board of directors of a woman's theater, helping them to grow in a professional way.

Step 4: *Write Down Your Thoughts*

As a therapist, I am not prone to using "gimmicks" to help a patient. However, I have learned from both my own and my patients' experiences that keeping a diary (or what psychiatrists call "process notes") is an important technique in uncovering Hidden Passions.[1]

THE OBSERVER'S LOG

All of my patients are encouraged to keep a log of their journey toward uncovering their Hidden Passions. I instruct them to keep as detailed an account as possible of all the events that transpire while they are in therapy. Nothing is to be excluded from the log—and, I literally mean, nothing. Lest you think that you might be writing drivel, may I remind you that the Pulitzer Prize–winning poet Anne Sexton started writing her poems at the suggestion of her psychiatrist. So for many of you aspiring writers (who of us is not?) this is your chance. And just think how profitable Woody Allen's psychoanalysis has been. I understand that a lot of the material in his movies arises from his therapy.

ACQUIRING DATA

The most obvious reason for keeping a log turns out to be the most important reason—data. Information. You would be surprised to see how much transpires in one day of your life. No, in one hour of your life. You have calls to make, people to see, projects to finish, obligations to meet, responsibilities to assume. So within any given period of time a lot is happening. With so much going on, there is just too much data to recall without recording it. This does not mean that you walk around your office or your home with your face buried in your notebook. I treated a Successful Woman who took my direction literally and tried to record everything. She was extremely compulsive anyway. One day when I asked her why she looked so exhausted and kept falling asleep in my sessions, she apologized and replied that in order for her to keep her diary up to date, she had to stay up an extra two hours a night transcribing the notes she had made during the day. That is not what I mean. At most, you should spend twenty minutes each evening writing down your thoughts, impressions, feelings, and events of the day. This information is the raw data from which we can work.

BAROMETER OF FEELINGS

Since the objective of this book is to mobilize those Hidden Passions that are buried beneath the busywork of everyday living, it is extremely important that you be able to recognize the particular *feelings* you experience during the day, and record them for future use. Writing down your feelings forces you to carefully observe what happens around you and to express what you feel about it. Similarly, keeping a log of your emotions allows you to look back over a period of time and see how a relationship arose and what that relationship felt like at the time. So writing about your feelings forces you to *notice* your feelings. A log also forces you to become a succinct observer of your life and all its relevant component parts. With the new role of observer, you have an ally (a part of yourself) who can help you to understand yourself so that you can begin to grow in the direction that you may want.[2] Most patients claim that once they get into the habit of sitting down at the end of each day to review the events of the day and record them in a book, they find the process quite pleasurable. They soon look forward to going over their day's activities. It's a way of reliving and reflecting upon them. You can call it a human video.

CORRECTING DISTORTIONS

Keeping a log is a good way of seeing what actually happened in a relationship. Most of us tend to distort or change past events or emotions, especially if they were painful or debilitating. Even pleasurable emotions become distorted, either exaggerated (in order to compensate for other pains) or negated (when viewed through anger).

Jocelynne, a forty-eight-year-old schoolteacher, had a tempestuous relationship with Craig, her on-again-off-again lover of four years. Whenever they were together, she would write,

> He made me feel complete, whole, sensuous, and (excuse the redundancy) sexy. There are times that I literally cannot live without him. He makes me feel alive. However, and I

emphasize however, he can also be a real *shit*! It doesn't take very much. He starts taking me for granted. He becomes entitled. He feels just because I enjoy sex with him that I should cater to his every whim. Guess what? We fight. He storms out. I don't see him for a couple of weeks, and then he returns. Because I miss him so much I weaken and invite him back into the relationship. I invariably forget why we even fought in the first place.

When Jocelynne was in therapy, she would often forget what brought her to see me. When I suggested that she begin to record her relationship with Craig, she balked. But then she began to keep a detailed account of how Craig would psychologically abuse her—withdraw his emotions, demand constant attention, yell at her. Jocelynne was extremely surprised to read, in her own log, how often she felt dejected, rejected, abused, and abandoned. Far more frequently and intensely than she ever could recall. I pointed out that in order for her to remain in the relationship, she had begun to rationalize away the pain, and memory lapse came into play. In the beginning she resented this observation. She thought I might be wrong. But when I asked her to bring in her log, and together we read the parts pertaining to their relationship, she became determined to terminate the relationship with Craig.

AN EMOTIONAL HELPER

The log for Jocelynne became a reference text in which she could check not only the distortions of her emotions, but also refer to those feelings, attitudes, or beliefs that could be useful in separating herself from her loved one.

Jocelynne needed to refer back to her log to an episode when she and Craig had "split up" once before. She wanted to understand the sequence of events as it had transpired. What she realized was that as soon as she announced that she would be leaving on a business trip, Craig would withdraw emotionally, become moody, sarcastic, and peevish. Reading the different excerpts of her log, she realized that what Craig needed more than anything else was a mother who could nurture him. Someone who could assure him that every separation was not an abandonment and every good-bye was not final. She began to realize that their relationship was becoming increasingly costly to her, both emotionally and physically. She literally was becoming ill, wondering whether or not he would show up for a designated appointment.

In preparing her final farewell to Craig, Jocelynne read over the passages that she felt would best help her to handle his emotional immaturity. As a result she approached him in a way that minimized the emotional trauma on *her*. She talked about the wonderful times they had together, but she emphasized that they had also come to a point in their relationship that was a dead end. There was no way to go but down. As predicted, Craig became vituperative. Jocelynne pulled back and braced herself for what she correctly knew would be an emotional onslaught. This time she was prepared. Her log was her textbook.

UNCOVERING PSYCHODYNAMIC PATTERNS

I was able to use Jocelynne's log as resource material to point out how she would consistently allow herself to enter into relationships that were potentially self-destructive. In the beginning she was incredulous. She saw herself as a highly maternal, nurturant woman who simply wanted to give to a man. When I told her that by giving in the way she did she was being highly manipulative and controlling, she got angry. But when we read specific passages from her log, she quieted down. In one session she read the following passage:

> I don't understand exactly what is happening. Last night, I prepared a wonderful meal of veal and spaghetti just the way Craig liked it—not too hard, not too soft. I had asked him to bring red wine, but he had forgotten. He seemed tense. Uncomfortable. The more I tried to make him comfortable, by making pleasant, light conversation or giving him more food, the more irritable he became. I had just the opposite effect on him from what I had intended. That's the way it always happens. He becomes silent and withdrawn, and de-

fensively I try to avoid the confrontation that I know will invariably arise. I knew this would happen. I had been putting it off for so long. I had to leave the day after tomorrow, and he knew that I was leaving, but instead of dealing with it directly, he withdrew into silence and I became more defensive and manipulative—all in an effort to avoid the kind of no-holds-barred confrontation that I had had with my father when I was a kid.

The psychodynamic pattern she usually followed in her relationships had been set down—by her.

What do I mean by psychodynamic patterns? Perhaps it's no more than a fancy way of identifying how we relate to people. If the Successful Woman is able to recognize her own needs, doubts, and ambivalences, and see how they interplay with her boss, her family, her lover, her friends, then she can read out a script about herself which, believe it or not, has a strong predictive capacity for the future.

Heather was a forty-one-year-old mortgage banker with one son. For the most part, she prided herself on being able to read her customers well. She was by all criteria a Successful Woman. Nevertheless she felt that her life was incomplete. She couldn't understand why she was not able to attract a man (she was divorced) into more than a three-month relationship. I asked her, as I would ask you, to list those characteristics of the men to whom she was generally attracted. She said all of them were impressive looking although not necessarily handsome. They were charismatic, independent, self-made men, who had a clear sense of themselves and where they were going. Then I asked her to pick out from her diary whether any of them had been previously married. She went down the list and found that two out of the three had been divorced. Each had been married not once, but twice. The third man had a stormy marriage and was in the process of divorce.

I could never have been more convincing to her than her own log. It was obvious that she was unwittingly picking men who, by their own history, were unable to form long-term relationships. What she subsequently uncovered about herself in therapy was that she needed this sort of man, who she found unthreatening. Furthermore, she uncovered another pattern in her choice of men. Each man had a major character flaw, whether it was drinking, gambling, or womanizing. When asked, she denied knowing anything about these flaws—until she went back to her log. There it was. On the first date with each of the men she had written down a notation to the effect that there was "something strange," with words in the margin such as "drink?" "gamble?" "sex?" But she had always decided to ignore her instincts and her inner voice. Her unconscious psychodynamics were playing out a pattern that was determined early in her life by her supportive relationship to a weak father. Over the years she continued to repeat that pattern by entering into relationships with and supporting weak, uncommitted men just like her father.

UNCOVERING PATTERNS IN RELATIONSHIPS: AN EXAMPLE

Your log, as you can see, can be of immense help in sorting out fact from fiction. It doesn't lie, like memory frequently does. It is a witness to history—your history—as you experienced it *at the time.*

There are many ways in which your log can be used, many questions that can be put to the content of its pages, and many patterns in your life that you can uncover. The following steps set out one approach to using your log to uncover patterns of interrelationships.

1. List Physical Characteristics

Go through your log and your memory, as far back as you can, and set down the physical attributes of the men and/or women with whom you have had a meaningful relationship (it does not necessarily have to have been an intimate one). List their:

> —Height
> —Weight
> —Complexion
> —Mannerisms
> —Unusual characteristics
> —Color of hair
> —Facial characteristics

　　　　—Physical characteristics
　　　　—Habits

See if there are any physical similarities among your choice of friends and lovers.

2. List Personality Attributes

Now review these individuals for their personality attributes. Which adjectives best describe him or her? Think carefully; the obvious traits don't always accurately reflect underlying dynamics. The list below contains examples of the traits you might include:

　　　　—Charismatic or self-effacing?
　　　　—Insecure or self-assured?
　　　　—Extrovert or introvert?
　　　　—Passive or aggressive?
　　　　—Aloof or engaging?
　　　　—Moody or stable?
　　　　—Dependent or independent?
　　　　—Lucky or unlucky?

　　(Some people always look as if they are losers—no matter what they do.)

　　　　—Dominant or submissive?
　　　　—Caring or indifferent?
　　　　—Persevering or a quitter?
　　　　—Emotional or controlled?
　　　　—Self-directed or externally directed?

Do you keep choosing friends or loved ones with similar personality traits?

3. List Patterns of Interaction

This is an extremely important category of questions because the answers will provide a very clear idea of how *you* interact with other people (not only men). To get the most out of this section, I would strongly recommend that you separate your answers about your patterns of interaction into the following groups: lover(s), husband, employer, coworker(s), friends, children, parents. Put in whatever other categories you might think are appropriate. And add to the list of questions below any others you think might be helpful in analyzing your patterns of interaction. I have structured the questions as if you were asking them of a lover.

1. How did the relationship start? Did you initiate it? Did someone else?

2. Did you have to chase him? Did he pursue you? Have the roles changed from hunter to hunted? If so, when and how?

3. Who was initially dominant in the relationship? Who was submissive? Did the roles change? When? How?

4. What were your feelings about him and yourself in the beginning of the relationship? In the middle? And at the end?

5. Do you feel you were in control of the relationship in the beginning? The middle? Or the end?

6. At the various stages of a relationship—beginning, middle, end—what were you feeling, and why?

—Content?	—Guilty?
—Elated?	—Nervous?
—Indifferent?	—Anxious?
—Depressed?	—Frightened?
—Numb?	—Needy?
—Angry?	—Uncertain?
—Sad?	—Bored?
—In love?	

7. What were your needs in the relationship?

—Love?	—Caring?
—Warmth?	—Romance?
—Connectedness?	—Intensity?
—Understanding?	—Compassion?
—Challenge?	—Passion?
—Security?	

8. Do you feel your needs were met at the beginning of the relationship? The middle? Or the end? How were they met?

9. What was sex like in the relationship? Did he fulfill your needs? Did you meet his needs? If not, why not?

10. How did the relationship progress? Was it stormy? Smooth? Challenging? Or was it predictably uneventful?

11. How did the relationship end? Was it painful? Why? Was it brutal? Why? Who left first? Why? Was anything tried to bring him back? Why?

12. Overall was the relationship worthwhile? (This, of course, can be answered with a yes or no; and if you believe that, I'll sell you the Brooklyn Bridge.)

As you look over the answers to these questions, I hope you will discern a pattern of interaction that will tell you just how you relate to the people around you. What these questions can help you to do is to force you to think about your style of relating to people as well as its implications for your personality. For example, the first question asks you who initiated the relationship. You or someone else? When you think about the answer to that question you are, in effect, forced to realize certain things about yourself. Are you passive or proactive? Are you someone who waits for things to happen to her or do you initiate events and relationships? Is passivity or aggressiveness a predominant characteristic of your personality? Is it something you might want to change?

The questions in this section of the chapter as well as in other parts of the book serve to focus the primary attention on only you. From that point on, you have only yourself to question and probe. Believe me, that's a powerful combination. As we say in the Orient, may a thousand questions blossom.

FINDING SELF-PATTERNS

The way you relate to yourself (as opposed to relating to someone else) is possibly more important than how you relate to others. I call these *self-patterns*. What do you expect from yourself? How does this expectation translate into your everyday behavior? As I pointed out earlier, many of the assumptions upon which a Successful Woman operates are based on self-perceptions that have no correspondence in reality. Unfortunately the self-perceptions generate self-patterns of behavior that frequently lead to a cycle of stress, disappointment, overreaction, more stress, and finally collapse. The positive part of this is that patterns of self-behavior are evident early on, even if you might not want to admit to them.

The following questions, and your honest answers, will provide you with a great deal of information on patterns you have formed, and that influence your own assessment of yourself.

1. Do you feel that whatever you have to do must be done as well as you can do it? And even then, you might want to do it again, better?

2. How do you feel when your employer or your husband or even your children ask you to do something? Do you respond positively most of the time? Do you respond with the feeling that you can't do enough? Do you ever become angry? When? Why?

3. When you have accomplished something, do you feel you've done enough? If not, what do you feel? Inadequate? Anxious? Do you feel you should be doing more? What more would you be doing?

4. During any part of the day do you feel tired or stressed? What does that feel like physically? Do you feel it in your neck (tightness), over your eyes (headache), in your stomach (upset), in your chest (tight)?

5. What do you do to relax? Exercise? Meditate? Massage? Time out? Hot bath? Do you relax?

6. When you are not working, do you feel guilty that you should be working?

7. Do you feel conflict between your obligations as a housewife, mother, and professional woman?

8. Is there ever a moment in time when you feel as if you have it all? Are you genuinely happy? Are you waiting to "have it all" before you can really enjoy yourself?

9. What is missing in your life? Action? Vitality? Love? Connectedness? Caring? Nurturance? With all your accom-

plishments, can you describe what it feels like to feel incomplete?

The questions aren't easy ones to answer, are they? And having answered them you may not be feeling too good about yourself, despite all of the obvious accoutrements of success.

If the collective answers to your questions add up to the fact that you never feel satisfied with your obvious accomplishments; that more is not enough; and that whatever you do seems to make you feel inadequate, insecure, anxious, and physically debilitated, then you are a stressed-out overachiever who should seriously consider changing her life-style. Drastic? Perhaps. But the problem, my dear reader, lies not in the stars—but with you. In part, your self-image is off kilter. The ideal image that you have of yourself is too unrealistic. You expect and demand too much from yourself. There is a little voice inside of your head (usually parental) urging you to keep trying harder. This judgmental, perfectionistic self-ideal can be corrected only if you can obtain accurate information about yourself. By answering these questions you can begin to see how you relate to the people around you. In particular, you want to see how demanding you are of others and try to relate that to your own expectations of yourself. My advice? Learn to let go. You don't have to be everything to everyone: the perfect housewife and the exemplary CEO, all rolled up into one. In order to let go you will literally have to learn how to relax as well as begin to refocus some of that intensity and drive away from your work. Learn to rely on others. Demand an equal distribution of responsibility. And, above all else, be grateful for your imperfections—they're what make you so lovable.

And please don't let this initial step toward uncovering your Hidden Passions be so frightening that you don't want to continue. I have faith in you!

Now we have completed some of the foundation work to making yourself the most important priority. You are beginning to listen to your inner voice. You are learning to become an observer through keeping a journal. You are learning to use that journal to tell you things about yourself and others. Let us proceed to the next phase— defining yourself. *Who am I?* From there we will try to find out how we go about answering *What do I want?* Quite an adventure, isn't it?

CHAPTER 8

The Problem of Self-Definition: Who Am I?

Before you can begin to ask the question, "What do I want?" you must first be able to answer the question, "*Who am I?*" What! you exclaim indignantly. What nonsense is that! Of course I know who I am! Well, if that is the case, then this chapter shouldn't concern you at all. So if you wish, you may proceed to the next chapter. However I will give you a fair warning. You proceed at your own risk. In my clinical experience I have discovered that most Successful Women do not see themselves as successful. They may be earning a good living. They may be highly respected both in their profession and in their community. They may be married to a successful man. They may have several successful children. But they do not necessarily see themselves as successful. As I pointed out earlier, the Successful Woman is confused and ambivalent with respect to self-definition. Most are genuinely uncertain about who they are. Is the Successful Woman a working professional who is able to manage thirty-five people and oversee a budget of forty million dollars? Or is the Successful Woman a housewife/mother who arranges her daughter's car pools and makes certain that her tap shoes fit properly? Or is the Successful Woman the one who has learned do all of the above and do them well?

The Successful Woman has certainly learned to take care of everyone but herself. In fact she has a very hard time talking about herself in the first person. I want. I think. I do. I know. I am. I need. She is a great talker in terms of "the company needs . . ." or "my husband and I went . . ." or "my children have always . . ."

We all need a clear, coherent, consistent sense of ourselves in order to live life with the least amount of stress and hassle. Nothing is more detrimental to one's psychological health than going through life confused about who or what you are about.[1] For all her successes, the Successful Woman does not feel comfortable; she feels that something is missing. Something doesn't allow her to feel complete or content. She has not yet learned to incorporate her achievements into a healthy sense of self-regard. She has not yet learned to say "*I am. Therefore I want.*"

How does she answer the question "*Who am I?*" There is clearly no one right answer. Who we think we are is a compilation of past psychological events, present-day interactions, and the internalized distortions of each. Our self-image frequently varies with the situation and the people surrounding us. Some days we feel great about ourselves. Some days not as good. Some people make you feel good about yourself. Others go out of their way to deprecate your achievements, or in surreptitious ways, make you question yourself. So called "friends" may be so threatened by your accomplishments that they feel uncomfortable; and in turn make you feel uncomfortable. Some people may respond to what you represent (i.e., the Successful Woman "who's got it all") with deep resentment and mixed emotions. In turn, this type of inconsistent behavior makes you feel angry, distant, ambivalent about that person, and, most important, about yourself.

The bottom line is that the psychological baggage from your past, plus other people's daily responses to you, have a major impact on how you see yourself. Equally disruptive to your sense of wholeness is the multiplicity of roles with which, as a Successful Woman, you are encumbered. Let us see if we can't describe some of those roles and help you to define yourself.[2]

SELF-DEFINITION EXERCISES: SORTING OUT ROLES AND MEASURING SATISFACTION

Exercise 1:
Evaluating Your Job as a Professional/Working Woman

Circle or provide a percentage for each question that best represents your feelings about your job.

1. What percent of your day do you spend at work?
   25%, 50%, 75%, 100%

2. Would you want to spend more time at work?
   no more, 25% more, 50% more, 75% more, 100% more

3. Would you like to spend less time at work?
   no less, 25% less, 50% less, 75% less, 100% less

4. How much of your work is *un*necessary to accomplish your job?
   25%, 50%, 75%, 100%

5. What percent of your capabilities are being utilized to accomplish your job?
   25%, 50%, 75%, 100%

6. How would you improve your job?
   Provide a percentage next to each category or zero if no change.

The Job	*% Increase*	*% Decrease*
Administrative tasks	_____%	_____%
Substantive aspects	_____%	_____%
People management	_____%	_____%
Overall responsibility	_____%	_____%
Contact with people	_____%	_____%
Scope of job	_____%	_____%
Variety of tasks	_____%	_____%

The Job	% Increase	% Decrease
Challenge	_____%	_____%
Stimulation	_____%	_____%
Pay	_____%	_____%
Change my employer	_____%	_____%
Change the people with whom I work	_____%	_____%

7. Your job fulfills what percent of your emotional needs?
   none, 25%, 50%, 75%, 100%

8. How much of your identity is tied to your job?
   none, 25%, 50%, 75%, 100%

9. How much of your pride is attached to your job?
   none, 25%, 50%, 75%, 100%

Self-Analysis

Question 1: **What percent of your day do you spend at work?**

Most Successful Women answer between 50 and 75 percent of their day. If you calculate a forty- to sixty-hour week as within the normal range, and subtract an eight-hour sleep (i.e., fifty-six hours per week), you find that you only have about fifty-two hours left. The weekend takes up a good thirty-two hours (remember you have to sleep sixteen hours). So that leaves you with twenty hours of free time during the week. Not much, if you want to spend time with your family and friends.

If you are spending more than sixty hours a week at work, I would say you are a workaholic! I don't care if you are a doctor, lawyer, accountant, or businesswoman. You have become your job. Your identity is determined by your job, and you are addicted to your work. So you will have to ask yourself some very tough questions. Do you want to continue working this way? If so, Why? And please, don't tell me it's for the money. What good is money to you if you discover that the major part of your life is engaged in working and you are unable to spend it?

Key Questions to Ask Yourself
If You Are Working Too Much

1. What are you afraid of? Losing your security? Loss of money? Loss of power? Loss of prestige? Boredom?

2. What are you avoiding? Going home? Spending time with your husband? Spending time with your kids? Spending time with yourself?

3. What else might you want to do if you didn't work as hard?

(Don't panic. I frankly don't expect you to know all the answers at this point.) You might want to seriously think about the Hidden Passions you have suppressed or sublimated under an overwhelming work week.

Question 2: **Would you want to spend more time at work?**

The answer to this question becomes self-evident. If you are working less than forty hours you might well want to increase the number of hours that you are working. But the key aspect here is not the number of hours as much as it is the quality of time you want to spend working. If you find the job rewarding, enriching, and enjoyable then it makes a lot of sense to increase your work time. Particularly if you feel that your work is fulfilling one or more of your Hidden Passions.

Key Questions to Ask Yourself
If You Want to Increase Work

Are you salami-slicing your way into an avoidance activity?

Question 3: **Would you like to spend less time at work?**

If you want to spend less than forty hours at work or you want to make your job part time, that's all right. Just be clear about your reasons for cutting back. If you want to spend more personal time, getting in touch with your own feelings, your own needs, or to spend more time at home with the kids—it's okay. If you want to start up another career because it's something you've wanted to do for a very long time (a Hidden Passion)—then do it! Don't worry about your guilt at working less on the job. You're doing a far more important job by defining and taking care of yourself. However, if you feel so guilty and anxious that you are neither able to do your work or proceed with your own self-assessment and program for change then simply back off and try again at some other more favorable time.

Question 4: **How much of your work is unnecessary to accomplish your job?**

If you find that your job consists of engaging in activities that in and of themselves will not lead to the concrete or enriching product you were hired to produce, then you are engaged in busywork. And it is time for you to get out—while you can.

Question 5: **What percent of your capabilities are being utilized?**

This question goes back to some of the previous questions but refines them. Many people who are having problems energizing themselves are basically bored at work. They are underutilized and feel completely unchallenged. The determining follow-up questions for you are: 1) How much of the time are you being underutilized? and 2) How long will the situation last? Every moment of every day cannot be challenging. There will be times when you are underutilized because there are fewer patients or clients. Don't worry. Things will pick up. And if they don't—maybe it's time to look elsewhere. A famous producer some twenty-odd years ago found himself without any work in the middle of a famous Hollywood writers and directors strike. So he decided to write a novel. It was initially rejected by several publishers, as I understand it, and then some young, courageous editor picked it up. It went on to become a best seller. The author's name was James Clavell; his novel was *King Rat*. He subsequently wrote *Shogun* and *Tai-Pan*. You get the idea. Use your capabilities. If you can't in your immediate situation, then let's get prepared to get out of it. If the immediate situation merely needs some improvements, tinker with it.

Question 6: **How would you go about improving the nature of your job?**

Review each area I have targeted and think about what it would really take to improve the job. If it turns out that you would like to see a major increase or decrease in one area, such as your overall responsibility, ask yourself if change is likely. If not, I would say that you've got some major problems in your job and you might want to think about making a change.

Question 7: **What percent of your emotional needs does your job fulfill?**

This is a double-edged question. If your job fulfills more than 75 percent of your emotional needs, then you have very little room left over for emotions that are typically found outside the work world, such as passion, intimacy, and connectedness.

Once the job goes, for whatever reason, your identity goes with it. And so will your self-respect and pride:

Then what's left? A sense of emptiness. A loss of direction and purpose. An inability to define yourself.

Exercise 2:
Evaluating Your Home Life as a Wife/Mother

Circle the percentage for each question that best represents your feelings about your home life, or write down your response.

1. What percent of your day do you spend being a wife?
   0%, 25%, 50%, 75%, 100%
   Being a mother?
   0%, 25%, 50%, 75%, 100%

2. How much more time would you want to spend as a wife?
   0%, 25%, 50%, 75%, 100%
   As a mother?
   0%, 25%, 50%, 75%, 100%

3. How much less time would you like to spend as a wife?
0%, 25%, 50%, 75%, 100%
As a mother?
0%, 25%, 50%, 75%, 100%

4. How would you describe your personal life (exclusive of being a wife or mother)? Is it rewarding? If not, why not?

5. How would you describe that part of your life that you spend as a wife? As a mother?

6. How does your family respond to you as a wife? As a mother?

7. What things, if any, would you change to make your personal life more vital?

8. How much of your identity is tied to being a wife?
0%, 25%, 50%, 75%, 100%
Being a mother?
0%, 25%, 50%, 75%, 100%

Self-Analysis

Question 1: **What percent of your time do you spend being a wife or mother?**

During the 1980s, more and more women were spending less and less time at home, with the majority of their days and weekends being spent on work and job-related matters. However, what I am presently seeing in my practice is a perceptible shift away from the five-day work week and the nine-to-five work day. The Successful Woman I see in therapy, if she can swing it at all, is beginning to insist on flexi-time and day-care facilities at the workplace.

Let me recount a recent episode that I think is typical of this trend. A neighbor of mine, an attractive woman in her mid-forties, was returning from work. She looked extremely distraught. Normally this woman is upbeat and cheerful. Resilience seems to be her middle name. But on this late afternoon, as I came jogging up the hill (I never realized that a hill could be so long) she ran crying into my arms. "Oh, God! How glad I am to see you. Of all the people in this world, you're the one I would have wanted to see first." After calming her down, I asked what was wrong. At which point she burst into tears again. After I helped her to recompose herself, she told me between deep sobs what had just transpired. After a five-year career as a high-powered investigative journalist at a major magazine, she had decided to call it quits. Without any forethought, she went to her boss, a man whom she respected but didn't particularly like, and told him she was leaving the job. When asked why, she looked at him and replied that she simply wanted to; work was no longer satisfying and she wanted to be involved in other activities. He was incredulous, but he told her that she could stay as long as she wanted. He considered her an excellent employee. She thanked him and left.

The truth of the matter, as she related it to me, was that as successful as she was, she felt she could no longer work in a large impersonal bureaucracy where hers was simply one more piece of anonymous paper output. When I told her that I thought that she had made the right decision, she replied fearfully, "I may have made the right decision for me. But the family is another matter. I earn a quarter of the revenue that is needed to run the household. How am I going to make up the difference?"

I asked her what was more important, earning less money or doing what she wanted to do? She looked at me thoughtfully and explained that the real reason for quitting (although the other reason was valid) was the simple but embarrassing fact that she wanted to spend more time at home with her children (a six-year-old boy and a nine-year-old girl). Although they were in a good elementary school and an equally good after-school day-care program, my neighbor felt that *she* was missing something very important by not being there with them, particularly during their formative years. She broke down crying again. "I feel so stupid. So silly. A grown woman who quits her job because she wants to spend time at home with her kids. I'm setting back the women's lib movement a good twenty years."

"I'm sure the women's movement would interpret your action as equally liberated and liberating."

She then talked about how upset she was one day when she was not there and her son was sent home because of an injury. She had never forgiven herself. But it was clear to me that her wanting to spend more time at home was not simply a function of guilt. This was not a woman who would spend much time on remorse. If anything, she would perk right back up and move on to the next item on the agenda. No, my instincts told me that what was working in her were Hidden Passions bubbling over. She wanted to reconnect to her family, especially her children. She wanted to use her vital energy to nurture and provide for her children. She had had enough of being a successful workhorse. She wanted to spend some time developing her singular talents as a mother.

She went from spending 25 percent of her time at home to spending 65 percent. The remainder of her time was spent as a free-lance journalist. The last time I heard from her she was extremely happy, (even though the money differential had not yet been made up).

Lest you think this was one abnormal case. . . . A few weeks later, an extremely successful mother of five children came to see me because she was no longer happy running her own business. It was too isolating, too lonely. She wanted to spend more time at home with the hurly-burly of her children. She appointed her vice president as CEO and resigned a few days later.

What's the moral? I don't really know. All I can envision as I write this passage is a magazine photograph that I recently saw picturing a properly attired mother holding her two young children. The magazine proudly announced the advent of a new era—the era of the neotraditionalists. Funny, but it sounded just right. More and more working women are beginning to return to traditional values—the home, the children, religion, spirituality, the family. For those who don't have children or husband, there is a desire to return to one's roots. Is this neotraditionalism? It's as good a term as any. And it may well be the trend for the next ten years.

Key Questions to Ask Yourself About Spending Time at Home

1. Do you have the feeling deep within you that you may want to spend more time at home with friends, children, and family? If so what are you going to do about it?

2. Does that feeling cause anxiety, guilt, or tension?

Question 2: **How much more time would you want to spend as a wife or mother?**

The answer to this question is clearly related to your reactions to question 1 on p. 148. Look carefully at this question and then put the book down. If the proposition is tantalizing, then attempt a gradual approach to the problem. Instead of shifting jobs suddenly (like my neighbor did), try out small increments of time away from work. Let's start by spending thirty minutes more at home. Then increase that amount by another fifteen minutes. You get the idea—increase the time you spend at home by small amounts and record your reactions (as well as the those of your family). I think that's where you may find the payoff.

Question 3: **How much less time would you like to spend as a wife or mother?**

Having said what I did in questions 1 and 2, I don't want you to feel intimidated by the fact that I am encountering women who want to return to the home setting. But if you feel that your passion for exploration, new experiences, or meeting new people and challenges has not been met by staying home, then you should very definitely examine the work world to see whether it can provide you with the necessary challenges.

Question 4: **How would you describe your personal life?**

This is the question that allows you to reflect on where you are right now in your life. Is this where you want to be? Do you feel comfortable that your identity is well-placed between your job and your personal life? If your personal life is not rewarding, what is holding you back? Do you find that you're not able to break out of the daily routines and habits of your life? Or, more important, do you feel that your needs are not being met in your present life? Do you feel stifled, unproductive, without life or vibrancy? Then write out on a piece of paper in detail all those things that are missing in your personal life, and then write out what you would like to have for yourself (love, excitement, fusion, connectedness). Think about these things. It's the first step toward trying to acquire them.

Question 5: **How would you describe that part of your life that you spend as a wife or mother?**

The answer to this question relates to the answers you may have provided to the previous questions. If you find that your life as a wife/ mother is rewarding, then be proud of it. If you suspect that in order for you to feel complete you need a part-time job, then put that down. But please, under no condition, feel ashamed or embarrassed that you are a wife/mother. Many people feel it is one of the most challenging jobs in this world. If you are already doing a terrific job at home, then you know that.

Let me recount another recent episode. At a lawyer friend's party, I met a couple, both of whom were also lawyers. The husband told me he was a professor of law at a local university, having already changed his life from that of a high-powered corporate attorney to the more contemplative (less financially rewarding) world of academia. His wife, on the other hand, became very apologetic when she announced that she was a wife/mother. I asked her why she sounded so defensive, and she replied that all the women in the room were working mothers and she felt "out of it." She flatly stated, however, that she was extremely happy being a mother of one daughter, and she added pridefully that she was expecting a second child. She had been a judge in the juvenile courts and after several years had found it both physically and emotionally debilitating and depressing. So she said good-bye to her job, married a man she loved, and had, by her own admission, a wonderful five years at home. Why did she sound so apologetic when, in fact, she was extremely happy to be a mother? In this instance she was responding more to what she felt were the perceptions of others, and less to her own satisfaction. But she wouldn't have changed anything!

Question 6: **How does your family respond to your identity?**

How much support you receive from your family often determines how you feel about yourself as well as how you identify yourself. If your family supports your activities as both a wife and mother, then you will see yourself comfortably situated in both of these roles. However, if your family doesn't approve of your work schedule, then it is more likely that you will be torn by your identity as a working woman. Most families, because of their vested interest, prefer mother to stay home and take care of them. Why not? But if the families are fair, they will apportion their support accordingly. It is up to you to elicit the type of support that you need and want. And, by the way, don't expect your family to be all that fair.

Question 7: What things would you change to make your personal life more vital?

The answer to this question goes back to whatever response you may have given to question 4 (p. 149). Before we get to the chapter called _What Do I Want?_, it would be a good exercise to enumerate some of the things you think might enrich your private life. Think of the chapters on Hidden Passions and write out which of those passions you might want: passion for living, physical passion, passion for uncovering the new and the different, passion for growth, passion for reaffirmation of self, passion for romance, passion for love.

Remember, when you think about some of the changes you might want to make, don't forget to include those activities that from the outside don't look too dramatic or earth-shaking. What do I mean? Take a simple thing like a hobby. What one thing do you like to do that distracts your attention from the daily monotony of life? Stamp collecting? Carpentry? Home improvement? Don't minimize their emotional impact. Many a client has expressed her passion for creativity by dedicating much of her free time to breeding and growing a particular flower. Several of these clients have even won awards. So at one and the same time they were positively reinforced for both creativity and achievement. Can't beat that combination. In another case, a young woman's passion for fusion was fulfilled by her having joined the management team of a religious organization, which in a spiritual sense allowed her to fuse her identity into the body of the church. There are many other types of examples that on the surface appear far less dramatic than they actually are. So, my recommendation is to begin by thinking of those activities you enjoy—those activities that we in the work world presumptuously call hobbies. Who knows? Yesterday's hobby may be tomorrow's vocation.

Question 8: How much of your identity is tied to being a wife or a mother?

During the 1960s and 1970s, when the majority of women spent most of their time as homemakers, that identity seemed negated. Many complained that they had no source of identity other than that they were somebody's wife or somebody's mother. It was a derivative identity based on someone else's existence. When they stayed at home they felt that they were consumed in a great void of anonymity, torn between the demands of husband and children. Then these same women entered the workplace where they were able to acquire a certain degree of prestige, power, and autonomy. But their identity was still derivative—completely dependent on their corporate title and position. Now many of these same women are returning to their respective homes in order to find a greater sense of meaning, purpose, and flexibility in their lives.

Those of you who will decide to change your workplace from a regimented, highly structured corporate style to one in which you control your own schedule, be prepared to enter into a period of emotional and intellectual disorientation. For the most part, the only meetings you will attend will be the ones that you set up. So it is safe to say that in the beginning you will be having "power breakfasts, lunches, and dinners" with yourself. Time will seem interminable, so you will have to find things to do. And last but not least, you will have to feel secure in appreciating the fact that what you do is far more important than how you are addressed. Loneliness is a companion you will have to learn to cherish.

A natural inclination is for you to want to fall back into old patterns—housewife, mother, general factotum. But if you feel that more than 60 percent of your identity is tied to being a wife or mother, and that you are uncomfortable with it, then it is time for you to start changing once again. Remember change is an everlasting process.

WARNING: BEWARE OF FREQUENT SELF-EVALUATIONS

A clear and positive self-image provides a strong psychological center to your life; a center that can stand being ravaged by personal, social, financial, or political vagaries. Therefore, it is important to conduct a self-evaluation on "who you are" before you can approach the problem of "what you want." But it is equally important for you to *take only periodic self-readings*. Let's say one every month. No matter how anxious or uncertain you feel about your present situation, don't attempt to evaluate the progress of your change every week. Don't! Frequent self-evaluations can actually cause you to become more anxious and distraught. It's a variation of what is known in physics as the Heisenberg uncertainty principle: the more closely you study a phenomenon, the more you distort it. Similarly, the more "readings" you take on your psychological well-being, the more you may actually impair your sense of self and, naturally, your self-esteem. What happens is that you begin to take in the "background noise" as well as the random fluctuations of your own change. Frequent readings distort your natural "down times" and give you a false sense of gloom and doom, paralyzing you even further. When you go on a diet for weight loss, you tend to want to check yourself every day. Well, you know what happens. You get discouraged. Depressed. And you want to go off your diet. I'm afraid that you will become discouraged and stop your exercises if you do more than one self-assessment every month.

IDENTIFYING THE SUCCESSFUL WOMAN

Exercise 1: Views of Me

Take a piece of paper and write down the ten major characteristics that you think a Successful Woman should have, whether she be a chief executive officer of a major corporation or a housewife in the suburbs with five small children.

Now make a list of ten characteristics that describe you as a working woman (for example, aggressive, assertive, commanding, etc.) and place it alongside the above list.

Place a third list alongside the other two, setting down the objectives that best describe you as a woman in your personal life. Make sure the adjectives correlate pretty closely.

Compare the three lists. What do you see? Are there discrepancies between the first list (definition of a Successful Woman), and your self-definition (as a working woman)? Where are the points of difference? Can you reconcile them?

How does the second list compare to your self-definition as a wife/ mother? If you are a single working woman without children, can you identify which of your traits are most compatible with becoming a Successful Woman (of course, as you understand it) or a wife/mother? Which traits in yourself would you have to emphasize or acquire in order to become the Successful Woman as the wife/mother?

We would expect some major points of difference. But can they be reconciled? How much underlying tension do you feel looking at the three lists? At two lists? What do you want to do about it?

Case Example

Ellen was the manager of a prominent toy store. She had two children and a pretty good marriage. But she felt anxious and nervous whenever she had to deal with her husband. He was portrayed to me as a domineering, authoritarian person who at times bordered on being abusive. Ellen would simply withdraw and remain silent when her husband looked as if he were about to explode. She came to see me because she didn't know whether she could continue in her "pretty good marriage." She was suddenly feeling pulled in too many directions. At work she felt self-assured, in control, and very much a professional. But at home she felt like the little girl who used to wait for her father to give her a lecture on proper behavior. I asked what she wanted for herself and she replied that her inability to answer the question was part of the problem. She knew that things had to change—her home life, her marriage, herself. But she didn't know how to change them.

I asked her to tell me how she saw herself as a person, as a professional, and as she would envision herself the Complete Woman.

She was hesitant. She had not gotten used to my "talking therapy." But she was quite prepared to deal with my written instructions. I asked her to write out a list of ten adjectives that would best describe her as a professional woman. She wrote with no hesitation. Then I asked her to describe the "who am I" in her personal life, and what she thought the Complete Woman would be like. The following were her responses.

Who Am I? (Business)	*Who Am I? (Personal)*	*Complete Woman*
confident	hesitant	well-rounded
assertive	nervous	honest
competitive	anxious	self-assured
professional	phony	comfortable
well-informed	insecure	effortless
disciplined	undisciplined	independent

Who Am I? (Business)	_Who Am I? (Personal)_	_Complete Woman_
tough	weak	demanding
persevering	undemanding	cosmopolitan
forthright	surreptitious	seductive
confrontational	avoid conflict	charming

Amazing, isn't it? Ellen was astonished to see the discrepancy between how she saw herself as a professional and how she saw herself in her personal life. It was like Dr. Jekyll and Mr. Hyde; or Ms. Jekyll and Ms. Hyde. How did she explain this discrepancy? The more she thought about it, the more her face lit up with insight. "That's exactly the way I felt when I was a kid. Particularly when I had to deal with my demanding father."

Exercise 2: Feelings About Me

I asked Ellen to list those adjectives that would describe her feelings toward her father when she was a "kid" and another to describe what she would imagine that her father thought about her. The following lists were set down.[3]

Feelings Toward Father	_Father's Feelings Toward Ellen_
Frightened	—I am spoiled
Nervous	—I am selfish
Anxious	—I am inadequate
Insecure	—I am weak
Angry	—I am untalented
Resentful	—I am sneaky
Overpowering	—I am cowardly
Unpredictable	—I am insincere
Abusive	—I am nervous
Avoid him	

The meaning of her lists is too obvious to spend time analyzing. You can see where Ellen's poor self-image came from. I ask you to complete the same exercise for a series of "significant others." Each set of comparisons will teach you about perceptions in relationships, as well as your development of a self-image. It is certainly not always a father who provides the basis for a negative self-image, or for a positive one. In this case Ellen had incorporated her father's negative image of her and carried the myth of her inadequacy into adulthood. She reinforced what she thought was her father's image of her by marrying a man who was somewhat similar to her father in temperament and style.

I told Ellen to rip up the list with her father's feelings about her; it wasn't true anymore. Now she would also have to give up that part of her that incorporated what she thought about her father's image of her and mourn its loss. How could she do that? Well, the second part of the exercise was to retrieve the list in which she described how she felt about herself as a professional woman. Where did those positive feelings of self-worth come from? As it turned out, this list incorporated many opinions about her that her mother had always expressed.

Exercise 3: Opinions About Me

I asked Ellen (as I would ask you) to construct a list of what she thought was her mother's opinions about her. The following list resulted.

Mother's Opinions of Ellen

—I am talented
—I am bright
—I am good
—I am disciplined
—I am a hard worker
—I am creative
—I am a people person
—I am a lot of fun
—I am kind

The discrepancy of opinions held by Ellen's mother and father is obvious. Unfortunately, few of her mother's opinions were incorporated into her self-image as a woman. Thank goodness some of them were incorporated into her self-image as a professional. Why this split? It was the safest way for her not to compete directly against her father, who was an extremely competitive man. By allowing herself to grow professionally she was able to feel good about herself (and didn't have to confront her father directly). But when she came home she had to deal with her husband, who, in part (and only in part), reminded her of her father.

This is not unusual. Many a Successful Woman has a split self-image. She often sees herself as one or another parent had seen her when she was a child. Unfortunately those impressions remain with a young girl for most of her adult life unless something is done about it. An extreme example is the beautiful model who came to therapy because rather than feeling confident during shooting sessions she saw herself as ugly and fat.

The work of therapy is to try to make sense of the inconsistencies, try to get rid of the Successful Woman's negative feelings, and try to accentuate her positive traits. We call these three steps reality-testing, which entails analyzing those parts of a personality that are part of the past and discarding those parts that no longer have relevance for present functioning.

Exercise 4: Acting Out You

Ellen liked the fact that she could be "tough" at work. So I asked her (as I would ask you) to imagine different types of scenarios (based on past experiences) in which she could "act tough" with her husband when he was being capricious, demanding, or inappropriate. We rehearsed those scenarios and she played them out at home. Within weeks Ellen felt that her husband was less intimidating and was learning to respect her for her toughness. Was he, really? Or did she just feel that way because she was getting stronger as a person. You know, it really doesn't matter. She was happier, more positive, and felt better about him. Later in therapy we began to concentrate on how he could become more supportive to her.

But you won't have me there to practice your scenarios. And I do suggest that you practice them in your head, and in the mirror, before you try them in real life. And the more you practice those positive traits that you like about yourself, in as many different settings as possible, the more those traits will become you. If you like the fact that you are humorous and entertaining, be it. If you like the fact that you are a good organizer or seller, be one. Attempt to expand as many of your positive traits as possible into as many different facets of your life as you can. Be flexible! Be creative! Be spontaneous! Be integrative! Strive to be the Complete Woman—your truly Successful Woman.

Exercise 5: The Hurtogram

Ellen had to learn to let go of the hurt, trauma, and anger that she experienced as a little girl.[4] As long as that hurt was there she would always act as if she were that little girl—withdrawn, frightened, anxious, desperately seeking male approval. She needed to let go of the child in her and see herself through words and thoughts that she would have liked to hear when she was young. So I asked her to send a Hurtogram, a telegram from her heart to her mind, telling her that she really was a good kid and that she was a unique, talented, loving girl.

The exercise was very meaningful to her, and I recommend it to you. Write a Hurtogram to some part of your childhood, telling yourself how sorry you as an adult are that you had to suffer so much as a child, and that whoever hurt you didn't do it intentionally. "They" were frustrated and took out their disappointments with themselves in the only way they knew how—by criticizing you.

Here was Ellen R's Hurtogram:

> Dear Ellie—
>
> Please excuse the rough way you were treated. Believe me, you were innocent. You were a great kid. I think Dad would also share that opinion of you. Although he didn't always tell you how much he loved you, I know for a fact that he was crazy about you. Unfortunately, he just didn't know how to show it. That was really his problem. There were times when he could be so loving and kind, but most of the time they were buried. Maybe you'll have to be big enough to excuse him. He did the best he could for the type of man he was.
>
> I just want you to know how much I love you. You can depend on me. I think you're great, talented, funny, and just a general knockout.
>
> > I love you baby—
> > From big Ellie

To say that Ellen cried as she wrote this would be an understatement. Ellen had a lot of hurt and pain and humiliation to release—and mourn. She had to erase a huge burden of guilt and self-blame that a hypercritical father had instilled in her. Her realization that she was an innocent victim of her father's frustrations was an insight that allowed her to free herself from her own critical judgments of herself. By placing the responsibility of the trauma back into the past, and onto the proper perpetrator (her father) she helped to release the hurt child (herself) from the bondage of pain and criticism, which allowed her to feel less vulnerable, anxious, and fearful in her personal life. Ellen learned that the more healing she could do of the hurt child, the less she would need to depend on her husband, children, or boss to reaffirm her self-worth. She could reaffirm her self-worth by her own actions and deeds.

I am suggesting that whenever you hear a harsh inner voice from the past criticizing you for things you know aren't true today, write yourself a Hurtogram and correct the situation.

Hurtograms! Do they sound silly? Sending letters or cables to the child in you. Excusing your past, soothing your present, forgiving your parents. Easier said than done! Platitudes! Palliatives! I can well understand how you might interpret these exercises as mental pablum. But, remember, I am at a distinct disadvantage. I must attempt to help you do in a few hours on a piece of paper what I do in therapy over months and years. Obviously nothing substitutes for the consistent concern and care of another person; particularly if that person happens to be a professional trained to deal with your problems. So the second best thing is to convey to you the human dimension of what transpires in therapy, the give-and-take process, through shorthand techniques. The techniques, in themselves, are not necessarily curative. But they definitely can help to put you in touch with your feelings, some of their causes, and some approaches to self-help.

You can tell someone that she has to mourn the loss of her anger and hatred. But what does that really mean? Is it simply a process of thinking about that hurt and anger, emotionally attaching onto it, and then going through a process of crying, reflection, acceptance, and letting go? In part, yes. But, only in part. A large part of mourning has something to do with the relationship between me and the patient.

As I often remind my patients, the relationship we establish in therapy is a mirror image of what happened between them and their respective parents or even the childish part of themselves. It is the genius of Freud and others to have understood that a patient plays out with the therapist those aspects of his relationship with his parents that have remained unresolved. Freud called this phenomenon "transference." Through the transference process I was literally able to see, feel, and work with the anger that my patient felt toward her father, because she unconsciously treated me as if I were her father. Believe me, transference is great to work with for both patient and therapist. Without it, I would have to reduce a lot of the therapeutic process into cognitive (intellectual) steps. But you are behind your book, and not in my office. What I am attempting to do is like trying to teach the mambo using a schemata—move your left foot to point 1, then place your right foot on point 2. I would rather hear the music, have the physical contact, and sway to the crisp Latin beat. But I will have to settle for second best; a method by which you can learn to dance. Although a Hurtogram may not substitute for the transference experience, it does allow you to play out several different roles, in any sequence you choose, to initiate the process of self-healing.

Exercise 6: Being a Square

This exercise is designed to allow you to view, in one geometric figure, the division between your professional and personal life.[5] It is also a technique that can be used to follow your own progress in integrating these two parts of your life.

Draw a square on a sheet of paper about three inches wide by three inches high. Using a straight line, divide the square into several segments: that portion of your identity that you attribute to being a professional woman, a wife, a mother, and "personal." Assume that the square represents the entirety of your psychological ego; that is, your identity and the totality of your feelings about yourself. Now look at the divisions in your life as you have represented them in that square. How much of your ego or identity is invested on your work life? How much is divided up into your role as a mother? Wife? Personal? Think of this diagram as a pictorial representation of the identity you already described in a previous section of this book. If you said previously that your work life consumed 50 percent of your identity, then I would expect to see half of the square assigned to your work life and the remaining half divided any way you want—personal, wife, mother, lover, etc. It's up to you.

Most Successful Women have designated a disproportionate amount of their square to their work life. From my experience with women in therapy I would like to see the personal part become larger. How much larger is, of course, strictly up to you.

Exercise 7: Who Am I?

When Ellen went through one period in therapy of seeming confused and uncertain about herself, I gave her the *Who Am I?* exercise. This exercise entailed completing sentences about herself. I asked her to list the first responses that came into her mind to complete each sentence.[6] Her responses follow.

1. I AM . . .
   Ellen
   a lady
   attractive
   a top sales manager
   forthright
   persevering
   tough

2. I WAS . . .
   Ellie
   a frightened girl
   always wearing running shoes
   a cheerleader
   nervous

3. I WILL BE . . .
   vice president of the company
   a wonderful lover
   a caring mother

4. I ENJOY . . .
   my children
   scuba diving
   my friends

5. WHAT I LIKE BEST ABOUT ME IS THAT . . .
   I'm caring

    I'm competent
    I can be tough

6. I RELATE TO MY FAMILY . . .
    warmly
    caring
    with fear toward my husband

7. IF MY RELATIONSHIP FAILS WITH MY HUSBAND . . .
    I will not fall apart
    I will ask friends to help me
    I will be me

8. I AM, THEREFORE I NEED . . .
    love
    caring
    attention
    warmth
    support
    self-assurance

Your responses to these questions are worth pondering. Are these the responses you are proud to see? Are there responses you've made that make you feel nervous? Are there things you are willing to try to change? This is an exercise to be used for yourself, to continue the internal dialogue with yourself that you have already started.

The last question, 9) I AM. I NEED. THEREFORE, I WANT, you will answer after you have completed the next section. And it will bring us to the second major question in your life, "What do I want?"

CHAPTER 9

What Do I Want?: The Problem of Indulging Yourself

How often do you hear yourself turn to your "significant other"—husband or lover—and ask him what you should take for dessert—the pie or the fruit? Or when you go shopping for clothes, do you ask the salesgirl if the garment really fits well on you, knowing fully well that it is her self-interest to sell you the merchandise? Clearly I am not talking about either desserts or dresses. I am addressing the issue of wanting something, but not being sure you deserve it.

Because the Successful Woman does not have a clear sense of who she is—her core self—she will identify with different parts of the world she encounters in order to determine what it is that she wants. At work she identifies with the attitudes, values, and behavior of her male counterparts, who are oriented toward achievement. In that setting she wants what all the men want—power, success, position, a sense of accomplishment, and the sense of being busy. At home she is the source of nurturance, the person to whom the rest of the household looks in order that *they* feel complete or integrated. In this setting she wants what she has been brought up to feel is important in the home—love, respect, warmth, dependency. If both settings, and the needs they elicit, could be "added" together, the result might seem to be a good balance of needs and goals. Yet somewhere in that addition, the Successful Woman falls into a void. She does not feel balanced. She does not feel whole. She is not able to say "I want . . ."

DENIAL OF DEPENDENCY AND NEEDS

Remember the dependency cycle I described in an earlier chapter, the one that begins with the little girl's denial of her own dependency needs because little girls are there to nurture little boys and not themselves? That self-denial led to that girl feeling needy and wanting, as if something were missing in her life. It is that cycle that contributes to the Successful Woman feeling inadequate, confused about her identity, and alienated from her own needs (Hidden Passions).[1] And it is that cycle that the Successful Woman will have to understand and break.

It is important to be able to visualize the sequence of events that could lead to such a present condition.

Exercise 1: Understanding Dependency

Sometimes it is easier to visualize cause-and-effect relationships than it is to have an internal dialogue about them. A good schemata can frequently allow you to pinpoint where you are in the cycle and, by comparison, know where you are heading. If you're going off course, it's there to see and correct. Think of this next exercise as a basic road map for dependency, showing you where you have been and indicating where you might want to go. I have simplified a long and potentially confusing discussion about dependency needs and created, instead, a small and potentially useful diagram. The diagram represents the psychodynamic events of the past (boxes 1, 2, 3, and 4) that have an impact upon the Successful Woman who feels incomplete (box 5).

Box 1 represents an early stage in development when, as a little girl, dependency needs were denied. This denial translated itself into a set of psychological consequences (box 2): decreased self-worth, identity confusion, and a feeling of not being entitled or worthy. As the young girl hides those dependency needs that are being ignored, she pursues objectives that others will find acceptable; in the process she becomes

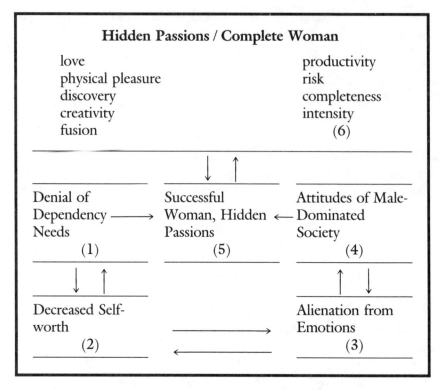

Hidden Passions / Complete Woman

love   productivity
physical pleasure   risk
discovery   completeness
creativity   intensity
fusion   (6)

Denial of Successful Attitudes of Male-
Dependency ⟶ Woman, Hidden ⟵ Dominated
Needs   Passions   Society
(1)   (5)   (4)

Decreased Self-   Alienation from
worth   Emotions
(2)   (3)

alienated from her own emotions (box 3). She also acquires the attitudes, values, and behaviors of a male-dominated society (box 4). The result is the Successful Woman with Hidden Passions (box 5). The woman who feels incomplete. The woman who has hidden her desires (the Hidden Passions enumerated in box 6). But when the Successful Woman incorporates her Hidden Passions, she becomes a Complete Woman (box 6).

I want you to notice that cause-and-effect is not necessarily unidirectional. The double arrows in the diagram show us that attitudes and values and emotions not only can lead to certain states of being, but that those states (e.g., accepting male-dominated work values) can also influence emotions (e.g., feeling further alienated from your emotions).

The diagram is useful as a reminder. Who you are is determined by a multiplicity of impacts (i.e., boxes). Although it is not always easy to determine which impact is most potent, or most timely, or most "blamable" for the outcome, it is frequently useful to think of an outcome (e.g., pay raise at work) in terms of those factors that had an impact on the outcome (e.g., support at home, long work hours, determination) and to diagram it as I have done above. It's a fun exercise, in addition to forcing you to think about "who you are" in different ways.

Exercise 2: Discovering What I Want

Let's take a fantasy trip. Sit in a relaxing chair or couch. Focus your attention on some object in the room—a rug, a plant, a wall hanging. Close your eyes (after you've read this entire passage) and imagine a beam of light emanating from the center of your forehead. As you focus more and more on that beam of light, it becomes bigger and bigger. The more you focus on that light the more clearly you feel it is a field of energy; a space where all of your Hidden Passions have been kept after you discarded them. Do you feel its life? Its vitality?

Envision your wants in that energy field, in whatever way you feel comfortable. As bold letters. As sculpted words. As images. Enactments. Dream. Fantasize. Let your mind wander to an image of something that you want or want to be. Remember, use any object in the room as a means of focusing attention on yourself.

One of the most common concerns I hear in my office whenever I ask one of my patients to engage in this exercise is that she feels foolish, childish, self-indulgent. If it helps you to fantasize your desires by thinking of yourself as a spoiled child, then do so! The outcome is what we are after.

You should be proud to embark on a path of self-discovery. It is frightening. It feels awkward. But take a minute, look around you, make certain that there is no one around, and scream (yes, scream) at the top of your lungs "I want!" Repeat it again. "I want!" Then follow up with: "*I am! I need! I want!*" Being able to do this places you squarely on the road to recovery. See it as an integral and vital part of developing the new you. Don't worry. You are not undertaking a life of hedonism or self-indulgence. You are just finally asserting yourself in a healthy way.

Remember, attempt this exercise whenever you feel ready to focus your attention on yourself—on the image of something that you may want or want to become. This is an exercise (which I invite you to modify in any way) that allows you to get in touch with your own desires.

WARNING: Be patient with yourself. Please! Identifying your needs and wants will take time. It is not a simple process of writing out a grocery list.

Don't be discouraged! You will discover that many of your wants are fuzzy, *uncertain*. You can't quite visualize or express them very well. That's all right. If we all knew what we wanted from the beginning we would never have undertaken this voyage of self-discovery. You may feel that you want passion. But you are not certain what kind of passion. Sexual? Artistic? Enduring? Sporadic? Don't get turned off! This is not an exam. There are no right or wrong answers.

You may also discover that many of the desires are *contradictory*. You may want to invest yourself in a social cause that pays very little money while at the same time you might want to engage in a financially successful entrepreneurial venture. On the surface these appear to be mutually contradictory. In reality they simply reflect two aspects of your personality, each of which is straining for some form of self-expression. With creative thought, the two could merge—or could be used as the basis for a long-term strategy for your life.

HOW TO FULFILL YOUR OWN NEEDS

Physical Needs

Let us begin with the most basic of all needs—physical needs. You are in your chair. Very relaxed. The beam of light is strong. What you need now is to have some of that wonderful nurturing energy that you give to others turned back on yourself.[2] It's your turn to treat yourself. What would you do to soothe someone who was in pain? Make up a list of different things you would do. I've started your list for you.

1. Hugging

I had a patient who felt that what the world needed most was hugging. She was a big, burly woman who enjoyed hugging her children when they went off to school and when they came back. According to her, they loved to be smothered in her all-encompassing warm hugs. She loved to hug her friends, particularly when they needed a pick-me-up. That's how she judged the closeness of her friendships—one- or two-huggies. "Those people who didn't like to be hugged like . . ." She paused and hesitated. I interjected, "Like your husband?" She demurred and went on to talk about how much she enjoyed having simple physical contact. Because, she added, it made her feel good.

I stood up from my chair, and I did something I do not often do—I grabbed her around the shoulders and gave her a big hug.

She started to cry. Without having said it directly, she communicated her deep need (passion) to be physically held. And this did not entail any notion of sex. All she wanted was a little physical TLC. But she could not ask for it because it would have threatened her self-image as a self-reliant, autonomous Successful Woman. In truth, any admission of that strong need would have been extremely threatening to her marriage. She would have to admit to herself that more than just a little hug was at stake in marriage.

Once she was able to talk to me about her physical needs, she began to talk about how emotionally starved she was. From that point onward, she opened up Pandora's box and began to talk about how miserable her marriage had been for the past ten years; since her husband had accused her of displacing most of her emotions onto her children. She said that it was an excuse to make certain that he didn't have to get close to her. Eventually she was able to accept that she would never have either her emotional or physical needs met unless she changed her marital situation. Her husband could not or would not provide the emotional nurturance that she needed.

One year later she was out of the marriage and happily ensconced as a single parent who was dating frequently. Not all hugging leads to such a dramatic denouement. Occasionally a little hug is all that's required to bolster the spirit or instill a little bit of courage.

Pamela, a thirty-three-year-old happily married woman, wanted to expand her parental responsibilities. She wanted to become more active in her six-year-old son's school by running for the Parent-Teacher Association (PTA), but she lacked the courage to stand up in front of an audience of her peers and announce in a self-assured manner her candidacy for the PTA seat. After showing her several techniques to relax herself (primarily desensitization therapy), I spontaneously gave her a firm hug, which assured her of both my confidence in her and her ability to handle her own anxieties. That evening she made her presentation and was elected by unanimous decision to be on the PTA board.

2. Gentle Stroking

Whenever either of my daughters are upset, I sit down next to her and gently begin to stroke her hair. It always amazes me how quickly they relax and place their heads on their father's shoulder. Believe me, whether you're ten or ninety, a gentle stroke can go a long way. Without belaboring the point, the gentle stroke connotes a controlled impassioned feeling; a combination of love, care, tenderness, and warmth all fused into one simple physical action.

3. Physical Exercise

I am always amazed at how many women (and men) overlook the pleasures of basic physical exercise, whether it be jogging, swimming, bicycling, or walking. It is ironic that I would have to say this in the sophisticated 1990s, when physical exercise has become a byword for taking care of oneself almost to the point of becoming a religion. But the sad truth is that I see many women who work out at a health club in order to avoid dealing with their Hidden Passions. Instead, these Successful Women use physical exercise as a way of obliterating tension, the emotional residue of the day, or as a way of venting frustration and anger (whether at themselves or someone else). These are all legitimate uses of exercise. But I am talking about using *physical exercise as a way of energizing you*; using it as an emotional spark plug.

Lee was a happily married forty-five-year-old school administrator with three children. She had ten wonderful years working in an elite private school for girls. But unlike many of her colleagues, she was ready to admit the need for a change in her life. Which way should she turn? Her husband was extremely supportive, suggesting that she return to school to continue her education in accounting and marketing. But she found that too sterile. She enjoyed moving about, talking to parents and children alike, and the feeling of being out of the office.

She came into therapy with what appeared to be a simple problem—she was having an increasingly more difficult time getting herself mobilized. For work. For her family. For her friends. She admitted that she might simply be depressed because she was so uncertain about her future. But other than her anxiety, depression, and some guilt she didn't really feel in touch with her body. So I suggested that she follow a videotape exercise program. She laughed away the suggestion until I challenged her. What did she have to lose? A few minutes of aches and pains? Her up-side gains could be impressive— a better-conditioned body and a psychological feeling of wellness.

She took my suggestion and began with stretching exercises, moving quickly onto calisthenics, jogging in place, and eventually aerobics. After three months of aerobics, I asked her how she felt. She replied "great." She was proud of the fact that she could master the intricacies of her exercises and feel so physically good. Working out, with the purpose of allowing her to get back into contact with her body, made a lot of difference in her body as well as in her feelings. For the first time in a long time she felt alive and vibrant. Furthermore, she derived an extra benefit from my initial suggestion. Since she enjoyed aerobics so much, she decided that she would like to become an aerobics instructor. And after doing that for a while, perhaps she would open her own studio. She received my full support and her family's. Eighteen months after she began exercising to videotapes, she opened her first exercise parlor. She called it Lee's. I attended once. My aching body didn't forgive me for several days afterward. But I was very much impressed by what she had accomplished for herself.

Clearly, not everyone has to become a professional exercise instructor. But in one way or another it is important to awaken your passions by the simple physical joy of moving, stretching, running. For those of you who have never run through the woods a few hours after it's rained, or danced in a nightclub, I strongly recommend it. It is a wonderful way to feel awake and alive and place your worries aside. Try it! You'll like it!

Make up a list of physical activities that you would suggest that others do for themselves—and then redirect it to yourself.

Remember, you are in need of love and attention from those around you who care. Even if you have some doubts (which I am sure you will), ask your children, your family and friends to answer your needs. How can a grown-up woman go to her ten-year-old-daughter and ask her for a hug? The answer is—very easily. And at times when you are uncertain, distraught, and anxious, a hug from a child can be extremely refreshing.

Remember the basic credo that runs through this book: *I am. I need. I want!* Simple! To the point! If you are in need of meaningful physical contact, I feel you are entitled to it. You have no one to fault but yourself if you don't treat yourself the way you have treated others, or the way you always hoped they would treat you.

It is extremely important to your mental health and physical well-being that you take care of yourself *now*. Please don't offer yourself any excuses. It may feel silly. It may be awkward. It may seem indulgent. All correct. But it's needed.

Exercise 1: Writing a Formal Agreement

I suggest you formalize the relationship between you and your body by making a *formal agreement* in which you list physical activities that you agree to do every week. You might want to do one activity each day, for the sake of simplicity. Once you have gone through your list, you might want to change it. **WARNING**: Do not approach the activities as if they were intended to punish you. This is strictly voluntary, although it carries the moral weight of a contract between the part in you that wants to change and the actual agent of change.

Write a contract with yourself along the following format:

A. *Parties Involved*: Jane Doe Fearful and Jane Doe Change.
B. *Subject*: Seven activities that I will engage in over a seven-day period.
C. The seven activities in which I will participate for at least *30* minutes per day include the following:

1. Walk through the park every morning at 7:00 A.M. before I go to work. (Walking or jogging may be one of those activities that you will want to participate in almost every day since both are so good for your cardiovascular endurance.)
2. Swim on Monday evenings at the YMCA pool between 8:30 P.M. and 9:00 P.M.
3. Take a massage on Tuesday during my lunch break. (Instead of eating a wonderfully nurturant slice of quiche, a sensuous, relaxing massage would make you feel equally as good—if not better.)

4. Fall into a hot bath on Wednesday evening after all the kids are in bed. (If you really want to treat yourself, make it a bubble bath.)
5. Work out at the health club on Thursday either during lunch break or early evening, right after work. (Have the attendants design a realistic work-out schedule for you and stick to it.)
6. Throw the Frisbee at lunchtime Friday with my colleagues.
7. Go horseback riding on Saturday. (Ask the local stable for riding lessons and proceed to enjoy an activity that combines two essential skills for life—daring and self-discipline.)

Get the idea? Participate in activities you know you've enjoyed in the past and seek out new activities that by their very nature will titillate you. For me, it was horse polo, something I had wanted to do for quite a long time. When I finally took it up, I realized that it was a far more dangerous sport than I had imagined. You had to be a talented horseback rider, which I wasn't. So I decided to start at the beginning—I settled for riding lessons, with polo reentering my plans in the future.

Uncovering a passion for physical activity serves several important functions. First and foremost it reminds you of the amount of latent energy that you have stored up either in the guise of anger, apathy, depression, or boredom. Second, physical activity literally allows you to dispel whatever other emotions have been debilitating or counterproductive (anger, depression, frustration). Third, physical activity allows you to feel free—not confined. Riding a bicycle through your town or city, if you have been cooped up all day long at home, allows you to feel expansive. One of the worst feelings that the Successful Woman complains about is her sense of confinement both at home, taking care of the household, and at work taking care of business. Women are complaining that their physical and emotional boundaries are becoming constricted by their obligations at home and at work. Consequently, the need for change becomes imperative. Physical activity can act as a booster rocket, by focusing pent-up emotions and feelings and allowing them to discharge in the process of motion. Think about it! Bustin' loose through bicyclin'. Catchy!

HOW TO UNCOVER
YOUR PASSION FOR LIVING

The passion for living is generic, primordial. It's that feeling that you have after a stormy relationship is over: "I am still alive and intact"; "I don't need so-and-so as much as I thought I did"; "I certainly don't need him to tell me what I should or shouldn't do." Sound familiar? Then you know what I am talking about. A feeling of liberation. A feeling of gratitude for being alive. That is the passion for living.

How to uncover it? What specific exercise could you do that would reaffirm your feelings, your sense of self, and your entitlements?

Exercise 1: Things I Want for Myself

Go to the nearest park. If the season isn't right, go to the florist and pick out one fragrant long-stemmed red rose. Place that flower in a vase of water on the desk or table in front of you. Smell it! Inhale it! Doesn't it smell wonderful—a soothing, sweet scent? Isn't it good to be alive?

Now take out a piece of paper and write down those things you want and deserve as an individual.[3] For example:

- I want people to listen to me.
- I want everyone to recognize my worth.
- I want people to accept me for who and what I am.
- I want to be able to say whatever I feel to whomever I want.
- I want to receive kindness from my friends and family.
- I want to understand what is being said to me.
- I want to be able to question people without the fear of rejection.

This last one is a doozy. In general I would say that women are still afraid to express themselves in a relationship with their intimate partner because they fear rejection, reprisal, or feel an overwhelming terror that the partner will leave them because of comments perceived as a personal attack or recrimination.

Rachel was a thirty-two-year-old litigator married to a forty-three-year-old martinet who ruled their household with an iron fist, if not a mallet. Although she was extremely articulate and forceful in the courtroom, she found herself restrained, if not mute, at home. Every time her husband opened his mouth, she shut hers. Although she knew better, she was intimidated by him. She realized that a long time ago in their relationship, she had given up the reins of control and abdicated her position as a mature adult. Now she was paying the price. She resented him for being a bully. But more important, she disliked herself for putting up with his behavior.

One day she felt that she had had enough, and she talked back to him. The argument that ensued was hot and heavy. But she had vowed that she would never again allow herself to feel oppressed by a man (not surprisingly, the way she had been oppressed by her father and stepfather). After a while in therapy she had decided that she wanted respect and a chance to be heard. She knew what she had to do. She filed for divorce. One year later she was living alone but feeling incredibly liberated. The tyranny of rejection and recrimination no longer hung over her head.

Lisa, a twenty-seven-year-old public relations consultant, felt intimidated by her boss who continuously deprecated her work, making her feel inadequate and insecure. One day, she finally confronted him and forced him to explain his rationale for treating her in such an inappropriate manner. He was so shocked by her newly found boldness that he admitted to her that he had no good reason or excuse for treating her in such a shabby fashion. Impressed by her forthrightness and courage, he immediately changed his own demeanor. He became both courteous and concerned, and in time, he made her a partner in the firm. Caring about oneself can often pay off.

Here are some additional items to think about for your wish list:[4]

- I want kindness, tenderness, and gentleness in my life.
- I want to be responsible for myself—for my feelings, for my actions.
- I want to be able to say no to those people to whom I feel closest without having to threaten them with rejection or abandonment.
- I want to be able to hold fast to my attitudes, beliefs, opinions, values, feelings, and desires without having to be contradicted or ridiculed.
- I want to be able to make mistakes without having to worry about failure.

- I want to be able to change my opinion about anyone or anything without being accused of being inconsistent.
- I want to be able to change my life or any part of it without having to be defensive or apologize to anyone, including myself.
- I want to negotiate any aspect of my life as I see fit, without having to acquire anyone's consent beforehand.
- I want to say no or walk away if I feel that I am being treated critically, unfairly, or abusively.

By now I think you have a clear idea of what this list is about. It is a list that reaffirms the rights, privileges, and beliefs of the Successful Woman as she proclaims her passion for living the type of life that she wants and is on her way toward becoming the Complete Woman.

HOW TO UNCOVER
YOUR PASSION FOR LOVE

Most, if not all passions may be learned; whether it be the passion for living, the passion for discovery, physical passion, the passion for growth, the passion for fusion, passion for reaffirmation of the self, passion for love (romance), or any other passion you might think of. Certainly individuals are born with different types and degrees of passion. But that is a normal variation within the population. The so-called "hot-blooded Latino" may or may not be more passionate than the cool, restrained WASP. Appearances and stereotypes are deceptive. A volatile personality is simply someone whose moods and temperament fluctuate over a period of time or in certain stressful situations. A passionate person possesses that passion over a sustained period. It just may not appear that way. Passion, as we know, may be hidden for many reasons. In the previous chapters we touched on some of the reasons: habit, fear of change, fear of creativity and spontaneity, fear of self-analysis, and fear of commitment. Not all of these reasons have a direct impact on our inability to feel passionate. Some of them, including the fear of commitment, relate more to taking the risks necessary to change one's life.

For the moment, I want you to remember that passions may be

learned (otherwise I would be wasting your time and mine) and that we are all conditioned by the norms of our society to conceal passionate feelings. Imagine a situation in a corporate boardroom where feelings of intensity or passion are considered inappropriate. Instead, a calm, collected composure is de rigueur. This image reminds me of one meeting of high-level officials at the State Department where everyone was acting calm, collected, and rational. It was one of those meetings where no one quite knew why they were there or cared what anyone else was saying. The tone of the meeting was passionless, until one senior department official, a man of Middle Eastern extraction and undisguised passion, tried to reduce the discussion to two highly charged issues: risk and choice. After he spoke, eloquently and passionately, the meeting was abruptly dismissed. His passion was too threatening. I know! I have often been accused of being frighteningly intense, too passionate—at work and at home. So, ladies, it's time to break out! Here you go. But, before you can become Passionate about Love, you must first learn how to become passionate in general. How to unleash the restraints governing your passions.

Exercise 1: Uncovering Your Passions

Make a list of all the things that inhibit you from being a passionate person. Let me help you along. I have just said that many of the people with whom I have worked feared my intensity. So let's assume that you might encounter a similar situation if your passionate self was unleashed. I've started a list of "passion inhibitors" for you. Remember that passions are emotions that have a strong activity component associated with them.

Passion Inhibitors

1. My passion is too threatening—too intense.

"My husband is unable to handle passion. He feels too threatened. How do I know? He withdraws or becomes sullen whenever I approach him and begin to initiate an emotional or physical overture."

Here are some of the reasons why he would be afraid: 1) unable to handle it, 2) fear of being overwhelmed, 3) fear of intimacy, 4) fear that he may not be able to reciprocate, 5) makes him feel anxious, 6) makes him feel guilty.

What can you do about it? —Run away? Unacceptable. —Withdraw? Unacceptable. —Tone down your passion? Unacceptable.

Confront! Sit down and talk to your spouse and discuss the problem as you see it. Don't hold back: Tell him that you feel there is a problem and that you feel it is a *mutual* (remember that word *mutual*) problem. And you would like to know what you can do about it. What he can do about it. What you two collectively can do about it. If he refuses to respond, or his answers sound evasive, insist that you both see someone professionally. If he replies that he does not understand what you are talking about, explain with specific illustrations exactly what you mean. *Remember, don't be coy or evasive or defensive.* You are entitled to feel passionate. Don't forget. *I am! I need! I want!*

2. Fear of being too personally exposed or vulnerable.

Ouch! This one hurts! No one likes to go on the line and bare his or her soul. But that is what it takes to be passionate or emotional. When I speak of passion I am talking about a sustained, intense feeling of aliveness or excitement; not a sudden, quick rush of adrenaline. That, too, is passion, and I am certainly not against it. But it's not the type we're talking about.

The truth is that you cannot feel passionate without feeling vulnerable. Ironic, isn't it? We feel passionate the moment we feel we must risk our self-esteem in order to obtain a particular level of emotional and physical intensity. We will discuss the problem of vulnerability more extensively in the next chapter. For the moment, I want you to feel that it is fine to feel vulnerable.

There is a lot of irony in this business of emotional "uncovering."

Passion is like salt. A little bit can pique the palate by adding flavor to a bland meal. However, too much salt can destroy the taste of the food (and create a potential medical problem—hypertension). Like the talented chef, you must discover the right amount of salt required to make your vulnerability arouse the Hidden Passions and not act as an emotional damper.

UNCOVERING THE EMOTIONS THAT HIDE OUR PASSIONS

Let us continue the exercise with which we began this section—listing those reasons that you felt inhibited you from being a passionate person. We've talked about your passion being too threatening to others, as well as your fear of becoming vulnerable. What other emotions might hide your passionate feelings?

Just for an experiment, assign to yourself those emotions that you attributed to your husband. Rejection. Anxiety. Guilt. Anger. Disappointment.[5]

Rejection

Reach inside of yourself and pull out rejection. What does it feel like? Think about it for a moment. You approach your husband, but he turns away. What images and feelings come to mind? Is it fair to say that you felt as if he had just kicked you in the solar plexus? Perhaps not so dramatic. But you feel injured. You exposed your vulnerability and he exploited it to hurt you. At least that's how you feel right now. So how can you feel passionate toward him when your basic emotions are layered over with hurt? I know it's hard to uncover your Hidden Passions, particularly the passion of love or romance, after it is buried in a morass of other feelings.

Rejection is a tricky emotion. One can often perceive rejection where it may not exist, as in the case of someone who feels so entitled that if she doesn't receive the proper respect or attention, she feels slighted or rejected. Or if one fears rejection, then one may set up a situation in which one may actually realize that fear, as in the case of the person who preemptively strikes out in an attempt to ward off a potential rejection. Then there is the help-rejector. The woman who continuously seeks assistance from others whether it is at home or at work, and as soon as someone attempts to help her, she immediately rejects that help. Paradoxical? Perhaps, but, in this particular type of reaction, rejection is used as a means of controlling other people.

So, as you can see, rejection is a complex issue. It is a strongly felt emotion with different strata of meaning. But remember, we all feel rejection at one or another time. Expect it! And, then, simply keep going.

Anger

Have you recently experienced a hurt or rejection? Do you feel that your husband has not been responsive to you? Or is your hurt, anger, and resentment from a distant past? Think back to when you first dated boys. Did they make you feel as if you were expendable or inadequate? Did you learn that if you felt sexy and passionate, you were automatically considered lewd, promiscuous, or cheap? Try to recall your parents' attitude toward sex. Did they approve? If so, how did they demonstrate their approval. Did they see sex as a normal part of a healthy development? Or did they view sex as an unfortunate necessity, which had to be at best tolerated?

I had a forty-one-year-old, attractive, single accountant in therapy who spent the first twenty-five years of her life trying to understand and undo her mother's vituperative indictments of her as "boy crazy." At first my patient was totally astonished by what her mother meant. If anything, she had always seen herself as shy and unassuming which, indeed, she was. How do I know? When she first came to see me she was a frightened, withdrawn junior associate in a major accounting firm. When I asked her what she wanted for herself she replied that she came to therapy to talk about her mother and try to understand how manipulative her mother was. Seven years later, after meeting twice a week in psychotherapy, she was finally able to answer "the" question. She also finally understood that the problem lay not with her mother, but with her. In an ironic twist of fate, as she began to emerge from her shy persona, she started to date men with a vengeance. Her explanation for not having been able to settle down was that there weren't any good men around. In fact, she eventually uncovered, through patient work and effort, that it was her need to keep her relationships at a distance and under control that made her unable to commit herself to any one man. Too much resentment and hurt had built up over the past toward the man she was dating. She could never really allow herself to let go. She could never again trust a man the way she had trusted her father, who left the family when she was eleven years old and never returned.

The moral of the story is to check your childhood baggage! Be very honest with yourself. Make certain that you explore your past hurts, resentments, and disappointments.

Anxiety

This emotion, as you must already know, is all-pervasive. It can come from any number of darkened corners, including how you feel about yourself.

Self-care is the first clinical sign I look for in a woman to tell me how she feels about herself. So look in the mirror and be honest with yourself about the person you see. Are you normally this attractive? If not, then why not. What cosmetic changes need to be made so that *you* will feel good about yourself? If your physical appearance doesn't cause you anxiety, then try to locate the focus of that emotion elsewhere. Is the anxiety coming from the way you project yourself to others? Are you too bold? Do you overwhelm people with your physical presence and domineering mannerisms? Or are you, conversely, too shy? Blushing at the least uncomfortable statement or situation; making others around you feel uncomfortable; and, they, in turn, make you feel anxious? Or is your anxiety arising from your doubts about yourself and your future? Then reassure yourself. You are on the road to solving that problem.

Mistrust

Mistrust is one of those emotions that can literally destroy passion. If he is ambivalent about his feelings toward you, and in the process keeps you swinging in the wind of uncertainty, mistrust develops. You begin to mistrust him, yourself, and the whole relationship. As this persists, you build up a reservoir of anger and resentment that no amount of understanding, caring, or loving can dissipate. Passion is built on trust. And trust requires time, patience, and lots of nurturance. Only you can determine when there is enough trust in the emotional reservoir. If your intuition and experience don't allow you to lower your defense barriers there will be no basis for a passionate relationship. So wait for a better time or person.

Irritation

Much like anger, irritation wells up and becomes significantly more important the longer you persist in keeping it out of the light of day.

It gnaws at you in small ways, but the reference point is never totally clear. Is it something he did? Was it recent or some time ago? Is there something he can do to help this feeling go away? Ask him! Tell him that you are irritated. You think it may be related to something he did to you. Talk about it. Like resentment and anger, the feeling of irritation must be flushed out into the open. Then it must be examined and discarded. The longer it persists the more quickly the relationship is heading for destruction.

Don't forget. When examining your relationship with your partner, question both your assumptions about yourself and the relationship, and his assumptions about you and the relationship. If the assumptions you both are working with bear no resemblance to reality—discard them quickly.

False Emotions

There is a great tendency among modern women to suddenly have an attack of shyness, self-consciousness, and self-doubt (what I call in this context "false emotions"). It is much easier to retreat behind a posture of flustered stammering and discomfort, than to simply recognize the fact that you are uncomfortable and nervous and get on with it. It is fine to be nervous. We all are nervous; if not during some part of the day, then certainly during some part of the week. I told you before that even as I write this book I feel terribly nervous about how it will be received. But I recognize that feeling; I accept it, put it into perspective, and proceed with the laborious act of writing.

Now that we have discussed some of the more prominent factors that inhibit the Successful Woman from being passionate, what shall we do about them? Let us proceed with an approach to uncovering your passions.

> **1.** Recognize and accept your fears and anxieties. Say to yourself that in order to change you must risk; and, in order to risk you must feel anxiety.
>
> **2.** Reaffirm that hiding behind the veils of shyness, self-doubt, and self-consciousness will only diminish your passion and seriously affect your ability to deal with people (particularly men).
>
> **3.** Be grateful (yes, grateful) you became nervous, anxious, and fearful. It means that you are vibrant, alert, and ready

to live. Only lobotomized people (through drugs, alcohol, work, sex) cannot really feel alive and awake.

4. Accept the fact that you will be awkward before you are graceful. A long journey begins with one fall to the ground (an old Chinese proverb I just made up).

5. Allowing yourself to be passionate requires time. Passion may be learned—as well as born. First you must get rid of your old baggage—the old precepts, assumptions, and values that inhibit your passion. Then you must give yourself the time, faith, and effort to take a risk on your feelings.

6. You must learn to become vulnerable, while at the same time reaching out to explore, grow, and try.

7. Imagine yourself sexy. Allow yourself the luxury of envisioning yourself as you would like to be and then acting accordingly. If you act sexy, if you think sexy, if you treat yourself and your loved one in a sexy manner, then you become a sexy woman.

8. Sit back and enjoy yourself. Close your eyes and see yourself as you would like to be. Don't worry about the awkward, frightening moments. They're par for the course. Just open your eyes and enact the very scene you had just visualized. Good luck!

Practical Considerations

There are also some very practical reasons why you may find it difficult to uncover your Hidden Passions. There is an old saying that I have adhered to since my student days in medical school: *When you hear hoof beats don't think of zebras.* What does this mean? After examining a patient one day, I had to formulate a differential diagnosis. At the top of the list would always be the disease I thought the patient had and not some esoteric illness. For example, if the patient had a fever, a cough, and aching muscles, I would have thought of a viral flu and not of some unusual muscular disease such as myositis (which could also exhibit similar physical symptoms). Similarly, one of the reasons it may be difficult for you to think about mobilizing your passions is the fact that you are presently immersed in what I call the "kitchen-sink-and-diapers syndrome." It is definitely not easy to think about your unfulfilled needs when your hands are immersed in cold water in the kitchen sink or changing the baby's diapers. Or any one of a number of real, demanding, everyday tasks that inhibit the expression of your emotions or the desire for you to grow. It is hard to think about yourself when you have a little baby in your arms. But think of yourself! You must! You must learn to be selfish because if you don't, then other people's selfishness will dominate your life. It is important to be able to identify those day-to-day concerns that constrain your development.

Exercise 1: Attacking Your Household

Imagine your household, with all its furniture, clutter, and bric-a-brac. Envision your husband, children, pets, cars, bills. The whole thing. Now write out, on a piece of paper or in your mind, which of your daily events inhibit you in uncovering your passions. And write down a number between 1 and 5 next to each daily chore that you feel has a *negative* impact on your passions—(1 being least impact, 5 being the most). Remember, there can only be a few 5s; otherwise, you are either completely flooded or you have lost your perspective and you should return to this exercise another day. If you feel that your evaluation may not be accurate, ask someone else in your family how he or she views the impact of your daily chores on your life-style.

Rating	*Activity*
_____	executive management of family
_____	cooking
_____	cleaning
_____	scheduling
_____	shopping
_____	car pooling
_____	children's homework
_____	planning social events
_____	home entertainment for business purposes
_____	home maintenance

If most of your answers are in the 3–5 range it is time for you to think about correcting an asymmetry of responsibility. If that is the case, confront the other responsible parties in your household, your husband and your children, and divide up the responsibilities. If anyone refuses to carry his or her load, then it is time to have a soul-to-soul conversation with that person. If your husband is fulfilling his obligation by "bringing home the bacon," tell him that it is only a start. If he still refuses, it is time to have a frank conversation about your basic discontent in the relationship. And his recalcitrance is a good example to use.

The point is that you must begin to tackle those aspects of your life that inhibit you from growth. Remember, you can't do it all in one day. Don't even try. Just mark them down according to priority.

HOW TO UNCOVER THE OTHER HIDDEN PASSIONS

Passion for Fusion

One strong aspect of love (and romance) is the unconscious (and sometimes not so unconscious) passion for fusion. Implied in this term is a deep desire to overcome an innate sense of loneliness and separateness, and to fuse with someone we love. As I mentioned before, there are clinicians who feel that this is a primitive drive arising from an incomplete childhood separation from mother, resulting in a deep need to fuse with a secure object (substitute loved one) to feel complete or whole. From my perspective the passion for fusion is a far more healthy manifestation of a deep desire to feel complete; not only with another individual but potentially with a group and its identity. By its very nature, this passion should be mutually satisfying. You can't fuse with someone who doesn't really want you.

Remember this desire? This is the passion that has to do with self-validation. How good do others make you feel about yourself? And of course the ultimate question, how good do you make yourself feel about yourself?

The example I used in chapter 4 was of a girl who ran home with almost a straight A report card. She was proud of her accomplishment. But more important than her own pride was her strong need to seek recognition of her accomplishment from either her mother or father or both. A pat on the back. A smile.

The passion for love has within it the passion for self-validation.

Because it is so strong, a need unto itself, I have broken it off into a separate entity.

Exercise 1: Who Makes You Feel Important?

Make a list of people at work from whom you seek validation of your self-worth. Or use my list. Next to each person or group write the percentage that represents that proportion of your total need for validation in the work setting that *you seek* from that person or group. Now make another list of the same individuals or groups. This time place beside each item a percentage that represents the portion of your need for validation that is *provided* by that group.

Groups from Which *I Seek Validation*		*Groups That Provide* *Me with Validation*	
Employer	_____ %	Employer	_____ %
Colleagues:		Colleagues:	
Male	_____ %	Male	_____ %
Female	_____ %	Female	_____ %
Clients:		Clients:	
Male	_____ %	Male	_____ %
Female	_____ %	Female	_____ %
Competitors:		Competitors:	
Male	_____ %	Male	_____ %
Female	_____ %	Female	_____ %
Vendors	_____ %	Vendors	_____ %

Compare the percentages you have filled (each list should equal 100 percent). The comparison should reveal whether the workplace is serving your needs, and the areas of greatest disjuncture among relationships at work. Make two similar lists, using family members this time (or use mine below), and place the percentage you feel is appropriate near each family member and how much he or she contributes to your sense of self-worth.

Family Members from Whom I Seek Validation		*Family Members Who Provide Validation*	
Husband	_____ %	Husband	_____ %
Children:		Children:	
Daughter	_____ %	Daughter	_____ %
Son	_____ %	Son	_____ %
Siblings:		Siblings:	
Sister	_____ %	Sister	_____ %
Brother	_____ %	Brother	_____ %
Parents:		Parents:	
Mother	_____ %	Mother	_____ %
Father	_____ %	Father	_____ %
Friends:		Friends:	
Female	_____ %	Female	_____ %
Male	_____ %	Male	_____ %
Lover:	_____ %	Lover:	_____ %

Think about your responses. Analyze them. Try to explain to yourself why someone is able to validate your image, or why you seek higher approval, or why that person withholds his/her approval. Is your need for validation from any one person too high? Ask yourself why. Would you like it to be less? What would you have to do to change it?

Remember, there is nothing wrong with the passion for validation. We all need it and want it to some degree. Measure your own response to validation. How much really satisfies you? How much makes you feel uncomfortable? Shift the proportions when necessary. Self-validation is a way of reaffirming all those positive traits about yourself that you felt good about in the first place. It implies your integral connectedness with your immediate surroundings. It allows others to feel a significant part of your life. This is your way of allowing those who are close to you to tell you how important you are to them. Self-validation is a way of reaffirming your love for others and their love for you.

Passion for Romance

This passion is the one that probably deserves the most attention and will be least listened to. Romance (and love) is a quasi-psychotic state;

a voluntary state of insanity. Whenever two people fall passionately in love with each other they are, in effect, entering into a state of loss of control, loss of reality, and loss of perspective. In short, madness. I say this neither with cynicism nor desperation. And I certainly do not evidence any signs of cool, clinical detachment. On the contrary, I am fully aware that there is a blissful state of romance, somewhere between purgatory and nirvana, that is sung about constantly on the radio. But it is a world characterized by partial insanity. In the case of mature love, the element of madness (that is, the distortion of reality) has markedly diminished.

What contributes to the insane quality? My answer is simple: an asymmetry of power. It is an axiom of human relationships that whenever two people come together in an intense way, there is an imbalance of giving, caring, and power. Usually the man has more power, the woman has proportionately less. In a mature relationship of love (versus romance) the power shifts back and forth at different times. But in a passionate romance, the power imbalance usually favors the dominant person—the man. (In a homosexual relationship the dominant person also determines the nature of the relationship.)

Too frequently, an emotionally intense romance is marked by neediness, excessive dependency, fear, terror, and outbursts of anger. The woman, who since childhood has been afraid of expressing her anger (learned helplessness), sees the dominant man as someone who is forceful, aggressive, and vibrant. But when his aggressiveness turns to abusiveness, and his forcefulness turns to outbursts of anger, and you still find him attractive, there is a good chance that you are addicted to romance. An unhealthy situation at best. His outbursts of anger serve the important function of ventilating his anger—an act with which the submissive, dependent woman vicariously identifies. He can do something that she cannot do. Therefore she will put up with all the "crap" in the relationship in order to be able to identify with the angry, dominant male. He, however, remains in this abusive, mutually destructive relationship because he can unconsciously identify through her (in a surreptitious way of course) with his childhood feelings of powerlessness, inadequacy, helplessness, and dependency, which she represents overtly. However, he is ashamed of himself for feeling that way and resentful of her for being so weak and helpless (even though that's the reason he remains in the relationship). In effect she is doing his dirty work. He manipulates her into expressing her helpless feelings and he then resents her for doing it.[6] You got it! It's a Catch-22!

There's no way out of this situation unless you, as the woman involved, first make a clear determination that you will do whatever is necessary to break this cycle of self-destructive behavior that we euphemistically call passionate romance. Caveat: not all romances are addictive or abusive; only those that play on the weaknesses of either lover.

IDENTIFYING CHARACTERISTICS OF PASSIONATE ROMANCE (OR AN ADDICTIVE RELATIONSHIP)

Exercise 1:
How to Tell Whether You Are Addicted

The following is a series of questions that *uncover* the addicted romantic.[7] If your answer to a specific question is yes, place a number next to it that measures its intensity (5 is maximum intensity, 1 is minimum).

1. Do you have a *compulsive* need to be with him?
   No _____ Yes _____ Intensity _____

2. When you are together do you find that it can be "heaven on earth" as well as "hell on wheels?"
   No _____ Yes _____ Intensity _____

3. When he isn't with you, do you experience pain you can literally feel in the pit of your stomach?
   No _____ Yes _____ Intensity _____

4. When he isn't with you, are you anxious and nervous?
   No _____ Yes _____ Intensity _____

5. Do you feel that you have no life without him?
   No _____ Yes _____ Intensity _____

6. As autonomous and independent as you may be at work or elsewhere, do you feel dependent on him when he's around?
   No _____ Yes _____ Intensity _____

192 _____ *My Life Is Great*

7. Do you feel an incredible high when you are together?
No _____Yes _____Intensity _____

8. Do you find that the more you are together the more you need to make him the principal feature of your life?
No _____Yes _____Intensity _____

9. Does he become increasingly more possessive and jealous as you spend more time together?
No _____Yes _____Intensity _____

10. Do you find yourself spending less and less time with other people?
No _____Yes _____Intensity _____

If you've answered yes to five or more questions, with an average intensity of 4, you are in a Catch-22 situation. The passion for romance for which you have searched so long has led you into the very entanglement you were trying to avoid. The very situation you worked so hard to obtain and preserve stands in serious risk of dissolving into a self-destructive dependent relationship. I know it's hard to believe. But nothing makes a Successful Woman more addicted to the passion for romance than the roller-coaster nature of the relationship. The wide mood swings, as disturbing and destructive as they are, provide her with the intense high for which she has been searching and obliterate the gnawing sense of incompleteness that she has been trying to avoid. The real hook that keeps the Successful Woman in this type of addictive relationship is the never-ending hope that her man will improve and the relationship will get better.

Unfortunately no such luck. If anything, things get worse. You start to lose confidence in yourself. Where once you had a clear sense of your own identity as a Successful Woman, now you must rely on a man to validate your self-worth. No matter how successful you may be or feel elsewhere, once you come home to this type of addictive relationship all your other accomplishments become demeaned within minutes.

Addiction doesn't characterize all romantic and love relationships. I am merely warning you about what might happen when a relationship is destructive and you are addicted to it. You must make a fast getaway!

Mildred was an extremely successful advertising executive in a large firm. She had been divorced for four years when she came to see me, and she was the sole custodian of her two children. She came into therapy because her self-image was very low. She felt that she couldn't do anything correctly. Her boyfriend, with whom she had been living for the past year and a half, continuously put her down. Why did she remain in the relationship? "Because I can't live without him," she replied indignantly. "He's the center of my life. He makes me feel alive!"

"But you seem to be dying slowly—your identity, your self-esteem, even your passion."

She started to cry. "What can I do?"

Before I went any further with Mildred, I wanted her to be able to ask herself some basic questions about what was happening to her. Before it was too late, I wanted her to gain some perspective on herself and the relationship she was in.

I asked her the following questions. I suggest you ask them of yourself.

1. Who is in control of the relationship?
2. Does he make you feel bad about yourself?
3. Does he criticize you no matter what you do?
4. Are you fair game for an attack anytime you say or do something?
5. In your heart of hearts, do you genuinely feel that he will change?

I rest my case.

HOW TO UNCOVER THE PASSION FOR MATURE LOVE

As I've mentioned earlier, mature love is part of a continuum of emotions, including infatuation and romance. But unlike the impetuousness of romance, mature love has a sustained warm feeling, a clear sense of give and take, earmarked by mutual respect and caring. On a gut level you can feel the difference between a mature relationship and the instability of romance.

Exercise 1: Evaluating Mature Love

Develop a list of ten characteristics that you feel describe a mature loving relationship. How does your current relationship rate? Place a percentage value on each characteristic, from 0–100.

Now that you've made your list, look at mine. How do they compare? To illustrate the usefulness of the exercise, let's work on my list (since I haven't seen yours).

Mature Love Characteristics	*% Value*
1. Mutual Trust	_____ %
2. Caring	_____ %
3. Tenderness	_____ %
4. Acceptance	_____ %
5. Responsibility	_____ %
6. Ability to negotiate differences	_____ %
7. Ability to accommodate each other	_____ %
8. Supportive of each other	_____ %
9. Sharing	_____ %
10. Sexual satisfaction	_____ %

Based on your percentages, how would you evaluate your relationship. What characteristics are lacking that should be there in greater strength? If five of your responses do not exceed 75 percent, you should begin to question whether you are in a mature love relationship.

The key to developing a mature love relationship is to allow reality to intrude very early on in the relationship. Begin by asking yourself relevant questions:

1. What are your expectations of this relationship?
2. What do you expect from yourself?
3. What do you expect from him?
4. How wide apart are your expectations and reality?

End by evaluating whether what you want is what you got! Mature love requires a transfer of energy and emotions away from yourself toward the other person. But in order to do that, you must first have a strong sense of yourself. You must be able to feel secure and fortunate in being able to give to others as you would want them to give to you. Remember, it is never a really equal relationship. Someone always has to give more and take less. But don't worry if you miss out this time. Next time it will be your turn.

Included in mature love are the important emotions of gentleness and tenderness. Nothing bonds a relationship more firmly than a feeling (followed, of course, by an act) of tenderness. Sex and tenderness is a winning combination. I often wonder that the true passions are those most often associated with the "soft virtues" of gentleness and tenderness. Love can only be passionate if the lovers stroke each other with the other's needs in mind and not their own.

CHAPTER 10

What Are You Willing to Pay for What You Want?

I am. I need. I want. Simple statements. Something every woman should be able to assert. And yet the Successful Woman in the 1990s is incapable of uttering them with conviction.

Two brave souls, however, are in the process of converting conviction into reality and changing their lives. As I write this book, their orientations, values, perspectives, and personalities were as different as anyone could imagine. Yet, they both arrived, at the same time, using the same reasoning process, at the same conclusion: life was too short. They both decided to change their lives drastically in order to satisfy the burning question within each of them—*What do I want?* Each made a very serious analysis of who she was, what she had accomplished, and each had asked herself what more she wanted to achieve. Independently, both came to the same conclusion: something in life that was missing could only be answered by completing the sentence—"I want . . ."

My friend on the West Coast, Deborah, is a thirty-six-year-old, single, bright, attractive movie agent who works for a major talent agency in Hollywood. She has been representing movie stars for well over a decade and is quite successful. From my contacts in the film industry, I know that she is a highly regarded mover-and-shaker who

196

drives a foreign sports car and lives beyond her means in a Beverly Hills condominium on Wilshire Boulevard. She dates regularly and is an extremely amiable, intelligent, articulate, self-possessed woman. As far as I knew she was happy as an agent. A few days before I started to write this chapter she telephoned me to tell me she was in the process of changing her life-style. She had stopped seeing her psychotherapist. After four years she felt she had gotten everything she could get. She had decided that her therapist would not be an asset to her during the change she was about to make. While supportive and caring, the therapist had been more of a friend than an objective evaluator. Deborah had decided that what she needed was someone who could help her take the risks necessary to make change. To see her through with her own choices. Quite frankly, she thought of me. But because I was not physically located in California and because I was a friend, she knew that my assistance would be limited. She decided she had enough internal assets (personal strengths) to rely on her own assessments and intuitions. If she ran into trouble she would seek out whatever help she might need at the appropriate time. But for the moment, she wanted to forge ahead with change on her own.

What did she do? And how did she go about making the necessary decisions?

First, she made an initial evaluation of her life. Her work. Her social life. Her ambitions. Her future. In looking at her life as an outsider she came to an outsider's conclusion: it was glamorous and exciting working with the stars. But at the age of thirty-six, what did she really want for herself? She was spending the majority of her life taking care of others—nurturing her clients, hustling for them, servicing their inflated egos and unrealistic demands. When she stopped to take a breath one day in her 450 SL Mercedes Benz she asked herself that one question that I had insisted she ask. Is this hurly-burly what I really want? All she could see was a sea of swarming narcissists, each insisting on being nurtured and fed, first and foremost. All she heard every day was "I want. I need. I want. More." Like many people who work in a service industry (doctors, lawyers, social workers, teachers, agents), she was burning out. Her identity as an individual was being submerged beneath the entitlements of her clients. And she was basically unhappy about what she had not accomplished in her life. Despite the surface appearance of dazzle and frenzy, she felt empty. She knew that she was still bright, witty, and creative. And now she wanted to utilize those attributes in a self-fulfilling way. In my terminology, her Hidden Passions were yearning to come to the surface. Despite a life that looked scintillating, she knew that she was going nowhere, only running in place.

She wanted a life-style that relied more on her creative resources—writing, humor, sarcastic wit. She had represented several prominent movie and TV writers and felt that theirs was a life-style she would enjoy: a combination of creative solitude and dynamic interaction. As a group, they seemed to be the most stable, emotionally and financially, although the down side to writing was extremely risky.

She weighed all the relevant variables—financial, emotional, social, professional, legal, personal—and decided that it would take her at least two years of very hard work to get herself established as a television/screen writer. She mapped out a plan of attack that would require her to attend writing classes and to spend some free internship time on the set of a television show. Three weeks after she had called me she resigned from her job as a talent agent and took up the new, more challenging persona of a television/screen writer.

As Deborah decided to go from the high-powered razzle-dazzle life of a movie agent to the more controlled, contemplative one of a writer, another friend, Randy, a forty-nine-year-old senior executive at a non-profit social agency, decided that she had not spent enough time with her family, particularly her two children, who would often come home from school to an empty house and feed themselves with dinner that had been prepared for them the day before. Her marriage was one that could best be characterized as an accommodation. She worked sixteen-hour days. Her husband, a senior member of a prestigious law firm, also worked sixteen-hour days. They both made certain, in their own quiet but nevertheless equally effective ways, that they never had to spend too much time with each other. When Randy's mother died suddenly, Randy surveyed her own life and didn't like what she saw. Her ninth-grade daughter was having serious difficulty at school and her eleventh-grade son was lost in the morass of precollege preparations. The guilt of having spent so much time at work, and so little with her children, caught her by surprise. When she asked herself what she really wanted for herself, she found her thoughts and emotions drifting toward her children and her home. At her mother's funeral, Randy cried. She realized that as a daughter she had spent very little time with her mother. They really didn't know each other well. Her mother had been a bright, caring woman who had given her daughter a sense of self-assurance and direction. She had taught her that being able to take care of oneself was important. But so was a family. And Randy had lost track of her family. She looked around her, trying to assess the psychological terrain. Why hadn't she given up on her marriage? There certainly was reason enough. Her sex life was both infrequent and unsatisfactory. She and her husband had lost any feelings of intimacy for each other a long time ago. The only thing they really had in common were the children; and they were losing them to adulthood. So what was left? She tried to weigh the pros and cons but discovered that the pros were evasive.

She decided that the best way to assess the strength of the pros was to ask her husband his opinion of their marriage. To her surprise, he was extremely pleased that she asked him. They talked for several hours about the problems of their marriage, their preoccupation with their respective jobs, and the fact that the vitality and zest had left their bed a long time ago. But they also agreed on several other points: that this was not unusual for people who had been married for close to twenty years; and that what kept the marriage together was mutual respect and caring. After that conversation, Randy decided that her priorities had to change. She would take off time from work, perhaps six months, and "move back" to her family. With the combination of her regrets about her negligence as a daughter, her absence as a mother, and her newfound desire to communicate with her husband, she decided that she now wanted to fulfill her Hidden Passion for providing nurturance. She had a strong desire to take care of her children in an intense, committed way. Her "absence" had caused a lot of damage to them, but now she wanted to make it up. So she left her job on temporary-leave status with the ostensible intention of returning in six months. But in her heart she knew that would not be the case. She sensed that as long as her children were at home and needed her, she would be there.

Two different cases and two completely different outcomes. One went on to obtain another more rewarding career. The other returned home to fulfill her own manifest destiny as a mother and wife. Each found her contentment in her own way; through a process of soul-searching and self-evaluation. Each in her own way assessed the cost/benefit ratio and decided that the cost of changing her life was worth the risk. Deborah made the change with the support of a few carefully selected friends. Randy did it with the support of her family. For each, life was too short. They couldn't afford too much more time in an incomplete, unfulfilled life.

COST/BENEFIT ANALYSIS: BECOMING AN EMOTIONAL ACCOUNTANT

Are you ready for a fulfilled life? The previous chapters should have convinced you that an assessment of your current situation is necessary periodically if you want to grow and develop as a person. Reality-test your wishes, desires, fears, anxieties. Try to determine what belongs to your childhood baggage, and what belongs to the present situation. Then question some of your basic beliefs about the situation. What are your assumptions? Where did your belief system come from? Who are the different players upon whom your changes would have an impact? By now you should feel comfortable with a method of quickly determining the intensity of your desire for change.

In this chapter I present a more systematic approach to deciding whether or not you should attempt change. I am going to make you into an emotional accountant, and you are going to assess the cost/risk ratio[1] of any decision you are contemplating.

Think of yourself as an accountant, someone who looks at figures on a sheet of paper and decides whether an investment will make money. In this case the investment is you. I don't expect you to be an expert in the technicalities of accounting. But I do want you to think of yourself as someone who will look at the benefits and costs of choices.

In effect what you are answering for yourself is one basic question: Do the benefits of the relationship outweigh the liabilities; or, do the liabilities of the relationship outweigh the benefits?

The answer to this question is essential to your decision-making process. However it is important to realize that your analysis of the situation and the conclusions that you reach are subjective. You are the one who has to determine that something is wrong (in a relationship, in your job, in your life) and that it is worthy of change. You have to decide which variables are the most important ones in assessing value of the current situation. You have to decide how to "load" each one of the variables so that you can "rate" your need for change.

Exercise 1:
Constructing an Emotional Balance Sheet

If you can identify a situation you want to change you can construct an emotional balance sheet. For the purpose of this discussion, we will be using a relationship that you want to terminate. On the top left of a piece of paper label a column *"Assets."* As you know, in accounting, an asset is anything that adds value or worth to your holdings. For example, a building, cash, inventory are all assets that have a definite financial value. In emotional accounting, assets will be the positive traits or positive aspects of a person or situation (e.g., caring, supportive). Frequently, people put a value on their assets (e.g., cars or friends) that does not correspond to their real worth. However, at this point we are only listing assets, not valuing them.

On the top right side of the paper create a column and call it *"Liabilities."* Since liabilities are negative, such as owing money to a bank, taxes to the government, or accounts payable to your creditors, in emotional accounting, liabilities will be negative traits or aspects of an individual or situation (e.g., abusive, manipulative).

When you subtract your liabilities from your assets, what is left over is your *"Net Worth."* For example, if your only possession is a house worth one hundred thousand dollars (an asset), but you have a mortgage of eighty thousand (a liability), your net worth is one hundred thousand dollars minus eighty thousand, or twenty thousand dollars. In terms of emotional accounting *Net Worth* can only mean one thing—the final value of your self-esteem. Has it increased or decreased after the transaction (i.e., change)? In principle, if you are making a change in your life in the direction of something you want (e.g., a divorce, a new relationship, or a new job) then your self-esteem (net worth) should increase after the change is made—if it is good for you.

There are two other accounting concepts that will prove useful in our discussion. As *"Cash Flow"* is the amount of cash generated by a business to keep it operating, I use the term *"Emotional Flow"* to mean the amount of emotional energy that is available for the process of change. *"Working Capital,"* the relationship between assets and cash flow or the amount of reserve financing available within a company to keep it running, becomes *"Emotional Capital,"* as a shorthand designation to signify how much emotional energy or reserve is available for whatever you will be undertaking. In other words, *Emotional Flow* measures the actual amount of energy or desire available for changing one's life; *Emotional Capital* measures the amount of emotion held in reserve or on call.

The purpose of the following exercise is to establish a format for evaluating your situation once you've made a decision that you might want a change.

COST/BENEFIT ANALYSIS OF A LOVE RELATIONSHIP: AN EXAMPLE

You and your husband are young professionals who are committed to your work life and have no plans to have children. For the past year you have been unhappy with your husband of five years. You have been silently debating whether you should start talking about a divorce.

In an attempt to take an *Emotional Accounting* of where your marriage stands, you have drawn up a list of feelings that are important to your "emotional" health and happiness (column 1). On a scale of 1 to 5, you have rated whether these feelings are assets (adds positively to your relationship) or liabilities (adds negatively) to your situation or a little of both (fractions are acceptable) (columns 2 and 3).

(1)	(2)	(3)	(4)
Emotions That Matter	*Assets*	*Liabilities*	*Net Worth* (Emotional Health)
Warmth	2.5	2.5	
Respect	4	1	
Passion	1	4	
Trust	3	2	
Fun	1	4	
Communicating	2.5	2.5	
Sexual Satisfaction	1	4	
Support (emotional)	1	4	
	16 +	−24	= −8

According to the above table, a score of 40 was possible for assets and liabilities combined. If we turn your husband's Emotional Assets into a percentage, his score is 16 or 40 percent (16/40); his Emotional Liabilities score 24 or 60 percent (24/40). In accounting terms, this *"Quick Ratio"* tells you at a glance whether there are enough assets to cover liabilities (assets/liabilities). In our example the answer is decidedly no. We have a 40/60 (2/3) ratio of assets to liabilities.

Now let's calculate the *Emotional Net Worth* you are deriving from this relationship—your emotional "health." According to our illustration, Assets (16) added to Liabilities (−24) lead to negative (−8) emotional health from this relationship. You may be in what I call *"Emotional Bankruptcy."*

You may certainly select other emotional variables to rate (e.g., love, kindness). You may increase the number of variables from the example given, to any number you choose. You may also want to rate your assets/liabilities on a scale of 1 to 10 (rather than on our scale of 1 to 5). The principle remains the same: when Liabilities outweigh Assets you are heading toward *"Emotional Bankruptcy."*

Certainly emotions play a major role in keeping a relationship together. But they may not play a deciding role in whether a change (in this case, a divorce) is the answer to unhappiness. For in addition to a category of items that we have called "emotional" variables, there may be a series of others that deserve consideration:

Social Variables	*Financial Variables*
Companionship	Living Standard
Mutual Interests	Property Ownership
Personal Growth	Retirement Account
Addictions	
Drugs	
Alcohol	
Food	
Sex	

In short, a cost/benefit analysis could be done with any one of these variables, which might alter your thinking about a potential divorce. It's up to you to determine whether emotional needs take precedence over financial ones.

CALCULATING EMOTIONAL FLOW

By definition, this calculation has to be a guestimate. How much energy do you have for the process of change? Only you can determine it. But as imprecise as it is, it is an interesting concept. For example, list those things that are "sapping" your emotional energy: a dying parent, a large student loan, an eighteen-hour work day. Each of these items taxes your energy level and influences how much is available for your relationship—let alone available to change it. If the idea of rating a variable appeals to you, then list those factors that influence your energy flow and rate them from 1 to 5 (5 = taxes energy maximally). This list and its ratings will always be a fuzzy way of visualizing your energy flow, but it will be helpful nonetheless in assessing your ability, if not your desire, to change.

In a similar vein, *Emotional Capital*, or your energy reserve, is a guestimate that is difficult to calculate. Your Emotional Capital might be your boundless energy, or your supportive friends. Again, a useful concept in your search for a method of assessing the need for change.

Now I must apologize for taxing you with numbers in the previous sections. But before I elaborate on my apology, I do want you to understand that you have seven procedures to follow if you want to employ a cost/benefit analysis.

1. Identify the specific problem in your life.
2. Divide the problem into Assets and Liabilities.
3. List those characteristics or variables that are relevant to your decision under the *Assets* or *Liabilities* columns.
4. Rate each characteristic on a scale of 1 to 5. Add up the lists so you have a total value under *Assets* and *Liabilities*.
5. Use the numbers in an assets/liabilities ratio.
6. List your Emotional Flow influences.
7. List your Emotional Capital.

You now have a good start at Emotional Accounting. But what about the emotions of others? What would happen if the problem was more difficult: You and your husband have a child. Now you've added several more relationships to evaluate in terms of assets and liabilities; in emotional terms, financial terms, etc. For example, we can write out a list of people who will be affected by your change (divorce) and rate specific situations on a scale of 1 to 5. In this instance, you might want to consider short- and long-term effects.

Impact of Divorce On	*Short-Term* *Assets/Liabilities*	*Long-Term* *Assets/Liabilities*

1. Children
—school attendance
—school performance
—relationship to siblings
—relationship with friends
—relationship with you
—relationship with husband

2. Husband
—relationship to you
—relationship to children
—relationship to his job
—relationship with his colleagues

3. Lover
—nature of relationship
—nature of commitment

4. Parents
—encouragement
—support

5. Friends
—relationship to you
—relationship to husband

6. Job
—change
—ability to enhance

7. Professional colleagues
—supportive
—detracting

8. Income
—increase
—decrease
—no change

While each of these categories will not hold equal importance for you in your determination, the list gives you an example of the types of impact you might be concerned with.

Exercise 1: Confronting Beliefs

When confronting any type of change in your life assume that even the contemplation of the possibility of that change is terrifying. Fear of change may strike at any time of the day or night. The basis of that fear is the fact you might confront several long-cherished beliefs that kept you in the relationship or job that you now want to change. What kind of beliefs? Well, you know the kind I'm talking about: love is forever; true love only comes once in a lifetime; marriage is until death do us part; you are together for better or for worse.

Kathy was a forty-two-year-old senior government official who came to see me because she felt her professional life was becoming stale. She wasn't going anywhere. But as it turned out, the problem was more severe. After several sessions she discovered that she not only had to change her job but her entire life. She was unhappy married to an authoritarian lawyer who prided himself on his anachronistic macho values: housework is for the woman who should be at home, and not at work. Nevertheless, Kathy found it extremely difficult to leave him because she had grown up in a strong Catholic family where certain values and beliefs were continuously inculcated: love and marriage are forever. Period. Although she knew her beliefs were antiquated, she nevertheless had a hard time relinquishing them. We probed, examined, and tore apart each one of her beliefs (about love or marriage) until she understood where they came from, why they were there, and what function they served. No concept or belief was sacred. After several months she realized that her beliefs were simply acting as a damper on her Hidden Passions (passion for discovery, romance) as well as her willingness to take a risk on herself. Two months later, she left her husband and found a new job in real estate.

Write out a list of beliefs[2] that have kept you in the relationship (or the job). On a scale of intensity (how strongly you hold that belief) of 1 to 5 (5 is maximum) rate each of the beliefs and how it affects you or your decisions. See which ones are most important and try to understand why. See which ones have changed and why. Who or what people, places, and events were the basis for these beliefs: sex, religion, family, friends, ancestors, school? Can you rate each on a scale of 1 to 5 on its role in accepting a belief?

Now look at these beliefs again—and where they come from. Do you still want to hold on to all of these beliefs or do you want to change them? Which ones do you want to change? Which ones do you want to keep intact? Which ones make sense? Which ones are superseded by your judgment and experience?

Now make a list of all those concerns or fears that might have an impact on whether you change a belief—or commit yourself to change. Rate each fear on a scale of 1 to 5 (5 is maximum) on its impact on your decision to change: e.g., fear of failure, anxiety, rejection, and humiliation.

Take a good hard look at the list. See how you've rated each one. Take one fear and work on it every day. Imagine what it would be like if you failed. What does that mean? Who will be affected? What effect would it have on your family, friends? What effect would your failure have on your future? On your ability to change?

Imagine the worst possible outcome. Then imagine what would happen if you got rid of that fear as if you could literally wipe it away or expunge it. Your most unrealistic fears will not happen because you won't let them. There is no failure because there is always another time. Another chance. Another effort. Tomorrow is another day.

CHAPTER 11

How to Get What You Want

BE SELFISH!

Whenever I encounter a Successful Woman who seems altruistic I get very nervous. You know the type I mean. She appears controlled and self-contained. She spends the better part of her free time working with charitable committees, worrying about the homeless, writing letters to her senator on behalf of the Third World, increasing membership for the church, organizing her childrens' after-school activities, and/or promoting her husband's career. A bit of a parody? The martyred woman, for the good of others. Molière, in *The Misanthrope*, didn't think so. According to this seventeenth-century playwright, he who loves all of man, loves no man.

Most people are not selfless. They do something for someone else because at some time in the future they expect something in return. Social scientists call this "Exchange" behavior. Not very complicated. I do something for you, and you do something for me. Sound mechanistic? Cold? Analytic? Perhaps. But it is also important in the give-and-take of everyday behavior. In case after case, Successful Women claim that they sacrifice their lives for their children, or for their hus-

208

bands, or for everyone but themselves. But once they've stopped sacrificing for the others, they become bitter and angry, wondering when it will be their turn to be on the receiving end. The longer they wait, the angrier they become.

What is the problem with this kind of martyr? First, she denies or puts off her own basic needs (for love, warmth, security, financial gain, personal fulfillment, etc.). Then she externalizes them (places them onto others) as a way of avoiding having to confront them directly. If she did, she might find that she has to do something about them strictly for herself. And that might be considered selfish!

Am I advocating a resurgence of the hedonism of the 1960s and 1970s? Not at all. The "me generation" of two decades ago advocated the supremacy of the self. They believed that "if it feels good, do it." In my opinion, this is self-centered hedonism. There was no concern for others or the collective good. I am advocating the importance of selfishness as a way of connecting with others, of breaking open the bonds of hypocrisy, self-delusion, and guilt that put most women in a role of submissiveness. I am advocating the need for selfishness because without it you cannot feel complete in a dyadic relationship. You cannot make your needs or desires known. And if they are not known—and explored—you cannot change and grow. I am not saying that you should not think of others. Or that sometimes the needs of others don't come first. But not all the time. More frequently than you think, your needs should take precedence. Why? Because selfishness can serve to expand you and make you into a more complete, fully enriched person. Being selfish *does not* mean being callous, indifferent, cruel, self-centered, boastful, uncaring, or unfeeling. Being selfish means to care about "me," without ignoring or hurting the ones I love. It means letting go of martyrdom. It means placing your work, friends, enjoyments, hobbies, free time, and relationships first, instead of last. Being selfish means that you expect your relationships with others will be equal in terms of results.

Use your selfishness as a tool of growth. Allow your selfishness to raise you above your daily concerns of life, to focus needed attention on your own development. Being selfish is a necessary tool for allowing you to uncover your Hidden Passions and potentials. Selfishness is the essential ingredient for allowing you to like, care for, and respect yourself. Selfishness means personal freedom. Perhaps not to the extent of the principal characters in Ayn Rand's *The Fountainhead*—but watch what happens to your family's dynamics when you inform them that you have needs, too. That they do not owe you anything, nor you them. While they feel deserted (for a short while), they also feel relieved from feeling responsible for or guilty about you. Plus, you are offering your children a model of behavior they can emulate. As you become more selfish, you eventually will attract people who are less needy; more healthy. These people, men and women, will be more nurturant and supportive of *your* needs. Nice switch! Believe me, it's worth the effort.

Exercise 1: Learning to Be Selfish

1. Make a wish list of things you want from significant others or situations.

2. Begin as many sentences, as you have wants, with "I want . . ." Then complete each sentence with one variable from your list.

For example:

> Day 1—Ask husband for a kiss.
> Day 2—Ask children for a hug.
> Day 3—Ask your boss for a compliment.
> Day 4—Ask your girlfriend for a favor.

By Day 10 you should be a "pro" at demanding something from someone. Congratulations, you're on your way to becoming constructively selfish.

3. Look at yourself in the mirror. Be honest. Do you take full responsibility for your own actions or do you tend to blame others?

4. List all the roles and activities in which you might be acting like a martyr and prioritize them.

> Wife—inquiring about *his* job all the time
> Mother—car-pooling kids on my one day free from work
> Sister—being the perfect aunt to her children
> Daughter—telephoning 3X per week
> Employee—working a 12-hour day (and getting paid for 8 hours)
> Colleague—buying lunch for the table

5. Which do you want to change? Repeat step 4; prioritize your changes and set up a change schedule.

Remember, changes you make may be threatening to others. A new group of women friends, for example, may threaten your relationship with your husband. A new exercise class may compete with car-pooling for your children's activities, and it may be viewed as a threat by them. Be prepared to receive and handle the following reactions from others: resentment, withdrawal, hurt, pleading, disapproval, sarcasm, annoyance, threats, surliness, and ordinary complaining.

You will have to learn to tolerate these reactions and not feel guilty about what you have chosen to do for yourself. "Stick to your guns," as they say. As time goes by, the reactions will decrease in intensity and frequency. And talking about those reactions with your husband and children can be an important learning experience for all of you. Don't feel as if you are in a contest of wills. Don't argue, apologize, rationalize, or justify yourself. The best you can do is continue your daily activities with equanimity and good humor. These are normal reactions that you must learn to recognize and tolerate. Yes, your family and friends will become uncomfortable with your change. Why not? They had a good thing going for them. The burden was on you.

Don't forget your inner voice. Trust it. Let it guide you through the surrounding turbulence. You will have to negotiate more through life on your own instincts and intuitions. Trust your ability to read people's nonverbal cues and emotions. Avoid those that make you uncomfortable.

COURAGE

Winston Churchill, the prime minister of England during World War II, was quoted as saying that of all the virtues that make a man great, the one that is by far the most important is courage. Why? Because with courage you can do almost anything—including failing (which is extremely important if you want to change). I've said previously that the major impediments to change are habit, ritual, and fear. Only one attitude and response can overcome all three impediments—courage. Instead of withdrawing from what is sure to bring on some pain and difficulty, the courageous woman faces and deals with the problems. Without courage, and its sister virtue, risk, there is no concept of life as exciting, demanding, or challenging. A life without courage is a life of boredom. As Thoreau said, "the mass of men lead lives of quiet desperation." Most people also fear the concept of change, and they try to rest quietly on a chaise longue of familiarity. They rest and they wait: for their pension, their IRA, their Keogh. All they have to do is just hang in there. They ignore their inner voice while they wait.

Courage is the ability to go against the norm and standard expectations, all the while relying on your intuition and feelings. It is no accident that the root of the word courage is the French word for heart—*coeur*.[1] Therefore, let's think of courage as a feeling that arises from the heart. Not the mind. We can discipline our fears through our intellect, but we cannot proceed forward with change without the feeling of courage.

For the most part, courage means the ability and desire to be vulnerable; that is, open to criticism and attack. Why would someone want to be vulnerable? Because without your willingness to expose yourself to ridicule, shame, rejection, and defeat there can be no gains. "No pain, no gain" is a very true aphorism. You must be willing to endure pain and loss in order to attain growth and inner peace. As one of my patients said, it takes courage just to be; just to exist in a world of uncertainty and contradictions.

Courage is often manifested by very mundane, nondramatic acts. For example, for over fifteen years I have been involved in all types of international crises, some of which might be construed as life-threatening situations. In Italy, I was exposed to possible assassination by terrorists while working on the kidnapping of a leader of the country. In Panama, my name was splattered all over the local newspaper, indicating that *I* was the head of an assassination squad sent to kill a major figure in the country. On several occasions I was chased out of the country and flown quietly out on a U.S. Air Force cargo plane. Did I exhibit courage? The exposure to risk was part of my job, and I never thought of my involvement as courageous.

My real moment of courage came quietly and went unnoticed. As I mentioned before, I have been writing poems, plays, and novels for years. But like all aspiring writers, I encountered a slew of rejections. At one point my agent stopped bothering to call; he simply sent four or five rejection slips together in one envelope. In my attempt to have one early novel published I received sixty-six rejections; not bad, considering there were only twenty-two publishers. But I kept persevering. I can't tell you precisely why, except to say that I had a dream. And in that dream I saw myself as a novelist and nonfiction writer. I just kept listening to my inner voice as I sat for countless lonely hours at my desk, writing. No promises. No guarantees. No advances. Only rejections. But I wanted to be a writer. And exactly on my fortieth birthday, I was given one of the great surprises of my life—my first book contract—for a novel. To me, those aching, lonely, painful days of writing were my real act of courage.

Ms. White, a forty-five-year-old divorced bookseller, came to see me because she was unable to break out of her well-protected insular existence. She knew there was something missing in her life. Well, what we uncovered was that because of a lack of courage she found herself living alone, going to work in an unfulfilling job, and leading a staid, predictable social life. Her life was bereft of passion or courage. On the surface she seemed a completely Successful Woman bedecked in financial and social security. Inside she felt empty, frightened, and devoid of emotion. It took months to teach her to trust her emotions and listen to her inner voice.

After many sessions of struggling, cajoling, and threatening, (but always caring), she came into my office with a big smile on her face. She announced that she had committed the most courageous act of her life. What was it? You won't believe it! She had worn a pair of abbreviated shorts to her exercise class. This, it turned out, was a major feat for a woman who had always been ashamed of her thighs. They were too big. Too unseemly. She could never wear shorts or abbreviated swimsuits because she was afraid that everyone around would laugh at her. The reality couldn't have been further from the truth. But that's the way she saw it and felt about it; so that's what she had to contend with. After her "debut" in exercise class, increasing courage allowed her to take ballroom dancing, meet a stranger on the bus with whom she developed a liaison, and most importantly, she was eventually able to change her job. Today she is a happier woman, all because she put on her shorts!

Exercise 1: Developing Courage

1. Make a list of those issues in your life that you fear. Let me assist you:

- Changing my job
- Divorcing my husband
- Making new friends
- Returning to school
- Ending my love affair
- Learning a new sport
- Confronting a humiliating experience

2. Take one of these fears, for example, changing your job. The questions you have to ask yourself are meant to help you confront your fear and examine it.

Are you afraid of the new job? Are you worried about your ability to handle it? Are new skills required? A new boss? Are you afraid to give up the security of the old job? Are you concerned about what your old and new colleagues may think of you? Perhaps the most important question you can ask is what is the worst thing that can happen to you if you make a change. Can you live with it?

You've just learned a principle about dealing with fear. Confront it directly. What are you are afraid of? Don't waffle, evade, or hedge. State it directly. *I am afraid of* . . . Then break down your fear into its component parts (e.g., boss, colleague, skills, self-assurance) and deal with each part separately. See if you can't understand it intellectually and master it emotionally. For example, your potential boss: Have you met him? Do you like him? What do you think he thinks about you? Will you be able to work with him easily? Do you know his style of management? Will you have to change your style of working? You will find that once you dissect your fears into their component parts, your fear itself will be lessened.

Exercise 2: Self-Guided Imagery and Anxiety

Now let's return to that quiet room in your house or office. Sit back and relax. Close your eyes and form an image of your new boss in your mind. What does he look like? Make him look evil and menacing. Now relax; take deep breaths, breathe slowly in and out, and let all the tension and fear travel down your body, from your shoulders, through your arms, and into your fingertips and toes and then outside of you. Can you feel all the stress and tension leave your body? Good. Visualize yourself at your new job, surrounded by new colleagues and your new boss. Conjure this image so that you can feel everyone watching you. Your anxiety level is at a peak. Now start your relaxation technique. Close your eyes. Breathe slowly in and out. Assure yourself that the worst that can happen is that they make fun of you or you lose your job; both of which are highly unlikely.

Conjure up a series of different images that will highlight the anxiety that you feel about this job. Don't forget scenes of making silly mistakes. Along with those images, practice your relaxation technique, breathing slowly in and out. Allow the tension and anxiety to flow down your arms, down through your body into the tips of your fingers and toes, and then outside of you.

What you are doing through this exercise is learning to associate your worst fears with a totally relaxed state. It is a principle of clinical psychology that two competing sensations cannot exist at the same time. One or the other has to dominate. If you learn to relax you stand an excellent chance of overcoming your imagined fears. Now I know it's not as simple as that. But this technique can help you to lower your fears while at the same time allowing you to become more courageous about your choices.

Exercise 3: Role-Playing Away Anxiety

I have found role-playing to be one of the most effective techniques for confronting fears directly and mobilizing courage. I usually assume the role of the terrifying person, for example, and my patient responds to a make-believe dialogue. Although this may sound childish, it works. What you are doing with this technique is re-creating those parts of reality you find frightening. By hearing out loud the very words you fear, the technique allows you to come to grips with how threatening they are and forces you to handle your fears directly. And, I hope, competently.

1. Write out a series of five to seven lines of dialogue that would capture the actual words that your boss might use that would frighten you.

2. Assign the role of your boss to your husband, friend, lover. Both of you should play act different versions of the scene in which your boss might be saying those lines that you wrote.

3. Monitor your reaction to those lines. Practice your reactions until you feel perfectly comfortable with the different variations of the problem. When anything like it does arise at work, you will be equipped to handle it. Courage is an emotion that can be learned and mastered, it controls your worst possible fears and anxieties. You can always try to play both parts, but it never quite works as well, so try and get help from a partner for this.

TAKE RISKS

Lest this book become too self-centered, I want to show you that "experts" are not necessarily immune to the very foibles we decry or try to avoid. Let me tell you a story about a man who dared to risk in certain areas of his life (job, emotions, creativity) but not in others (finances):

Several years ago, the state of Maryland had a major bank crisis. A crooked owner of a major savings and loan had a liquidity crunch that precipitated a major crisis in his bank. After three savings and loans (S & Ls) folded, I still hesitated to withdraw my savings from my own savings and loan. I felt that the uncertainty of a possible bank freeze didn't warrant the risk of pulling all my savings out of the bank and incurring a substantial penalty. A little voice inside of me said that I was making a mistake. But I went against my inner voice (my better judgment) and left my money in the S & L. The events that unfolded were worse than I could ever have imagined. I lost a substantial amount of time, energy, and money trying to get my own money out of the bank. In the process, I became entwined in a two-year lawsuit that was filed against the S & L and lost a considerable amount of money. And it all began when I didn't want to risk the interest on my savings. What followed was a sad human story, because after all state savings and loans were closed by the governor, countless numbers of people had no money with which to pay their housing and medical bills. A few committed suicide. I saw the chain of events unfold.

What is the point? Nothing is certain. Not money. Not a job. Not a relationship. Don't lead your life as if everything were certain—if only you didn't make any changes. For the most part we all tend to live too cautiously, holding out for the promise of security.

Those who earn their livelihood through risk ventures are often the ones who understand best of all that nothing is assured.

Many of us seek comfort and assurance of our viability and safety in the achievements and memories of the past. Nostalgia becomes the shibboleth for security and complacency. Arthur Miller's brilliant play *Death of a Salesman* underlines for me the fragility of the past and the incredible uncertainty of the future.

Not surprisingly, many a Successful Woman continues her rituals and habits despite the fact that she admits to being depressed or disconsolate. How a false sense of security can be intoxicating. She doesn't risk because she is afraid of changing. She continues to lead an incomplete and empty life. That seems to be more reassuring than a life filled with some (manageable) anxiety, fear, and uncertainty.

Without belaboring the obvious—life is filled with risks. Every second of every minute of every day is literally a crap shoot. I recently learned of an American friend of mine who, while crossing a street in London, was struck by a taxi. He had forgotten to look the other way. Another acquaintance, a man in his early forties, was unexpectedly diagnosed as having lymphocytic leukemia. Another acquaintance developed a brain aneurysm and when neurosurgeons opened his skull, they discovered another one. You get the point!

I am always amazed by how much we all take for granted on a daily basis. We live life as if we were destined to be immortal. But every time I fly on a plane to some far-off seemingly exotic place, I can feel my immortality dissolve in the first twenty seconds after takeoff.

Many of you live your life in a futile effort to insure yourself against potential dangers, uncertainties, and insecurities. We earn money in order to insure our long-term health and well-being. We jog so that we can protect ourselves against coronary artery disease. We pay incredible life insurance premiums in order to insure ourselves against what we thought we had personally just insured ourselves—our immortality.

All of life represents a risk. And a life without risk is a life of the living dead. Those who complain of an empty life or boredom are simply afraid to live. *The greatest risk I know is not taking a risk.* For then you are at the cruel mercies of the gods. Anything can happen —and often it is the very thing you fear most.

Lucy, a thirty-year-old divorcee, couldn't have been more accommodating to her future husband. Whatever he desired she made possible. His wishes were her commands. When asked why this otherwise independent woman was acting so fearful, she replied that she felt she had no other choice. She didn't want him to leave her the way her former husband had. She wanted to hold on to the feeling of security this man provided. He had bought her an apartment, a car, and even placed her in a job. She saw this as his way of providing for her needs. She never dared to question her own discomfort at feeling increasingly stifled, controlled, and dependent. The one time she wanted to reduce his "largess" she was rebuffed. Then and there she should have known she was in trouble. She admitted later on that this was a turning point for her. She had to risk her relationship in order to gain back her personal freedom. But she decided not to. Instead she assumed the course of least resistance—don't rock the boat.

One day it all stopped, as you would have expected. He took back the house, the car, and left the relationship without so much as "I'm sorry." His reason: she was too staid for him. So she was the one to realize the very thing she had feared—his loss. No one can say what would have happened had she dared to risk for her independence, but we can say for sure that it was no worse than the reality that prevailed. So how do we learn to risk? The answer is really quite simple: By risking. Taking small risks in the beginning and then increasing the seriousness of the risks as you go along.

Exercise 1: Risk and Courage Go Hand in Hand

Please don't feel offended if I repeat most of the format I outlined in the previous exercise on courage. It's not that I'm lazy. It's simply that risk and courage go hand in hand. One needs courage to overcome the fears of risk. And one needs to have risked in order to overcome the fears of courage. A little circular but apt.

1. First identify your risk factors by making a list of all of the areas in which you find difficulty taking a risk.[2] I told you that my particular area was financial. Yours may also be financial or it may be something else. But confront *directly* those areas in which you know that you are not able to risk. For example:

- Financial
- Personal
- Marital
- Professional
- Maternal
- Filial
- Spiritual (yes, there is such a thing as risking spiritually)

Let's take the "marital" area. Let us assume that like most marriages, yours is asymmetric. You tend to do most of the household chores (as well as earn a living). You want to risk asserting yourself with your husband in order to realign the power balance; but you are afraid. Your fears, as you will subsequently uncover, are well grounded in his past innuendoes that he may leave. So do you dare risk a relationship so that you may feel more equal within that relationship?

Or, let's take the financial area. You are making a good salary, which allows you a comfortable life-style. Perhaps, too comfortable a life-style. What do I mean by that? Well, in some ways it may be self-evident. You like your job, but you realize that in reality you are a hostage to that salary. Without that steady income, you or your family can't afford those amenities of life that have become the prerequisite of a comfortable life-style—the skiing vacation during Easter break; the trip to the islands during Christmas. Not quite the essentials of life, but meaningful enough so that you have second thoughts about developing your own financial base independent of your salary. Like what? Managing your own financial investments; developing a transitional career that will allow you to move from your present job to an uncertain but potentially lucrative future (like real estate). Take the time and initiative to identify those areas for financial growth that would only require your part-time attention in the beginning and could eventually lead to a new, lucrative yet meaningful second career.

2. List all those things that you most fear would occur if you told him that you want him to do more of the chores at home.

- rejection
- abandonment
- anger
- physical beating
- verbal abuse
- humiliation
- being ignored

3. Which of those feelings make you most fearful? Examine that feeling, e.g., fear of abandonment. Did it come from your childhood? From your mother? From your father? Did someone whom you loved dearly die or disappear suddenly? In short, try to analyze why you are fearful.

4. What will it cost you if you don't risk confronting your husband? Will you lose your self-respect and self-esteem? Is it worth the loss?

This exercise is simply another attempt at helping you to identify important elements: What is the nature of your fear to change? Is it primarily based on the changes you will make in your surroundings (are you afraid of forfeiting a large sum of money)? Or is it psychological—fearful of releasing the pain of the past and assuming the uncertainties of the future? Or is it both? Again, remember, there are no right, wrong, or foolish answers. There are only those turbulent emotions that require both a method of understanding and using them. I hope these exercises will give you a better way of coping with the fear of change.

Exercise 2: Self-Guided Imagery and Risk

Let's take that trip back to the quiet dark room. Make yourself comfortable. Close your eyes and imagine your husband. Imagine him enraged. Imagine the worst possible scene; he may shout, threaten, and even be physically abusive. Now do your relaxation techniques. Breathe in slowly and rhythmically. Feel the tensions and anxiety travel down your neck, all the way down to your fingertips and toes. Create a gradient of desensitization starting with the least threatening image of you and your husband, then gradually work your way up to a full confrontation scene. Go over it enough times so that you feel comfortable and relaxed with the idea of confronting him.

Exercise 3: Talking Yourself Down

Make two separate columns. One entitled *Frightening Thoughts*, the other labeled *Soothing Responses*.[3] Look them over carefully and then start to work on your internal monologue. Practice it in your thoughts. Say the soothing words out loud. Try to dispel those fears that prevent you from taking the risk. Here's an example of the two lists:

Frightening Thoughts	*Soothing Responses*
"Don't push me too hard."	"I have the right to demand what I need."
"I've given you everything you've ever needed. But you're never satisfied."	"I feel I deserve more in our relationship. I've given at least in equal, if not greater shares."
"You are a castrating bitch."	"I'm sorry you feel that way. Most people with whom I deal like me very much and find me quite reasonable."
"I'm leaving you. And I will never return."	"If that's the way you feel, I am sorry. I think we have a lot of good things going for us but if you run away we'll never know."
"You'll never find someone like me again."	"I hope I'll find someone who cares enough about me to stay and love me with full equality."

Go over your two columns and compare them. Play out different scenarios. Enact one scenario constructed on the fact that you are taking greater and greater risks to confront him directly.

Exercise 4:
Create a Behavioral Hierarchy of Risk-Taking

This section is a little different from the section on courage, but it is based on the same behavioral principle. In order to overcome one's basic fears about any activity or emotion, the Successful Woman should first desensitize herself to that fear (through imagery and desensitization) and then develop a hierarchy of responses to practice before directly confronting fears.

Risk-taking is an activity that lends itself to role-playing. Probably one of the quickest ways to overcome the fear of risk is to act *as if* you have already achieved your desired goal. If equality with your husband is your desired goal, then act as if you have already obtained it, and you will see that your underlying attitudes, values, and expectations will follow suit—and so will your husband.

I know women who have spent a fortune on their personal comforts, acting as if they were millionaires. And their reason? If you act like a millionaire, you're forced to make money like a millionaire. Unbelievable, isn't it? But it is true. Insights and attitudinal change often follow behavioral change even when that change is specifically contrived for the occasion.

We'll use the example of sharing chores in a marriage. Start with a simple activity that you could practice without your husband being there. And when you get to the point of confronting your husband directly, you might want to role-play this first with a friend. If you find this procedure too complicated, modify it so it suits your own comfort level.

1. Face yourself in the mirror. Imagine you are your husband. What would you want to tell him? This takes the least amount of risk. Now go one step further.

2. Stop doing one activity at home that you would normally do (e.g., cleaning, cooking). Evaluate his responses. If

the response is quizzical, use that for your simulation exercise and role-playing. If the response is angry, try to desensitize yourself to it through imagery and role-playing simulation.

3. Resume the activity, but *ask* him if he would mind sharing the activity with you. If he says yes, wait a few days and then proceed to the next step. If the response is no, examine your reaction to it; and proceed onto the next exercise. Remember—be gentle with yourself.

4. Sit down with him and tell him that you would like to talk about the relationship in general. What you feel is good, what you feel is lacking. Monitor his response. Then again determine whether you want to continue.

5. Tell him that you are unsatisfied with the division of labor at home and that for your own self-esteem you need it to be more equitable. He has to do more of the household chores. Monitor his response.

6. Then present a list of activities that you are doing and a list of activities that he is doing. Ask him which one of the activities that you are doing he will be willing to share with you. Suggest a few that you might think he would enjoy. If his response is positive or uncertain, take the final risk.

7. Present him with a contract of equality, specifically spelling out what he will do and what you will do. If he becomes angry back off, and then decide whether you can really stay with a man like this.

Remember, risk-taking can be learned. You must start slowly and proceed gradually. Imagine yourself preparing for a marathon—pace yourself. Your speed. Your distance. Your effort. And always monitor your breathing and pulse rate (i.e., your emotions and beliefs).

One of the most important fears is the fear of failure. You may feel ashamed, foolish, humiliated, and incensed. Not the least of which, you will be extremely angry with me. In any case, *I hope you fail!* You read me right. I not only want you to fail once, *but fail over and over again*. Failure is the best antidote I know to fear of taking risks. Once you've gone through the humiliation of feeling foolish or inadequate and realizing that you do recoup and bounce back, then you can quickly get back into the arena of courage and risk-taking and try it all over again until you obtain your desired goals. You might even program some failure into your behavioral hierarchy. Screw up. You'll see that it ain't so bad! And it isn't.

Think of failure as your best friend.

HOW TO RECHARGE YOURSELF

Throughout these mechanistic exercises you will tend to feel somewhat sterile and robotic. It is only natural! I'm asking you to do things that are not very creative or spontaneous. However, I assure you that I would find nothing wrong with your acting spontaneous and breaking away from these exercises. Remember, the point of all these exercises is not to be right, correct, perfect, or appropriate. They are simply intended to help you develop a way of dealing with a lot of mixed and often contradictory emotions. We are still human, remember, and no one I know has, yet, found the golden norm.

Develop Creative Dreams

What I propose here is that you take some time out from your structured exercises, and sit down in the little dark room, or better yet, take a walk in the park among the flowers, the birds, and the bees and just let your mind wander. Imagine a flower! What are your thoughts? Jot them down. Associate to that barren tree! What are you thinking? Or, more important, what are you feeling? Concentrate on any part of the day's activity, including the exercises. What are you thinking? What are you feeling?

Don't be afraid to be spontaneous, wacky, or bizarre.[4] You know where I go to recharge my creativity? To the movies! That's right! Sitting there enjoying the film I can allow my mind to wander. And what I discover while watching that movie are interesting plot twists or characters that have nothing to do with that movie. I find I am able to reach inside myself and draw out emotions like sadness, passion, joy, which are elicited by the story line or a certain musical theme running throughout the movie.

Recharge yourself wherever you go. During sleep! Try to remember your dreams and your immediate associations to those dreams—especially those hidden emotions associated with the dreams. Use this emotional energy creatively. In the car while driving to work. At work. On the jogging track.

All these freely generated emotions and associations become part of the rich reservoir of hidden passions and secret desires. They work on one another in a mysterious, wonderful way. Don't try to understand it—just enjoy it!

Develop a Support Group

When embarking on a scary journey of uncovering your passions where you have to mobilize your courage and risk-taking, make certain that you have a group of friends around with whom you can share your concerns, your dreams, your frustrations, your hopes. It's extremely important that you not feel isolated or alone, particularly when things don't turn out the way you want. And they may not. Be sure you know how to reach your friends and be sure your friends are kept abreast of what you want to do.

Develop Spirituality

Go to your house of worship, whatever it may be. Sit there. Meditate. Think about the wondrous joy of being alive. And marvel at the community of man that is a joy to behold. You don't have to pray if you don't want, but I do want you to communicate with something greater or larger than yourself.

If you don't believe in God, then go outside, look up to the skies and enjoy the beauty and wonder of such natural timelessness. Get outside of yourself. Let your spirit soar and imagine what it would see. Welcome to the larger community of man.

I would be negligent if I didn't tell you to seek out professional help wherever you are wont to do it. Don't be ashamed or afraid. Ask your local doctor, hospital, minister, or professional association for the name of a qualified psychotherapist who can deal with the wonderful, complex problem of being a Complete Woman. Don't be afraid to see a male or female psychotherapist—as long as he or she is licensed and certified to practice by a professional association. Above all else, have an open mind as well as an open heart. No one person (including myself) has all or even most of the answers. But I do know I wish you all that you wish yourself. I hope that someday you will be able to say these simple sentences: *I am. I need. I want. Therefore, I am complete.*

CHAPTER 12

Rules for Becoming a Complete Woman

At this point in the book, you are either enchanted, grateful, bemused, confused, annoyed, perplexed, or disgusted. You either understood what I have said and appreciate the basic litany of "I am. I need. I want!" or you think it's all hogwash. That's all right. It's really up to you. Take exactly what you want or need. Discard the rest. Above all else—be gentle with yourself. It's not easy to be happy—to feel complete. It takes work! But it's worth it, simply because *you want it.* Care enough about yourself—no one else will. Take the necessary time. Make the effort. You can't escape the fact that you know there is something missing in your life. You feel incomplete. The more you achieve or acquire, the greater the status, the bigger the car, the more numb you feel within yourself. You would like to reach inside and pull out whatever feelings or passions you need in order to feel whole. But, it's not easy. It's even harder to admit that something is missing within you; and it is downright frightening to decide to do something about it.

As you, the Successful Woman, enter the twenty-first century you will find yourself pulled in different directions by the demands and expectations of the multiplicity of roles you have assumed. Your life will be busy, filled with events, people, and processes. In business, you will eventually become the majority of America's entrepreneurs. While, at the same time, you will choose to spend more time at home, in your role as mother. Increasingly, you will be torn by the conflicting values, attitudes, and behaviors of the nurturant caring mother and the aggressive, achievement-oriented businesswoman. Everyone will expect everything from you. And you, in turn, will toss yourself into a dizzy whirlwind of activities and accomplishments.

Your passage into the twenty-first century will also be characterized by an inexplicable feeling that *something is missing in your life*. In spite of all the accoutrements of success—power, prestige, money, status —you feel incomplete. Some will say you are just a mite depressed. Others will say you are needy. I will say to trust only yourself and your feelings. Something *is* missing in your life and will continue to be missing until you choose to reclaim your own identity.

You now know that what is missing is the realization that there are Hidden Passions which are buried in a childhood socialization process designed for producing a derivative identity, learned helplessness, and selfless nurturing. Absent are the clarity of your own identity and the intensity of your own entitlements. Instead of asking yourself "*What do I want?*" you were taught to cater to the needs of others, asking "What do they want?" Instead of learning "*How do I get it?*" or "*How much is it worth?*" you rush immediately into the predigested course work of professional schools. Where once you wanted to be an artist, instead you have become a litigator. Where once you dreamed of the impossible, now, you are satisfied with the limits of the probable. Gone is the exhilaration of tomorrow—of what could be—in a day without an agenda; in a day blocked by your own thoughts, actions, and emotions. Gone is the childhood defiance that you could and would do anything you wanted. And gone is the sense that you could become the Complete Woman living life with passion.

To regain those Hidden Passions requires the courage to risk and the conviction to feel. You must learn to accept the basic tenet of the book: *I am. I need. I want.* And you must learn *how* to ask and answer the three basic questions: *What do I want? What is it worth? How do I get it?*

The journey into becoming the Complete Woman is an arduous but joyous one. It requires the boldness of youth and the discipline of maturity. It is an adventure that requires your full commitment as well as the willingness to question all assumptions. It is a constructive journey into uncertainty where the outcome of becoming whole is apparent to only you. I wish you *bon voyage* and safe journey.

RULE 1
Your Life Will Remain Status Quo As Long As You Let It

A comfortable life is simply that—a comfortable life. For most people it means a house in the suburbs, two cars in the garage, a household of children, and one or two planned vacations a year. Nothing wrong with that! Correct! Except that for an increasingly greater number of Successful Women the status quo does not seem to be sufficient. You feel that you spend the better part of your life in a frenzy of activity primarily fulfilling the mandates imposed from without. If you were to ask your friends if they felt anything was wrong with your life, they would look at you quizzically; either threatened by the presumption of your question or bemused by your apparent ingenuousness. Rest assured that what is around you will remain as it is, except the children will become older, the cars will be exchanged, the marital relationship will course through accommodation and compromise, and you will remain busily content. But within, you know and feel something is wrong. Something is missing. If you do not pursue your emotions, then you must accept Rule 1—the status quo will remain. And you will realize that your today is a mirror of your tomorrow.

RULE 2
Trust Your Feeling That Something Is Missing

One of the best ways of knowing what you might really want in life is to ask yourself that childhood question: "What would I do if I had only twenty-four hours to live?" The sage and somewhat pretentious answer is that "I would live it hour by hour." But if time really were to be limited—a month, a year, a few years—what would you want to do? And if the answers are entirely different from what you are doing now, something is missing.

Another cursory test of incompleteness is how you feel as you acquire more of the accepted accoutrements of success. My suspicion is that you will not feel commensurately content. If anything, as the veneer of success becomes more polished, the validity of your sense of incompleteness becomes more real. The extra Mercedes, the new job title, the vacation in exotic places such as the Himalayas—all these are nice. But something is still missing. And you don't know what it is. At best, you sense it as a feeling—a gnawing sensation of wanting to be more alive and awakened to your passions. At worst, it is a teasing moment, mocking your discontent.

Above all else, trust *that* feeling. It is the most true feeling you will have about yourself at any time in your life.

RULE 3
Only You Can Change Yourself

Many Successful Women who feel this sense of incompleteness look around and attribute it to everyone else but themselves. It's her husband who hasn't been attentive. It's her children who are demanding. It's her boss who is basically insensitive. Instead of focusing on herself she focuses on changing the people around her. Too much time and energy that could have been used for self-exploration is dissipated in the futile effort of changing her surroundings when instead, her interior should have been remodeled.

RULE 4
Learn to Love Yourself

No one else will ask you what you want. No one else will provide you with what you need. You must do it all by yourself, and for yourself (with this helpful guide, and some assurances from loved ones and friends). But before anything can happen, you must be able to look at yourself in the mirror and be pleased with the person you see. In time, through compassion and diligence, you will learn to love yourself.

From that basic love arises the first premise for change: "I am." And from that clear sense of identity arises the second premise: "I need." If you love yourself, you will need respect, caring, equality, attention, support, guidance, and, yes, nurturance. The circle must make a full turn. You began as someone who nurtured others, now you must demand that the others nurture you.

RULE 5
Deeds Speak Louder Than Words

To desire something without following through is at best an empty, if not self-indulgent, gesture. But to quietly state that you want to change, and then follow through with actions required to implement your desires, is both a courageous and noble act, worthy of everyone's respect and attention.

It is in our deeds and not in our words that people will judge us. For that act of self-change is one of the most difficult things to do. We can invent, create, fix, improve. But to change ourselves into something that we want to be is an act worthy of dedication, commitment, time, and energy. It is an act worthy of a lifetime. But it is an act which only you can choose to implement.

RULE 6
Courage and Intuition Can Save You

In an increasingly more mechanized world where the logic of the computer comes precariously close to supplanting man's innate intelligence and judgment, there is a basic audacity to the notion that the nonrational aspects of our being—courage and intuition—can be the basis of our personal salvation. But only by trusting that inner voice telling you it is time to change can you proceed to the next step—daring to change. And for that you need a healthy dose of courage, often missing or reconfigured.

Courage can be learned, as can risk and daring. These are behaviors that have been hidden by your very successes. You were *courageous* for your country, your company, your school, your team—but not yourself. You dared to *risk* for your country, your company, your team, your school—but not for yourself.

Return the courage and the intuition to where it belongs—to yourself, for yourself. Only then will others prosper.

RULE 7
Fear Is the Panacea for the Cowardly

We are all afraid at one or another time. We are afraid of what we've done, what we are doing, and what we will be doing. So there is no shortage of fear around. Or the excuse of fear behind which to hide.

For those who don't, can't, or won't change, fear is both a convenient and convincing panacea. It can excuse all of our inactions, resistances, and procrastinations. It is the one emotion with which we can all identify because we all have it.

To overcome fear you must have more than a façade of false bravado. It calls for determination, discipline, and courage. All three require self-love and patience. A lot of self-love and patience. But it can be done. And once fear disappears there is no more need for a panacea. Each problem begins to have its own solution. Each solution requires its own attention and dedication.

RULE 8
Respect Your Hidden Passions

It is one thing to talk about wanting to change in order to get in touch with your needs for growth, creativity, and love. But it is another thing to be able to handle these explosive emotions. There is a good reason that they have remained hidden for so long. To release them prematurely, without the proper preparation or attention, is to literally play with dynamite. Above all else, you must be very respectful of your emotions and understand why they are where they are.

Be respectful of these emotions but don't be afraid of them. Handle them with care, and they will serve you well for the rest of your life. Experiment with them as you would with a bunsen burner—the flame may be used to catalyze a lot of different chemical (read emotional) reactions. If improperly used it could blow up in your face.

RULE 9
Life Is a Continuous Change:
You Are Simply a Voyager

If you take the attitude that life is filled with challenges and risks, you can begin to assume a more relaxed attitude toward daily living. I said *relaxed*. I did not say *lazy*. To understand that there are no certainties other than change is to arrive at the very essence of this book. Then you can assume the comfortable posture of the bus rider who will "leave the driving to us."

This doesn't mean that you will work any less. It simply means that you won't have to replay the myth of Sisyphus over and over again. Once is enough, thank you.

RULE 10
To Be Complete Does Not Necessarily
Mean to Be Happy—There Are No Guarantees

What? You are incredulous. All of this time, energy, and effort to find out that all this daring, self-analysis, and change may lead to further discontent? That's true—it might. And, then again, it might not. The outcome really depends upon you.

What you have learned in this book is not that you are deserving of a once-in-a-lifetime chance to change or that there is only one type of change in which you should engage. On the contrary, if you need to self-correct several times, then do it. Remember, *there are no guarantees*. Most people don't believe that. They feel that simply making an effort is really good enough. Once that effort is realized, then all good things should befall them. Unfortunately that is not the case. I wish it were. If I made that claim I would be telling you a lie, and that is precisely what you do not need now or later. But I hate to end this book on a down note. What this rule really means is that if you don't succeed then try . . . try again. You can't be more hopeful than that.

PERSONAL NOTE

Now that we've come to the end of the book, I would just like to say how much I've enjoyed working with you. As I write I carry a mental image of you. Of the countless "yous" I have had the privilege to treat, know, and love. And so I hope that you in turn have learned to appreciate me—to know my strengths, my weaknesses. For it is in this type of relation that personal change can occur. I hope you will use the different parts of this book as you see fit. These last ten rules were written as a reminder about what I consider to be the most relevant issues for you. As you already know, they are simple: Be kind to yourself; dare to be what you're not; and, have the courage to uncover what is rightfully yours—your passions. Ask yourself the three basic questions as a way of monitoring yourself as you navigate your way through your hectic work and personal lives: *What do I want? What is it worth? How do I get it?* Through these questions you can affirm and reaffirm the basic precepts of your existence. *I am. I need. I want. Therefore, I am complete.*

NOTES

INTRODUCTION: *Yearning for Self: Awakening the Hidden Passions*

1. Halpern, Howard M., Ph.D., *How to Break Your Addiction to a Person* (New York: Bantam Books, 1982), pp. 135–88.
2. Rusk, T., M.D., and Read, R., M.D., *I Want to Change but I Don't Know How* (Los Angeles: Price Stern Sloan, Inc., 1987), pp. 130–60.

CHAPTER 1: *The Problem of Becoming a Complete Woman*

1. Eichenbaum, L., and Orbach, S., *What Do Women Want: Exploding the Myth of Dependency* (Toronto: Coward-McCann, 1983), pp. 29–86.
2. Braiker, H. B., Ph.D., *The Type E Woman* (New York: New American Library, 1986), pp. 1–8.

CHAPTER 2: *The Successful Woman: Contradictory Realities—Why She Feels Incomplete*

1. Braiker, op. cit., pp. 80–113.
2. Mahler, M. S.; Pine, F.; and Bergman, A., *The Psychological Birth of the Human Infant: Symbiosis and Individuation* (New York: Basic Books, 1975), pp. 3, 33, 34, 54.
3. Eichenbaum and Orbach, op. cit., pp. 51–57.
4. Braiker, op. cit., pp. 113–38.
5. Ibid., pp. 151–54.

235

CHAPTER 3: *Warning Signs: How to Recognize That Something Is Wrong*

1. Gaylin, W., M.D., *Feelings* (New York: Harper and Row Perennial Library, 1988), pp. 89–164.
2. Ibid., pp. 98–100.
3. Ibid.
4. Ibid., pp. 103–5.
5. Ibid., pp. 105–12.
6. Ibid., p. 116.
7. Ibid.
8. Ibid., pp. 118–23.
9. Ibid., pp. 131–34.
10. Ibid., pp. 140–41.
11. Ibid., pp. 142–43.
12. Ibid., pp. 54–74

CHAPTER 4: *Discovering the Different Types of Hidden Passions*

1. Gaylin, op. cit., pp. 204–23.
2. Ibid.
3. Cowan, C., Ph.D., and Kinder, M., Ph.D., *Women Men Love/Women Men Leave* (New York: Clarkson N. Potter, Inc., 1987), pp. 143–60.
4. Ibid., pp. 147–48.
5. Ibid., pp. 153–61.

CHAPTER 5: *What Prevents the Successful Woman from Feeling Complete?*

1. Rusk and Read, op. cit., pp. 101–33.
2. Peck, S., M.D., *The Road Less Travelled* (New York: Touchstone Books, 1978), pp. 131–54.
3. Ibid., pp. 71–75.
4. Ibid., pp. 155–60.
5. Ibid., pp. 140–50.

CHAPTER 6: *The Un-Successful Woman: A Hostage to Herself*

1. Halpern, op. cit., pp. 1–10.
2. Person, Ethel S., M.D., "Love Triangles," *Atlantic Monthly*, February 1988, pp. 41–52

CHAPTER 7: *How to Make Yourself Number One*

1. Halpern, op. cit., pp. 188–200.
2. Ibid., pp. 188–95.

CHAPTER 8: *The Problem of Self-Definition: Who Am I?*

1. Braiker op. cit., pp. 80–84.
2. Ibid., pp. 84–88.

3. Forward, S., Ph.D., *Men Who Hate Women/The Women Who Love Them* (New York: Bantam Books, 1987), pp. 191–203.

4. Ibid., pp. 188–208.

5. Braiker op. cit., pp. 84–88.

6. Halpern, op. cit., pp. 213–15.

CHAPTER 9: *What Do I Want?: The Problem of Indulging Yourself*

1. Eichenbaum and Orbach, op. cit., pp. 51–97.

2. Forward, op. cit., pp. 188–91.

3. Ibid., pp. 212–15.

4. Ibid., pp. 213–15.

5. Cowan and Kinder, op. cit., pp. 216–23.

6. Forward, op. cit., pp. 41–52.

7. Halpern, op. cit., pp. 7–10.

CHAPTER 10: *What Are You Willing to Pay for What You Want?*

1. Halpern, op. cit., pp. 136–38.

2. Ibid., pp. 170–77.

CHAPTER 11: *How to Get What You Want*

1. Rusk and Read, op. cit., pp. 172–84.

2. Ibid., pp. 102–19.

3. Forward, op. cit., pp. 251–55.

4. Garfield, Patricia, Ph.D., *Creative Dreaming* (New York: Ballantine Books, 1974), pp. 172–76.

BIBLIOGRAPHY

Braiker, Harriet B., Ph.D. *The Type E Woman*. New York: New American Library, 1986.

Cowan, Connell, Ph.D., and Kinder, Melvyn, Ph.D. *Women Men Love/Women Men Leave*. New York: Clarkson N. Potter, 1987.

Eichenbaum, Luise, and Orbach, Susie. *What Do Women Want: Exploding the Myth of Dependency*. Toronto: Coward-McCann, 1983.

Forward, Susan, Ph.D. *Men Who Hate Women/The Women Who Love Them*. New York: Bantam Books, 1987.

Garfield, Patricia, Ph.D. *Creative Dreaming*. New York: Ballantine Books, 1974.

Gaylin, Willard, M.D. *Feelings*. New York: Harper and Row Perennial Library, 1988.

Gilligan, C. *In a Different Voice: Psychological Theory and Women's Development*. Cambridge, Mass.: Harvard University Press, 1982.

Halpern, Howard M., Ph.D. *How to Break Your Addiction to a Person*. New York: Bantam Books, 1982.

Mahler, Margaret S.; Pine, F.; and Bergman, A. *The Psychological Birth of the Human Infant: Symbiosis and Individuation*. New York: Basic Books, 1975.

Peck, M. Scott, M.D. *The Road Less Travelled*. New York: Touchstone Books, 1978.

Person, Ethel S., M.D. "Love Triangles." *Atlantic Monthly* (February 1988): pp. 4–52.

Rusk, Tom, M.D., and Read, Randy, M.D. *I Want to Change but I Don't Know How*. Los Angeles: Price Stern Sloan, Inc., 1987 (6th printing).

INDEX